D1258714

CliffsTestPrep®

California High School Exit Exam: English-Language Arts

by

Jerry Bobrow, Ph.D.

Contributing Authors/Consultants

Robert DiPietro, M.A.

Jean Eggenschwiler, M.A.

Christina M. Heredia, M.A.

Michele Spence, B.A.

WILEY

Wiley Publishing, Inc.

About the Author

Jerry Bobrow, Ph.D., is a national authority in the field of test preparation. As executive director of Bobrow Test Preparation Services, he has been administering the test preparation programs at over 25 California institutions for the past 30 years. Dr. Bobrow has authored over 40 national best-selling test preparation books, and his books and programs have assisted over two million test-takers. Each year, Dr. Bobrow personally lectures to thousands of students on preparing for graduate, college, and teacher credentialing exams.

My loving thanks to my wife, Susan, and my children, Jennifer, Adam, and Jonathan, for their patience and support in this long project. I would also like to give a special thank you to Dr. Suzanne Snyder, for final editing and careful attention to the production process.

Publisher's Acknowledgments

Editorial

Project Editor: Suzanne Snyder

Acquisitions Editor: Greg Tubach

Production

Proofreader: Arielle Mennelle

Wiley Publishing, Inc. Composition Services

CliffsTestPrep® California High School Exit Exam: English-Language Arts

Published by:
Wiley Publishing, Inc.
111 River Street
Hoboken, NJ 07030-5774
www.wiley.com

Copyright © 2005 Jerry Bobrow, Ph.D.
Published simultaneously in Canada

Library of Congress Cataloging-in-Publication Data

Bobrow, Jerry.
  CliffsTestPrep California High School Exit Exam-English language arts /
by Jerry Bobrow; contributing authors Robert DiPietro . . . [et al.].--1st ed.
      p. cm. -- (CliffsTestPrep)
  ISBN 0-7645-5938-9 (pbk.)
1. Language arts (Secondary)--California--Examinations, questions,
etc.--Study guides. 2. California High School Exit Exam--Study guides.
I. Title: California High School Exit Exam-English language arts. II.
Di Pietro, Robert J. III. Title. IV. Series.
  LB1631.5.B63 2005
  373.126'2--dc22
2004028566

Printed in the United States of America

10 9 8 7 6 5 4 3 2 1

1B/QY/QS/QV/IN

WILEY

Table of Contents

PART II: REVIEWS

PART IV: FINAL PREPARATION AND SOURCES

Preface

**We know that passing the CAHSEE
English-Language Arts is important to you!**

And we can help.

As a matter of fact, we have spent the last 30 years helping over a million test takers successfully prepare for important exams. The techniques and strategies that students and adults have found most effective in our preparation programs at 26 universities, county offices of education, and school districts make this book your key to success on the California High School Exit Exam (CAHSEE) English-Language Arts.

Our easy-to-use CAHSEE English-Language Arts Preparation Guide gives you that *extra edge* by

- Answering commonly asked questions
- Introducing important test-taking strategies and techniques
- Reviewing the California English-Language Arts standards
- Analyzing sample problems and giving suggested approaches
- Reviewing the writing process
- Providing a quick review of grammar and usage, prefixes, suffixes, and roots, and literary terms
- Providing three simulated practice exams with explanations
- Including analysis charts to help you spot your weaknesses, including Essay Checklists
- Giving you lots of strategies and techniques with plenty of practice problems

There is no substitute for working hard in your regular classes, doing all of your homework and assignments, and preparing properly for your classroom exams and finals. But if you want that *extra edge* to do your best on the CAHSEE English-Language Arts, follow our Study Plan and step-by-step approach to success on the CAHSEE.

Best of Luck,

Jerry Bobrow, Ph.D.

Study Guide Checklist

Check off each step after you complete it.

❏ 1. Read the English-Language Arts Study Guide available from your school or from the California Department of Education

❏ 2. Review any information materials available online at cde.ca.gov.

❏ 3. Look over the "Format of the CAHSEE English-Language Arts" (p. 1).

❏ 4. Learn how you can do your best (p. 1).

❏ 5. Read "Questions Commonly Asked About the CAHSEE English-Language Arts" (p. 4).

❏ 6. Carefully Read "Part I: Working Toward Success" focusing on the sample problems and suggested approaches.

- Reading (pp. 7–44)
    - Word Analysis (pp. 17–19)
    - Reading Comprehension (pp. 20–31)
    - Literary Response and Analysis (pp. 32–44)
- Writing (pp. 45–82)
    - Writing Strategies (pp. 45–49)
    - Writing Conventions (pp. 50–54)
    - Writing Applications (pp. 55–82)

❏ 7. Carefully review "Part II: Reviews," which covers grammar and usage, prefixes, suffixes, and roots, and literary terms (pp. 85–124).

❏ 8. Take Practice Test 1 (pp. 125–159). After you take the test, check your answers and analyze your results using the "Answer Key" (pp. 160–161), the "Reviewing Practice Test 1" section (pp. 163), and the "Explanations for Practice Test 1" (pp. 165–171).

❏ 9. Have a teacher, tutor, or another knowledgeable adult review your essay using the Essay Checklist.

❏ 10. Review any basic skills that you need to review.

❏ 11. Take Practice Test 2 (pp. 175–209). After you take the test, check your answers and analyze your results using the "Answer Key" (pp. 210–211), the "Reviewing Practice Test 2" section (pp. 213), and the "Explanations for Practice Test 2" (pp. 215–222).

❏ 12. Have a teacher, tutor, or knowledgeable adult review your essay using the Essay Checklist.

❏ 13. Review any basic skills that you need to review (p. 85–124).

❏ 14. Take Practice Test 3 (pp. 225–258). After you take the test, check your answers and analyze your results using the "Answer Key" (pp. 259–260), the "Reviewing Practice Test 3" section (pp. 261), and the "Explanations for Practice Test 3" (pp. 263–270).

❏ 15. Have a teacher, tutor, or knowledgeable adult review your essay using the Essay Checklist.

❏ 16. Review your weak areas and then selectively review the strategies and samples in "Part I: Working Toward Success" (pp. 5–82).

❏ 17. Read "The Final Touches" (pp. 273–274).

Format of the CAHSEE English-Language Arts

The test consists of 79 multiple-choice questions and one essay; 72 of the multiple-choice questions actually count toward your score. The following areas are covered (but the questions will **not be labeled or in this order**):

Areas Covered on the CAHSEE English-Language Arts	
Reading	
Word Analysis (WA)	7 questions
Reading Comprehension (RC)	18 questions
Literary Response and Analysis (LR)	20 questions
Writing	
Writing Strategies (WS)	12 questions
Writing Conventions (WC)	15 questions
Writing Applications (WA)	essay
Total multiple-choice questions that count on score	**72 questions**
Plus "trial" multiple-choice questions for future tests	7 questions

Total questions on the English-Language Arts Test	**79 multiple-choice questions**
	Plus 1 Essay

Because this is a new test, the number of questions and the types of questions may be adjusted slightly in later tests. Also note that the "trial" questions could be scattered anywhere on the exam.

The CAHSEE English-Language Arts is divided into two sessions as follows:

CAHSEE English-Language Arts	Approximate Working Times	Number and Kinds of Questions
Session 1	2 hours	21 multiple choice, 1 essay
Session 2	1 hour, 30 minutes	58 multiple choice

How You Can Do Your Best

A Positive Approach

Since every question is worth the same number of points, do the easy ones first. To do your best, use this positive approach:

1. First, look for the questions that you can answer and should get right.
2. Next, skip the ones that give you a lot of trouble. (But take a guess.)
3. Remember, don't get stuck on any one of the questions.

Here's a closer look at this system:

1. Answer the easy questions as soon as you see them.
2. When you come to a question that gives you trouble, don't get stuck.
3. Before you go to the next question, see if you can eliminate some of the incorrect choices to that question. Then take a guess from the choices left!
4. If you can't eliminate some choices, take a guess anyway. Never leave a question unanswered.
5. Put a check mark on in your test booklet next to the number of a problem for which you did not know the answer and simply guessed.
6. After you answer all of the questions, go back and work on the ones that you checked (the ones that you guessed on the first time through).

Don't ever leave a question without taking a guess. There is no penalty for guessing.

The Elimination Strategy

Sometimes the best way to get the right answer is by eliminating the wrong answers. As you read your answer choices, keep the following in mind:

1. Eliminate wrong answer choices right away.
2. Mark them out in your question booklet.
3. If you feel you know the right answer when you spot it, mark it. You don't need to look at all the rest of the choices (although a good strategy for some questions is to scan the choices first).
4. Try to narrow your choices down to two so that you can take a better guess.

Remember, getting rid of the wrong choices can leave you with the right choice. Look for the right answer choice and eliminate wrong answer choices.

Here's a closer look at the elimination strategy.

Take advantage of being allowed to mark in your testing booklet. As you eliminate an answer choice from consideration, make sure to mark it out in your question booklet as follows:

$$\cancel{A}$$
$$?B$$
$$\cancel{C}$$
$$?D$$

Notice that some choices are marked with question marks, signifying that they may be possible answers. This technique will help you avoid reconsidering those marked-out choices you have already eliminated and will help you narrow down your possible answers. These marks in your testing booklet do not need to be erased.

Avoiding the "Misread"

One of the most common errors is the "misread," that is, when you simply misread the question.

- **A question could ask,**

  What does the word *lifting* mean in the context of the passage?

  Notice that this question asks for the meaning of *lifting* in the *context of the passage*.

- **A question could ask,**

  Which of the following is the main point of the essay?

  Notice that here you are looking for the *main point*.

- **A question could ask,**

  Which of the following BEST illustrates what the author believes?

  Notice that here you are looking for that which *BEST illustrates* what the *author believes*.

- **A question could be phrased as follows:**

  Based on information contained in the article, which statement is NOT accurate?

  Notice that the word NOT changes the above question significantly.

To avoid "misreading" a question (and therefore answering it incorrectly), simply circle or underline what you must answer in the question. For example, do you have to know the meaning of the word *lifting* or can you find its meaning in the passage. Are you looking for what statement is accurate or is NOT accurate? To help you avoid misreads, circle or underline the questions in your test booklet in this way:

What does the word *lifting* mean in the <u>context of the passage</u>?

Which of the following is the <u>main point</u> of the essay?

Which of the following <u>BEST illustrates</u> what the <u>author believes</u>?

<u>Based on</u> information contained in the <u>article</u>, which statement is <u>NOT accurate</u>?

Note that sometimes the test will capitalize a key word in the question for you.

And, once again, these circles or underlines in your question booklet do not have to be erased.

A Quick Review of Basic Strategies

1. Do the easy problems first.
2. Don't get stuck on one problem—they're all of equal value.
3. Eliminate answers—mark out wrong answer choices in your test booklet.
4. Avoid misreading a question—circle or underline important words.
5. Take advantage of being allowed to write in the test booklet.
6. No penalty for guessing means "never leave a question without at least taking a guess."

Questions Commonly Asked about the CAHSEE English-Language Arts

Q. What does the CAHSEE English-Language Arts cover?

A. The CAHSEE Language Arts tests state content standards in grades 8 and 10. The exam covers **Reading** (**Word Analysis**—discovering meaning; **Reading Comprehension**—understanding main idea, purpose, tone; and **Literary Response and Analysis**—understanding characters, relationships, fiction, theme, and poetry) and **Writing** (**Writing Strategies**—finding and correcting errors; **Writing Conventions**—using tense, word placement, and punctuation correctly; and **Writing Applications**—writing an essay).

Q. How much time do I have to complete the test?

A. The test is given in two sessions. There is no time limit for the test, but the first session will be approximately 2 hours and the second session will be approximately 1½ hours. If you do not complete the section in the time period given, simply ask the proctor for additional time.

Q. When will I first take the test?

A. You will take the exam for the first time in the second part of tenth grade.

Q. What is a passing score?

A. Raw scores (actual number right) will be converted to scaled scores ranging from 250 to 450. A passing score is 350 or higher. Since this is a new exam, you may wish to check with your school district to confirm the passing scores.

Q. When do I find out if I passed?

A. Score reports are mailed to the school district and your home about two months after you take the test.

Q. What if I don't pass the exam in tenth grade?

A. You will have several chances to take the test as a junior and senior.

Q. How should I prepare?

A. Keep up with class work and homework in your regular classes. Read, read, read. There is no substitute for a sound education. As you get closer to your exit-level tests, using an organized test preparation approach is very important. Carefully follow the Study Guide Checklist on page xi in this book to give you that organized approach. It will show you how to apply techniques and strategies and help focus your review. Carefully reviewing the Study Guide for each exit-level exam available from your school district or the California Department of Education will also give you an edge in doing your best.

Q. What should I bring to the test?

A. You should bring 3 or 4 sharpened No. 2 pencils, a good eraser, and a picture I.D. All of your answers and your essay must be written in No. 2 pencil. No pens or scratch paper are allowed.

Q. Should I guess on the test?

A. Yes! Since there is no penalty for guessing, guess if you have to. If possible, try to eliminate some of the choices to increase your chances of choosing the right answer.

Q. Can I write in the test booklet?

A. Yes. You can mark in the test booklet. Use the test booklet to mark questions, circle important points, and make notes. Your answer sheet must not have any stray marks, but your test booklet can be marked up.

Q. How can I get more information?

A. More information and released exam questions can be found on the California Department of Education's CAHSEE Web site at http://www.cde.ca.gov/statetests/cahsee/.

PART I

WORKING TOWARD SUCCESS

CAHSEE English-Language Arts: Reading

The Reading questions of the CAHSEE English-Language Arts are composed of Word Analysis questions, Reading Comprehension questions, and Literary Response and Analysis questions. The number of questions that actually count toward your score in each of these categories is as follows:

Word Analysis	7 multiple-choice questions
Reading Comprehension	18 multiple-choice questions
Literary Response and Analysis	20 multiple-choice questions

Remember, these question types are not in any particular order. Of the 79 questions on the CAHSEE English-Language Arts, 72 actually count toward your score. Although there will be more than 45 Reading questions, only 45 will count toward your score. The Writing Multiple-Choice questions and one essay will account for the remaining questions.

A special note: The reading passages and the questions following the reading passages are NOT in order of difficulty.

Before you look at the following suggested approaches, keep in mind that there is no substitute for reading widely. Knowing what to look for when you read and knowing how to read and mark a passage actively and efficiently can be very helpful.

Suggested Approaches with Sample Passages

This section will provide you with some general and specific reading strategies followed by sample passages. The sample passages will be followed by suggested approaches, questions, and a careful analysis of each question.

General Strategies

- **Read actively.** Read the passage actively, marking main points and other items you feel are important, such as conclusions, names, definitions, places, and numbers. Make only a few such marks per paragraph. Remember, these marks are to help you understand the passage.

- **Preread a few questions.** You may want to skim a few questions first, marking words that give you a clue about what to look for when you read the passage. This method, called *prereading questions,* can be especially helpful on unfamiliar passages. Try it on a variety of passages to see how it works for you.

- **Pace yourself.** Don't get stuck on the passage or on any one question. If you have difficulty with one question, take a guess and return to it briefly before you read the next passage. If possible, try to eliminate some of the choices before guessing, but never leave a question without at least taking a guess.

- **Remember that answers are from information given or implied.** Base your answer on what you read in the passage, the introduction to the passage, or any other information given with the passage. The passage must support your answer. All questions can and should be answered from information given or implied in the passage.

- **Be sure to answer the question.** Some good or true answers are not correct. Make sure that the answer you select is *what the question is asking for according to the passage*.

- **Read all choices.** Be sure to read all of the choices to make sure that you select the best of the ones given. Some other choices may be good, but you're looking for the best.

- **Avoid the attractive distractor.** Watch out for *attractive distractors,* that is, answers that look good, but aren't the best answer. These attractive distractors are usually the most common wrong answers, but they are carefully written to be close to the best answer. When you narrow your choice down to two answers, one is probably the attractive distractor. Reading the question again can help you find the best one.

- **Eliminate.** Use an elimination strategy. If you know an answer is incorrect, mark it out immediately in your question booklet.
- **Take advantage of information given.** Some questions will give you part of the text along with the question. These questions will often start with "Read this sentence from the passage," or "What does the word ___ mean in the sentence below taken from the passage?"
- **You can skip passages.** If you are having trouble with a passage, you may wish to skip it and come back to it later. Be careful, however, if you skip a passage to mark your answers in the proper place on your answer sheet.
- **Remember that you can ask for more time on the test if you need it.** If you are not finished with the test when the suggested time is up, simply raise your hand and ask the proctor for more time.

Specific Strategies

- Read the passage looking for its main point and its structure.
- Make sure that your answer is supported by the passage.
- As you read, note the tone of the passage.
- Take advantage of the line numbers or paragraph numbers, if there are any.
- Use the context to figure out the meaning of the words, even if you're unfamiliar with them.
- Read all the choices, since you're looking for the *best* answer given.

The Approach

Read the passage actively, marking the main points and other items you feel are important. You can mark a passage by underlining or circling important information. But be sure you don't overmark, or you'll defeat the purpose of the technique. The following passage shows one way a test taker might mark a passage to assist in understanding the information given and to quickly return to particular information in the passage when necessary. You may find that circling works better for you or using other marks that you personally find helpful.

Sample Marked Reading Passage

Read the following passage and answer questions 1 through 8.

The Coming Climate

by Thomas R. Karl,
Neville Nicholls, and Jonathan Gregory

Human beings have in recent years discovered that they may have succeeded in achieving a <u>momentous</u> but rather <u>unwanted accomplishment.</u> Because of our numbers and our technology, it now seems

(5) likely that we have begun <u>altering</u> the climate of our planet.

Climatologists are confident that over the past century, the global <u>average temperature</u> has <u>increased</u> about half a degree Celsius. This warming

(10) is thought to be at least <u>partly</u> the <u>result</u> of <u>human activity</u>, such as the burning of fossil fuels in power plants and automobiles. Moreover, because populations, national economies, and the use of technology are all growing, the global average temperature

(15) is <u>expected to continue increasing</u>, by an additional 1.0 to 3.5 degrees C by the year 2100.

Such warming is just one of the many consequences that climate change can have. Nevertheless, the ways that warming might affect the

(20) planet's environment—and therefore, its life—are among the most <u>compelling issues</u> in earth science. Unfortunately, they are also among the most difficult to predict. The effects will be complex and vary considerably from place to place. <u>Of particu-</u>

(25) <u>lar interest</u> are the changes in <u>regional climate</u> and local weather and especially extreme events— record temperatures, heat waves, very heavy rainfall, or drought, for example—which could very well have staggering effects on societies, agricul-

(30) ture, and ecosystems.

Based on studies of how the earth's weather has changed over the past century as global temperatures edged upward as well as on sophisticated computer models of climate, it now seems probable (35) that warming will accompany <u>changes</u> in <u>regional weather</u>. For example, longer and more intense heat waves—a likely consequence of an increase in either the mean temperature or in the variability of daily temperatures—would <u>result</u> in public <u>health</u> (40) <u>threats</u> and even unprecedented levels of <u>mortality</u>, as well as in such costly <u>inconveniences</u> as road buckling and high cooling loads, the latter possibly leading to electrical brownouts or blackouts.

Climate change would also affect the patterns of (45) rainfall and other precipitation, with some areas getting more and others less, changing global patterns and occurrences of droughts and floods. Similarly, increased variability and extremes in precipitation can <u>exacerbate existing problems</u> in water quality (50) and sewage treatment and in erosion and urban storm-water routing, among others. Such possibilities underscore the <u>need to understand</u> the <u>consequences</u> of humankind's effect on global climate.

Researchers have <u>two main</u>—and complementary—(55) <u>methods of investigating</u> these climate changes. Detailed <u>meteorological records</u> go back

about a century, which coincides with the period during which the global average temperature increased by half a degree. By examining these measurements (60) and records, climatologists are beginning to get a picture of how and where extremes of weather and climate have occurred.

It is the <u>relation between these extremes</u> and the <u>overall temperature increase</u> that really interests scientists. (65) This is where <u>another critical research</u> tool— global ocean-atmosphere <u>climate models</u>—comes in. These high-performance computer programs simulate the important processes of the atmosphere and oceans, giving researchers insights into the <u>links</u> (70) <u>between human activities</u> and <u>major weather and climate events</u>.

The <u>combustion</u> of fossil fuels, for example, increases the concentration in the atmosphere of certain <u>greenhouse gases</u>, the fundamental agents (75) of the global warming that may be attributable to humans. These gases, which include carbon dioxide, methane, ozone, halocarbons, and nitrous oxide, let in sunlight but tend to insulate the planet against the loss of heat, <u>not unlike the glass of a</u> (80) <u>greenhouse</u>. Thus a <u>higher concentration</u> means a <u>warmer climate</u>.

Pre-read a Few Questions

Pre-reading can give you a clue about the passage and what to look for. Quickly reading a few of the questions before reading the passage may be very helpful, especially if the passage seems difficult or unfamiliar to you. *In pre-reading, read only the questions and NOT the answer choices* (which aren't included in the following examples). Notice that you should mark (underline or circle) what the question is asking. After you read the passage, you'll go on to read the questions again and each of their answer choices. The following questions give examples of ways to mark as you pre-read.

1. **Which of the following is the <u>main idea</u> of this passage?**

   Notice that *main idea* is marked. This is a main-point question and tips you off that you should be sure to read for the main point in the passage.

2. **Which of the following <u>inferences</u> is <u>NOT supported</u> by information in the passage?**

   Notice that *inferences. . . NOT supported* is marked. To answer this question, you'll need to draw information from the passage by "reading between the lines."

3. **According to the passage, which of the following terms <u>BEST describes</u> the <u>effects of global warming</u>?**

   Notice that *best describes . . . effects of global warming* is marked. You now know that the passage involves the effects of global warming.

4. **What <u>tone</u> does the <u>author</u> establish in the passage?**

   The words *author* and *tone* are marked here. You now know to pay special attention to the tone of the passage.

After pre-reading and marking the questions, you should go back and read the passage actively. The passage is reprinted here without the marking. Try marking it yourself this time before you go on to the sample questions that follow.

Read the following passage and answer questions 1 through 8.

The Coming Climate

by Thomas R. Karl,
Neville Nicholls, and Jonathan Gregory

Human beings have in recent years discovered that they may have succeeded in achieving a momentous but rather unwanted accomplishment. Because of our numbers and our technology, it now seems

(5) likely that we have begun altering the climate of our planet.

Climatologists are confident that over the past century, the global average temperature has increased about half a degree Celsius. This warming

(10) is thought to be at least partly the result of human activity, such as the burning of fossil fuels in power plants and automobiles. Moreover, because populations, national economies, and the use of technology are all growing, the global average temperature

(15) is expected to continue increasing, by an additional 1.0 to 3.5 degrees C by the year 2100.

Such warming is just one of the many consequences that climate change can have. Nevertheless, the ways that warming might affect the

(20) planet's environment—and therefore, its life—are among the most compelling issues in earth science. Unfortunately, they are also among the most difficult to predict. The effects will be complex and vary considerably from place to place. Of particu-

(25) lar interest are the changes in regional climate and local weather and especially extreme events— record temperatures, heat waves, very heavy rainfall, or drought, for example—which could very well have staggering effects on societies, agricul-

(30) ture, and ecosystems.

Based on studies of how the earth's weather has changed over the past century as global temperatures edged upward as well as on sophisticated computer models of climate, it now seems probable (35) that warming will accompany changes in regional weather. For example, longer and more intense heat waves—a likely consequence of an increase in either the mean temperature or in the variability of daily temperatures—would result in public health (40) threats and even unprecedented levels of mortality, as well as in such costly inconveniences as road buckling and high cooling loads, the latter possibly leading to electrical brownouts or blackouts.

Climate change would also affect the patterns of (45) rainfall and other precipitation, with some areas getting more and others less, changing global patterns and occurrences of droughts and floods. Similarly, increased variability and extremes in precipitation can exacerbate existing problems in water quality (50) and sewage treatment and in erosion and urban storm-water routing, among others. Such possibilities underscore the need to understand the consequences of humankind's effect on global climate.

Researchers have two main—and comple- (55) mentary—methods of investigating these climate changes. Detailed meteorological records go back

about a century, which coincides with the period during which the global average temperature increased by half a degree. By examining these measurements (60) and records, climatologists are beginning to get a picture of how and where extremes of weather and climate have occurred.

It is the relation between these extremes and the overall temperature increase that really interests sci- (65) entists. This is where another critical research tool— global ocean-atmosphere climate models—comes in. These high-performance computer programs simulate the important processes of the atmosphere and oceans, giving researchers insights into the links (70) between human activities and major weather and climate events.

The combustion of fossil fuels, for example, increases the concentration in the atmosphere of certain greenhouse gases, the fundamental agents (75) of the global warming that may be attributable to humans. These gases, which include carbon dioxide, methane, ozone, halocarbons, and nitrous oxide, let in sunlight but tend to insulate the planet against the loss of heat, not unlike the glass of a (80) greenhouse. Thus a higher concentration means a warmer climate.

Read the passage looking for its main point and structure.

As you read the passage, try to focus on "what the author is really saying" or "what point the author is trying to make." There are many ways to ask about the main point of a passage.

---

1. Which of the following is the main idea of this passage?
    A. The history of climate should be carefully explored and documented.
    B. Fossil fuels and greenhouse gases may be linked.
    C. The earth's temperatures have been rising.
    D. Human activity and global warming may result in a changing climate.

Asking for the main point, or main idea, is a very common question type. Now take a careful look at each answer choice. Choice A is too broad; also, the passage doesn't actually deal with the *history* of climate. Choices B and C, on the other hand, are too narrow and not emphasized in the passage. While it's true that all of these topics are touched upon in the passage, the main idea should cover the passage as a whole or be clearly emphasized in the passage. The best choice is Choice D.

Make sure that your answer is supported by the passage.

Every single correct answer is in the passage or can be directly inferred from the passage.

---

2. Which of the following inferences is NOT supported by information in the passage?
    A. Computer models of climate have proved superior to old meteorological records in helping climatologists pinpoint changes.
    B. Changes in climate are affected by both natural and human activities.
    C. Whatever the changes that occur in North America's climate over the next one hundred years, it is unlikely they will be accompanied by cooler average temperatures.
    D. Dramatic changes in precipitation could have negative effects, producing both droughts and floods.

This is a tricky question, since it asks you which of the answer choices is NOT supported by the passage. The author mentions two ways of researching climate changes but describes them as *complementary*, not as superior or inferior. Therefore, Choice A is not supported by the passage. You might be tempted by Choice B, but notice that lines 9–11 state that warming is thought to be at least *partly* the result of human activity, suggesting that natural forces are involved as well. Choice C is supported in lines 12–16, and Choice D in lines 44–47. The best choice is Choice A.

Make sure that the answer you select "answers the question."

Some good or true answers are not correct. Even though more than one choice may be true, you're looking for the *best* answer to the question given.

---

3. According to the passage, which of the following terms BEST describes the effects of global warming?
    A. complex
    B. disastrous
    C. predictable
    D. inconvenient

Although it's true that some effects will cause inconvenience, making Choice **D** a possible answer, the passage indicates that more far-reaching effects are probable as well. Another possible answer is Choice **B,** but according to the passage, effects will vary from place to place; *disastrous* is too strong a word and not as accurate as Choice **A** *complex* (line 23). Choice **C** can be eliminated, since the passage states that the effects can't be predicted easily (lines 22–23). The best choice is Choice **A.**

As you read, note the tone of the passage.

The words that the author uses to describe events, people, or places will help give you an understanding of what and how the author wants you to feel or think. Pay careful attention to the types of words—are they emotional, calm, positive, negative, subjective, or objective?

4. What tone does the author establish in this passage?
    A. alarmist
    B. irate
    C. concerned
    D. accusatory

Although the author does mention some possible *staggering* effects, the tone is calm and concerned, not emotional as in Choice **A.** Nor is the tone *irate*, Choice **B,** or accusatory, Choice **D;** the author presents facts about fossil fuel's role in global warming but doesn't place blame. The best choice is Choice **C.**

Take advantage of the line numbers, if there are any.

A few poems, articles, or passages may have the lines or paragraphs numbered, which, in questions that mention specific line numbers or paragraph numbers, give you the advantage of being able to quickly spot where the information is located. After you spot the location, be sure to read the line(s) before and after the lines mentioned. This nearby text can be very helpful in putting the information in the proper context and answering the question.

5. The name "greenhouse gases," first mentioned in line 74, is appropriate because these gases—
    A. are hot.
    B. are produced in controlled circumstances.
    C. filter the sun's harmful rays.
    D. prevent heat loss.

Although *greenhouse gases* are first mentioned in line 74, the answer to the question is actually found in lines 78–79. You can eliminate Choice **B;** even though it is true that a greenhouse is a controlled climate. Also, nothing in the passage suggests that these gases are hot, Choice **A,** or that they filter out harmful rays, Choice **C.** The best choice is Choice **D.**

Use the context to figure out the meaning of words, even if you're unfamiliar with them.

Some of the questions deal with "vocabulary in context," that is, with understanding the meaning of a word as it is used in the passage. Even if you don't know the meaning of the word, the passage will give you good clues. You can also read the sentence from the passage, leaving the word space blank, and plug in each choice to see which answer choice makes sense in the sentence. The phrase or sentence that includes the word is usually displayed in a box with the question.

6. What does the word *exacerbate* mean in the following sentence?

> Similarly, increased variability and extremes in precipitation can exacerbate existing problems in water quality and sewage treatment and in erosion and urban storm-water routing, among others.

    A. worsen
    B. change
    C. cause
    D. complicate

As it is used in this sentence, *exacerbate* means to aggravate or irritate (make worse). The passage describes the problems as already existing; therefore, Choice **C** could not be correct. From context, it is also clear that choices **B** and **D** are too mild; neither of them includes the concept of an existing problem (such as water quality) becoming *worse* because of variable and extreme precipitation. In this case, a common meaning is the correct answer, but remember that the common meaning of the word is not always the meaning used in the passage. The best choice is Choice **A.**

Read all the choices, since you're looking for the best answer given.

Best is a relative term; that is, determining what is best may mean choosing from degrees of good, better, or best. Although you may have more than one good choice, you're looking for the best of those given. Remember, the answer doesn't have to be perfect, just the best of those presented to you. So don't get stuck on one choice before you read the rest.

7. According to the passage, scientists are most interested in the link between global warming and extreme changes in regional climate because—

    A. such a link has never been made and cannot be easily explained.
    B. establishing the link will prove their current theories about the causes of global warming.
    C. it could help explain the effects of natural forces, such as gravitational pull, on climate.
    D. it could help pinpoint which human activities are involved in climate extremes.

It is possible that choices **A** and **B** are peripheral reasons for their interest, but not their main reason and, therefore, not the *best* answer. Choice **C** is not the best answer because scientists are more interested in the effects of human activities than those of natural forces on global warming. Notice that some of the choices here are possible, but Choice **D** is the *best* because it is clearly supported in lines 67–71. The best choice is Choice **D.**

Use an elimination strategy.

Often you can arrive at the right answer by eliminating other answers. Watch for key words in the answer choices to help you find the main point given in each choice. Notice that some incorrect choices are too general, too specific, irrelevant, or off topic or that they contradict information given in the passage.

8. If true, which of the following would call into question current theories of global warming?

    A. a dramatic increase in world precipitation
    B. a dramatic decrease in world precipitation
    C. an increase in the rate of global warming following the elimination of the use of fossil fuels
    D. below-normal temperature recordings in Canada for two years

Since experts believe that the use of fossil fuels is partly responsible, one would expect the elimination of that use to lead to a *decrease*, not an increase, in the rate of global warming. Both increases and decreases in precipitation are expected, and, therefore, choices **A** and **B** are incorrect and can be eliminated. Two years of decreased temperatures in a particular area wouldn't disprove global warming; its effects vary considerably from place to place, according to the passage; thus, Choice **D** can be eliminated. The best choice is Choice **C.**

Now that you've reviewed some general reading strategies with samples, let's take a careful look at the specific Reading Strands.

The Word Analysis Strand (Grade 10)

There are 7 questions involving word analysis that actually count toward your score on the CAHSEE. The questions will typically ask you the meaning of a particular word or phrase. These questions are spread throughout the test and can refer to reading comprehension informational passages and literary response and analysis passages. The passages and questions are not in order of difficulty.

Questions are taken from the following standards:

Standard Set 1.0—Word Analysis, Fluency, and Systematic Vocabulary Development

Standard Set 1.1—Understanding the Meanings of Words

Understand the literal and figurative meanings of words and their derivations.

Distinguish between the denotative and connotative meanings of words.

Standard Set 1.2—Demonstrating Comprehension of Materials Through Original Analysis

Read several pieces from a single author, paraphrase the ideas and connect them to other pieces of literature that deal with related topics.

Extend ideas from the text into original analysis.

Now let's take a look at some of the common question types.

Examples of Typical Word Analysis Question Types
The author uses the word *fleet* to describe the animals in order to suggest—
What does the word *eradicate* mean in this sentence from the story?
What does Rafael mean when he says, "You can lead a horse to water, but you can't make him drink"?
Which of the following is NOT a correct rewording of the following sentence?
Read this sentence from the selection. What does the phrase *across the divide* mean in the above sentence?
Read the sentence from the selection. What does the word *deplete* mean in this sentence?

Sample Passages and Questions with Strategies

Read the following selection and answer questions 1 and 2.

Zora Neale Hurston

Zora Neale Hurston (1891–1960) died unnoticed in a welfare home in Florida and was buried in an unmarked grave. Her books went out of print for thirty years. Hurston had been a leading figure in the Harlem Renaissance but fell out of favor with African-American intellectuals, who felt she played to black stereotypes. A folklorist at heart, Hurston didn't shy away from using rural black vernacular in her writing. But unlike most important African-American writers, she evaded the question of race as a major aspect of American identity. In the 1970s, Hurston's work enjoyed a renaissance, largely because of another African-American writer, Alice Walker, who reawakened interest in her work. Today, Hurston's novel *Their Eyes Were Watching God* is widely read and highly regarded.

---

1. What does the word *renaissance* mean as it is used in this sentence from the selection?

> In the 1970s, Hurston's work enjoyed a renaissance, largely because of another African-American writer, Alice Walker, who reawakened interest in her work.

A. notoriety
B. success
C. rebirth
D. republication

The historical period known as the Renaissance was a time of revival of humanistic values and a flowering of arts and literature. The term is used generally to describe a rebirth or revival, and is appropriate here. *Success* (**B**), may seem like a good choice, but knowledge of word roots makes *rebirth* correct. The best answer is **C**. (**Word Analysis**)

---

2. Read this sentence from the selection.

> A folklorist at heart, Hurston didn't shy away from using rural black vernacular in her writing.

What does the word *vernacular* mean in this sentence?

A. foreign terminology
B. everyday language
C. rhythmic language
D. colorful discriptions

The word *vernacular* usually refers to native, hometown, or everyday language of ordinary people in a particular locality. Hurston didn't shy away from using rural black everyday language in her writing. The best answer is **B**. (**Word Analysis**)

Read the following selection and answer question 3.

Charles Dickens and the French Revolution

Charles Dickens was influenced by Thomas Carlyle's *The French Revolution* when he wrote his novel *A Tale of Two Cities* in 1859. Dickens claimed to have read the historian's book "500 times," and critics have noted Carlyle's influence in the narrative technique and imagery associated with the Revolution. But unlike Carlyle, Dickens ultimately didn't see the justice in the violence of the revolutionaries, though he always sympathized with the plight of the poor. Dickens' novel, not Carlyle's history, is in large part responsible for the popular image of the French Revolution today. When *A Tale of Two Cites* was filmed in 1935, the filmmakers capitalized particularly on the scenes depicting the revolutionary mob.

---

3. Read this sentence from the selection.

> Dickens claimed to have read the historian's book "500 times," and critics have noted Carlyle's influence in the narrative technique and imagery associated with the Revolution.

What does the phrase *narrative technique* mean in this sentence?

A. methods of description
B. use of poetic devices
C. creation of a narrator
D. way of telling the story

"Narrate" means to tell, and a "narration" is a story; "narrative technique" means the way in which an author tells a story. Choice **C** may be tempting, but how a narrator is used in a novel is only part of an author's narrative technique. Choice **A** is related to the descriptive passages in a novel, not the way the story is told, and Choice **B** is not relevant. The best answer is **D**. **(Word Analysis)**

Remember: These questions are spread throughout the test and can refer to reading comprehension informational passages and literary response and analysis passages.

The Reading Comprehension Strand

There are 18 multiple-choice reading comprehension questions associated with informational text that actually count toward your score.. The passages, informational materials, and questions are not in order of difficulty and are spread throughout the exam.

You may be asked to read informational text from articles, magazines, journals, newspapers, editorials, warranties, instruction manuals, contracts, etc.

Questions are taken from the following standards:

Standard Set 2.0—Reading Comprehension (Focus on Informational Materials)

Standard Set 2.1 (Grade 8)—Consumer Documents

Focuses on obtaining information from consumer documents like warranties, contracts, brochures, and instruction manuals.

Standard Set 2.1—Workplace Documents

Analyzes the structure and format of ordinary workplace documents.

Standard Set 2.4—Several Sources/Single Issue

Combine and analyze content from several sources by a single author and about a single issue.

Standard Set 2.5—Extension

Extend the ideas read in the various primary and secondary sources through analyzing the ideas in the text, applying them to new circumstances and evaluating their usefulness.

Standard Set 2.7—Document Logic

Critique the logic and examine the sequence of information and procedures.

Standard Set 2.8—Argument Credibility

Evaluate the author's argument or defense of a claim by assessing the relationship between generalizations and evidence, the extensiveness of the evidence, and how the author uses structure and tone in the text. (Primary source materials, journals, editorials)

Now let's take a look at some of the common question types.

Examples of Typical Reading Comprehension Question Types

What is the main purpose of this passage?

What is the main purpose of the article?

The main idea of this essay is that airplanes—

Which statement BEST summarizes the author's main point?

Which of the following BEST summarizes the information given in the article?

Which statement from the passage BEST describes the narrator's reason for writing the passage?

Which of the following is suggested by the article?

Based on the article, which of these statements is true?

Based on the regulations, which of the following is allowed during the inspection?

Which of the following strategies does the writer use MOST frequently to describe the village?

This document provides the MOST information on—

This document provides the LEAST information on—

Which of the following is NOT discussed in this pamphlet?

Which of the following would make this passage easier to understand?

What information from the article supports the writer's claim?

Based on the information in the passage, which of the following is MOST likely to occur?

What evidence does the author provide to show the speed of the SKX Mach 7?

Which of the following BEST illustrates the need for safety valves?

The narrator MOST likely placed the bottle on the shelf so that he—

What tone does the author establish in the article?

The words ----, ----, and ---- in paragraph 4 suggest a feeling of—

Which of the following MOST accurately indicates the author's attitude toward hunting?

The chart at the end of the article illustrates information that is found primarily in which paragraph?

A library patron is looking for a particular work of modern fiction. Considering the way the information is cataloged, what is the BEST way for the patron to find this book?

Sample Passages and Questions with Strategies

Some Word Analysis questions have been included in this section, since they are interspersed throughout the reading section on the actual exam.

Read the following selection about Woodrow Wilson and answer questions 1 through 5.

Woodrow Wilson

Woodrow Wilson is usually ranked among the country's great presidents in spite of his failures to win Senate approval of the League of Nations. Wilson had yearned for a political career all his life; he won his first office in 1910 when he was elected governor of New Jersey. Two years later he was elected president in one of the most rapid political rises in our history. For a while Wilson had practiced law but found it both boring and unprofitable; then he became a political scientist of great renown and finally president of Princeton University. He did an outstanding job at Princeton but lost out in a battle with Dean Andrew West for control of the graduate school. When he was asked by the Democratic boss of New Jersey, Jim Smith, to run for governor, Wilson readily accepted because his position at Princeton was becoming untenable.

Until 1910 Wilson seemed to be a conservative Democrat in the Grover Cleveland tradition. He had denounced Bryan in 1896 and had voted for the National Democratic candidate who supported gold. In fact, when the Democratic machine first pushed Wilson's nomination in 1912, the young New Jersey progressives wanted no part of him. Wilson later assured them that he would champion the progressive cause, and so they decided to work for his election. It is easy to accuse Wilson of political expediency, but it is entirely possible that by 1912 he had changed his views as had countless other Americans. While governor of New Jersey, he carried out his election pledges by enacting an impressive list of reforms.

Wilson secured the Democratic nomination on the forty-sixth ballot after a fierce battle with Champ Clark of Missouri and Oscar W. Underwood of Alabama. Clark actually had a majority of votes but was unable to attract the necessary two-thirds. In the campaign, Wilson emerged as the middle-of-the-road candidate—between the conservative William H. Taft and the more radical Theodore Roosevelt. Wilson called his program the New Freedom, which he said was the restoration of free competition as it had existed before the growth of the trusts. In contrast, Theodore Roosevelt was advocating a New Nationalism, which seemed to call for massive federal intervention in the economic life of the nation. Wilson felt that the trusts should be destroyed, but he made a distinction between a trust and a legitimately successful big business. Theodore Roosevelt, on the other hand, accepted the trusts as inevitable but said that the government should regulate them by establishing a new regulatory agency. The former president also felt that a distinction should be made between the "good" trusts and the "bad" trusts.

---

1. The author's main purpose in writing this passage is to—

- **A.** argue that Wilson is one of the great U.S. presidents.
- **B.** survey the differences between Wilson, Taft, and Roosevelt.
- **C.** explain Wilson's concept of the New Freedom.
- **D.** discuss some major events of Wilson's career.

Always look for the main point in the passage. Remember that there are many ways to ask about the main point of a passage. What is the main idea? What is the best title? What is the author's purpose? Choice **A** is irrelevant to the information in the passage, and choices **B** and **C** mention secondary purposes rather than the primary one. The best choice is Choice **D**. (**Reading Comprehension**)

---

2. Which of the following is suggested by the author about the New Jersey progressives?

- **A.** They did not support Wilson after he was governor.
- **B.** They were not conservative Democrats.
- **C.** They were more interested in political expediency.
- **D.** Along with Wilson, they were supporters of Bryan in 1896.

Be aware of information not directly stated in the passage. Read between the lines. Suggested or implied information can be valuable in understanding the passage and in answering some questions. In the second paragraph, Wilson's decision to champion the progressive cause after 1912 is contrasted with his earlier career, when he seemed to be a conservative Democrat. Thus, it may be concluded that the progressives, whom Wilson finally joined, were not conservative Democrats, as was Wilson earlier in his career. Choices **A** and **D** contradict information in the paragraph, while Choice **C** is not suggested by any information given in the passage. The best choice is Choice **B**. (**Reading Comprehension**)

3. **Which of the following conclusions about the progress of Wilson's political career is supported by the passage?**

   A. Few politicians have progressed so rapidly toward the attainment of higher office.
   B. Failures late in his career caused him to be regarded as a president who regressed instead of progressed.
   C. Wilson encountered little opposition once he determined to seek the presidency.
   D. The League of Nations marked the end of Wilson's reputation as a strong leader.

Watch for information that supports an author's claim or a conclusion. This choice is explicitly supported by the third sentence in the first paragraph in which you are told that Wilson was *elected president in one of the most rapid political rises in our history*. The best choice is Choice **A**. **(Reading Comprehension)**

4. **Read this phrase from the first paragraph of the passage.**

   > . . . his position at Princeton was becoming untenable.

   The word *untenable* in the phrase above means—

   A. unlikely to last for ten years.
   B. filled with considerably less tension.
   C. difficult to maintain or continue.
   D. filled with achievements that would appeal to voters.

Learn to determine the meaning of words or phrases in context. Be alert to the positive and negative connotations of words and phrases in each passage, as well as in the questions themselves. In the case of *untenable*, the prefix *un-* suggests that the word has a negative connotation. The context in which the word occurs does as well. Wilson *left* his position at Princeton; therefore, you may conclude that the position was somehow unappealing or something else was more appealing. Only two of the answer choices, **A** and **C**, provide a negative definition. Although Choice **A** may attract your attention because *unlikely to last for ten years* looks like it might be a definition for *untenable*, it is not. The correct choice is **C**, which, in this case, is the conventional definition of *untenable*. **(Word Analysis)**

5. **According to the passage, which of the following was MOST likely true about the presidential campaign of 1912?**

   A. Woodrow Wilson won the election by an overwhelming majority.
   B. The inexperience of Theodore Roosevelt accounted for his radical position.
   C. Wilson was unable to attract two-thirds of the votes but won anyway.
   D. There were three nominated candidates for the presidency.

Eliminate choices that are not supported by the passage. Your answer choice must be supported by information either stated or implied in the passage. Choices **A, B,** and **C** contain information that is not addressed in the passage and can be eliminated as irrelevant. The discussion of Taft and Roosevelt as the candidates who finally ran against Wilson for the presidency supports choice **D**. The best choice is Choice **D**. **(Reading Comprehension)**

Read the following article and answer questions 6 and 7.

Elephants

It would seem that because of their size and huge appetites elephants would be destructive to the environment. But elephants actually use only half of the foliage they obtain from the tops of trees, leaving the rest on the ground as a food source otherwise unavailable to ground animals. By "pruning" parts of plants and trees, they also stimulate new growth. In the dry season they dig holes with their forefeet, tapping into underwater springs and providing new watering places for themselves and other animals. Inaddition, elephants' droppings provide food

for many insects, and these insects in turn become a food source for birds. Indeed, scientists classify elephants as a "keystone species" because of their significant role in ecology.

---

6. According to the passage, a "keystone species" is one that—

   A. is essential in maintaining an ecosystem.
   B. provides food for insects.
   C. distributes nutrients through dung.
   D. creates new habitats for other animals.

The passage makes it clear that elephants are essential to an ecosystem and therefore play a significant role in ecology. The "key" in "keystone" is also a good indicator or the importance of the species. Choices **B, C,** and **D** are only part of the reason scientists classify elephants as a "keystone species." The best choice is Choice **A. (Reading Comprehension)**

---

7. Based on the passage, which of the following is an accurate statement?

   A. Elephants' role in providing food for other animals makes up for their destructive size.
   B. Although elephants are an endangered species, they survive in a poor environment.
   C. Elephants show concern for other animals by leaving foliage for them to eat.
   D. Indirectly, elephants provide food for birds.

Nothing in the passage suggests that providing food "makes up for" elephants' size; in fact, there is no evidence that elephants are destructive (**A**). Also, nowhere in the passage is the elephant classified as an "endangered" species (**B**). At first glance, Choice **C** might seem possible, but although the passage does say elephants leave foliage on the ground for other animals, the leavings are a by-product of their own food gathering, not a generous donation because they are "concerned" for other animals. The best choice is Choice **D. (Reading Comprehension)**

The following excerpt from an article is about the demise of the check. Read the article and answer questions 8 through 12.

Marked for Extinction

by Kim Clark

A new law hastens the check's demise. But is that a good thing?

The check, that slip of valuable paper that is an ingrained part of American financial life, is headed toward cancellation.

(5) The rise of cheaper and faster payment alternatives such as credit cards, debit cards, and online banking started eating into the check's market share in the 1990s. And next month, a new law takes effect that will eliminate many of the check's few remaining advantages for consumers. As a result, (10) the current 4 percent a year decline in check writing is expected to accelerate. Within a generation, checks are likely to be a rarity, used only by a few stubborn oldsters or in special situations, such as giving a nephew money as a graduation gift.

(15) Many consumers and businesses say checks are so antiquated and expensive that their demise can't come soon enough. But some consumer advocates and fraud experts warn that while paper checks are vulnerable to forgers, they nevertheless provide (20) more privacy and security than many of today's electronic alternatives. "There aren't a lot of strong controls on all the doors into checking accounts," says Avivah Litan, vice president of Stamford, Conn.–based research firm Gartner. "And there are (25) a lot of doors."

Still, the fate of the check seems sealed. Americans wrote a peak of 50 billion checks a year in the mid-1990s but this year will very likely pen only about 37 billion. Meanwhile, the use of electronic (30) payment methods is skyrocketing. Credit cards are now used 23 billion times a year, according to the *Nilson Report*, which monitors the payment industry. In the 1990s, debit and check cards became popular. Debit cards, also known as ATM cards, require (35) a personal identification number, while check cards require only a signature (and sometimes not even that). Both immediately withdraw funds from your bank account. Consumers have doubled their use of debit cards in the past four years and now use them (40) nearly 19 billion times annually, the *Nilson Report* estimates.

In addition, banks and businesses eager to cut down on paper formed a cooperative in the mid-1970s called the Automated Clearing House that
(45) allows members to electronically transfer funds. That spurred a boom in all kinds of E-payments such as direct deposit, online banking, and automatic bill payment, where consumers give businesses permission to debit their checking accounts to pay monthly
(50) bills like mortgages. This year, the ACH says it will handle nearly 8 billion payments, up 40 percent from 2000.

As a result, last year, for the first time, more shoppers chose plastic over paper for payments.
(55) The reasons for the switch are clear. Electronic payments are faster, easier, and cheaper for shoppers, merchants and banks alike. Banks, for example, have to transport an estimated 101 million checks—weighing 163 tons—each day, at a cost of about 16
(60) cents apiece. Clearing an E-payment through the ACH costs banks only about 2 cents. So banks are using all kinds of carrots and sticks to herd consumers onto the electronic payments highway. Wells Fargo, for example, offers frequent-flier miles to
(65) customers who buy, say, their groceries with debit cards instead of checks. And many lenders, such as student loan giant Sallie Mae, give discounts to those who have monthly loan payments automatically debited from their checking accounts.

(70) **Digital trail**. The drive to go electronic will most likely shift into hyper-speed when the "Check Clearing for the 21st Century Act," or "Check 21," takes effect on October 28. The law, inspired by the snafus caused by the grounding of planes after 9/11, will
(75) allow banks, retailers, and others to replace paper checks they receive with electronic versions.

The potential savings thrill bankers, but Check 21 voids many of the things that check writers like. The law, for example, will allow banks, retailers,
(80) and businesses to destroy the original paper checks they receive. That will be a disappointment to the more than 45 million banking customers who currently get their checks back with their monthly statements. They will be able to get copies of the
(85) "substitute checks," as the new E-checks are called, but often only if they ask. And consumers who write a check to the dry cleaners on Wednesday hoping to take advantage of the float until payday on Friday are in for a shock: Their accounts will be
(90) debited much sooner.

The big question: How safe are the new electronic payments? Many in the banking industry insist that eliminating paper increases security.

Checks printed with a name, address, and account (95) number have long been notorious aids to identity thieves. And banks lose about $700 million to spurious checks each year. Retailers suffer even more from bad checks, says John Hall, spokesman for the American Bankers Association. Speeding up (100) clearing will cut down on scams such as check kiting, where con artists play the float of one bank against another. "Banks will be able to stop payment quicker and have a better chance of apprehending the criminal," Hall says. In addition, the (105) rate of bogus E-checks is far below that of paper checks, he says.

But some consumer and fraud experts say the very things that make checks a hassle also serve as a protection against the kind of privacy invasions (110) and scams that are becoming rampant. By turning checks into electronic images, banks could collect the kind of financial data about consumers that credit card companies have long amassed. And those files will be at least as vulnerable to hackers as credit card (115) databases have been. A computer filled with hundreds of credit card numbers at the headquarters of B.J.'s Wholesale Club in Natick, Mass., for example, was hacked earlier this year.

Perfect con. Frank Abagnale, whose life as a (120) check swindler was portrayed in the recent movie *Catch Me If You Can*, says the digitization of payments "is a forger's dream come true." For all their faults, paper checks can at least be dusted for fingerprints and provide other clues. Abagnale, who (125) now lectures on financial security, says that Check 21 and recent technological advances are making it harder to prosecute financial fraud. His payment choice? A credit card, because federal law caps its liability at $50 in unauthorized charges.

---

8. **All of the following illustrate why electronic payments are becoming so popular EXCEPT—**
   A.   banks are offering incentives to use them.
   B.   they are faster than checks.
   C.   they are cheaper than checks.
   D.   the databases that serve them cannot be penetrated by hackers.

Remember to underline the word *EXCEPT*. Choices **A, B,** and **C** are all true. But the article states that because these are electronic images, the files that contain them are as vulnerable to hackers as are credit card databases. The best answer is **D. (Reading Comprehension)**

9. **Based on the article, which of the following statements is true?**

    A. Most states provide refunds of unauthorized demand drafts.

    B. Electronic bill payments allow banks to stop payments quicker.

    C. Debit card use has decreased in recent years.

    D. Almost no one in America gets their cancelled checks back with their monthly statements.

Many states don't supply refunds for unauthorized demand drafts. Debit card use has increased, not decreased in the last four years and over 45 million people get their checks back from their bank. The best answer is **B. (Reading Comprehension)**

10. **Which of the following BEST summarizes the information contained in the article?**

    A. The popularity of the check is waning, but there are dangers in the move toward electronic banking.

    B. Forgers believe that the check users are more susceptible to fraud than are those who opt for electronic banking.

    C. The Automated Clearing House is one of the most important developments in finance in the last decade.

    D. The weight of checks alone is enough to ensure their demise.

This question is very close to the main idea type question. Choice **A** encompasses the main idea of the article most succinctly. There is reason to believe that checks offer some protection against fraud, so Choice **B** is not the answer. Choice **C** is purely speculative and is somewhat extreme at that. Choice **D** is a detail and therefore wouldn't serve well as a summary. The best answer is **A. (Reading Comprehension)**

11. **The word *pen* in the following sentence means—**

> Americans wrote a peak of 50 billion checks a year in the mid-1990s
> but this year will very likely pen only about 37 billion.

    A. to write.

    B. to erase.

    C. to imprison.

    D. to enclose.

If you plug the choices into the original sentence, the only one that really makes sense is Choice **A.** While you can erase a check, you can't really imprison or enclose it. The best answer is **A. (Word Analysis)**

12. **The article provides the LEAST information on—**

    A. why shoppers find electronic banking attractive.

    B. what incentives banks and businesses use to lure customers to switch to electronic payments.

    C. why banks are eager to change.

    D. the impact of counterfeiting on national economies.

Choices **A, B,** and **C** are all included in the article. The article doesn't talk about counterfeiting. The correct answer is **D. (Reading Comprehension)**

Read the registration information that follows and answer questions 13 through 17.

Registering Your New IQuick Computer

Registering your new IQuick computer is quick and easy.

You can register your computer by visiting us online at **www.IQuick.com**

Or by mail to: IQuick Computers, Inc.

Registration Division

3133 Reseda Blvd.

Reseda, CA 91335

IQuick Support

Once you've registered your computer, you are eligible for a wide variety of service and support options that are available around the clock. If you have a question or a problem with your IQuick computer, you should seek assistance from IQuick service and support in the following manner:

- **Use the Help and Support** features that are installed with your product. Refer to your product documentation for specific instructions and troubleshooting information.

- **Contact your local IQuick dealer's service department** open 9am to 5pm Monday through Saturday.

- **Visit the IQuick online service and support** at www.IQuick.com. IQuick online service and support is available to all IQuick customers for the life of their IQuick computer. It is always available and is your fastest source for up-to-date product information and expert assistance.

- **Contact IQuick Customer Care** by phone 24 hours a day, seven days a week in both English and Spanish at 1-800-IQuick1. When you call please have your computer's model number, serial number, and date of purchase available. Telephone support is free during your limited warranty period.

---

13. A consumer who is experiencing difficulties with her computer should FIRST—

    A.   contact the local IQuick dealer's service department.
    B.   call 1-800-IQuick1.
    C.   bring the computer back to the store from which she purchased it.
    D.   make sure the computer is registered.

All services are contingent on the computer being registered. Choice **C** is not mentioned anywhere in the instructions. The correct answer is **D. (Reading Comprehension)**

14. A consumer calling the IQuick Customer Care center by phone should have all of the following EXCEPT—

    A.   the computer's model number.
    B.   the computer's original packaging.
    C.   the computer's serial number.
    D.   the computer's date of purchase.

The packaging might presumably be useful if the item were to be shipped back but is not required for phone contact.

The other items are all listed as necessary when the Customer Care center is contacted. The correct answer is **B. (Reading Comprehension)**

15. A Spanish-speaking person would be best advised to use which of the support options at IQuick?

    A.   the service department
    B.   the online option
    C.   the Customer Care phone
    D.   the Help and Support features

The information regarding the Customer Care phone explicitly states that help is available in both English and Spanish. The others options *might* have language support for Spanish speakers, but the existence of such support is not stated in the information. The correct answer is **C. (Reading Comprehension)**

16. What is the purpose of this document?

    A.   to advertise the features of the IQuick computer
    B.   to encourage people to purchase extended warranty plans
    C.   to inform customers of the support/customer service options available
    D.   to avoid the inevitable lawsuits

The registration process enables the customer to access the company's customer service network. None of the other choices are either stated or implied. The correct answer is **C. (Reading Comprehension)**

17. The word *troubleshooting* in the sentence below means—

> Refer to your product documentation for specific instructions and troubleshooting information.

    A.   to locate and eliminate sources of difficulty.
    B.   to create a disturbance.
    C.   to end an altercation or argument.
    D.   to target and fire an artillery piece.

The word *troubleshooting* means to locate and eliminate sources of difficulty. The correct answer is **A. (Word Analysis)**

The Literary Response and Analysis Strand (Grade 10)

There are 20 multiple-choice questions involving literary response and analysis that actually count toward your score on the CAHSEE. These passages and questions are not in order of difficulty and are spread throughout the exam.

Questions are taken from the following standards:

Standard Set 3.0—Literary Response and Analysis
Standard Set 3.1—Characteristics, Traits, and Conflicts

Understand the relationship between the purposes of literature and the characteristics of different types of literature (comedy, drama, tragedy, and dramatic monologue).

Standard Set 3.3—Interactions of Main and Subordinate Characters

Analyze the interactions of characters and explain the affect on the plot. Interactions include internal and external conflicts, influences, relationships, and motivations.

Standard Set 3.4—Characters' Traits

Determine characters' traits based on the information given in the text. This information can come from the characters' narration, dialogue, dramatic monologue, and soliloquy.

Standard Set 3.5—Works with Universal Themes

Compare works' themes and provide support for the ideas expressed.

Standard Set 3.6—Time and Sequence

Analyze and trace the time sequence of a piece of literature. This includes the use of complex literary devices such as foreshadowing and flashbacks.

Standard Set 3.7—Literary Devices

Identify and understand various literary devices including figurative, allegory, imagery, and symbolism.

Standard Set 3.8—Impact in a Text

Understand and evaluate the impact of subtleties, ambiguities, contradictions, and ironies in a text.

Standard Set 3.9—Point of View

Clarify how point of view can affect the text. How does voice, persona, or choice of narrator affect the tone, plot and credibility of a text?

Standard Set 3.10—Functions of Types of Dialogue

Recognize and explain the function of types of dialogue, scene designs, and character foils in a piece of dramatic literature.

Standard Set 3.7 (Grade 8)—Biographical Approach

Analyze a piece of literature and show how it reflects the type of person the author is—attitude, heritage, beliefs, traditions.

Standard Set 3.11—Aesthetic Approach

Evaluate the impact of aesthetic style on a piece of literature. Use the terminology of literary criticism to evaluate diction, figurative language, tone, mood, and theme.

Standard Set 3.12—Historical Approach

Examine a work of literature as it relates to a historical period.

(The last three standards, involving the three different approaches, will be rotated through different exams.)

Some Specific Strategies for the Literary Response and Analysis Questions

Before you take a careful look at the samples and suggested approaches, let's review some specific test-taking strategies for the Literary Response and Analysis questions. These strategies can be very helpful.

- **Read Thoroughly.** Make sure you read the introductory lines at the top of the page, the passage, the questions, the footnotes (if there are any), and the choices in their entirety. A single word can make a difference in the answer, so do not skim or skip anything.

- **Read Carefully.** Pay attention to keywords. Words such as *best*, *most*, *main,* or *least* should make certain answers jump out at you. These words are asking you to make a judgment call. Even if another answer looks as though it could be correct, ask yourself, is that really the *best*, *most*, *main,* or *least*. Many of these words are often capitalized in the question to make them easier to spot.

- **Review Vocabulary.** The test questions assume you know the definitions of some basic literary devices. Words such as *metaphor*, *simile*, *alliteration*, *allegory*, and *foreshadowing* are used throughout the test. In Part II, the review section, a list of key literary terms and definitions is provided. The back of any literature book will also have a list of such definitions in an appendix usually titled something like, "Literary Terms."

Now let's take a look at some of the common question types.

Examples of Typical Literary Response and Analysis Question Types

What is the author's main purpose in this passage?

Which of the following is the main theme of the passage?

Which of the following BEST describes the theme of this poem?

Which of the following BEST supports the story's theme?

Which of the following BEST describes what happens in the story?

Which one of the following themes is developed in the article?

Which sentence is an example of a simile?

Which sentence from the passage is an example of figurative language?

What makes the statement above ironic?

The author conveys which of the following in the sentence above?

Which term BEST describes the narrator's tone in the passage?

Which phrase from the poem creates a tone of despair?

Which of the following BEST describes the mood of the poem?

Which of these sentences from the story BEST illustrates the spirit of Fury?

Which of the following describes the attitude change during the play?

Which phrase BEST represents the organization of the poem?

The selection is BEST described as fiction? Essay? Biography? Article?

This story is an example of which of the following genres of writing? Narrative story? Persuasive essay? Biographical essay? Informational text?

How does the reader know that the story is a dramatic monologue?

How is Lee a foil character in the drama?

Where does the drama take place?

Where does the story take place?

Which of the following best describes the setting of the play?

What is the main effect produced by repeating the word *slower*?

What does the use of flashbacks accomplish in the story?

How does Billy react to the use of slang?

Which of the following illustrates the time sequence?

Which of the following BEST describes the relationship between Tom and Phil?

Why does the narrator whistle during the ceremony?

According to lines 10–15, the man's life is—

Sample Passages and Questions with Strategies

Some Word Analysis questions have been included in this section since they are interspersed throughout the reading section on the actual exam.

Read the following story and answer questions 1 through 3.

Boy on a Dolphin

by Horace E. Dobbs

Of all the creatures in the sea dolphins have a unique place: for centuries they have been renowned for their friendliness towards man. Telemachos, the legendary son of Ulysses, was saved from drowning by a dolphin and pushed ashore. Many sculptures and ancient coins, such as the didrachma from Tarentum (331–302 BC) have depicted boys riding on dolphins. Were the stories of rescues and rides that have been passed down through the ages simply myths? Before 1974 I had some reservations about the authenticity of these tales. But now I have none, and I will tell you why.

It started, as these things so often happen with me, by events not working out as planned. I had arranged to run a short course on underwater photography at Dale Fort, on the remote tip of south west Wales. It was to incorporate a short family holiday, and we were to be joined by our Italian underwater photographer friend, Luciano. A few days before he arrived I received a message to say the photography course was cancelled due to unrelenting south westerly gales.

It was Luciano's first diving visit to Great Britain and I was resolved that he should not go back to Milan without seeing something of the wealth of underwater life that the British Isles has to offer. The question was, where could we go? A visit to Douglas the previous year had brought me into contact with the Isle of Man Branch of the British Sub-Aqua Club. Two members of the club, Mike and Maura, had met my plane on arrival and the few dives I had there were memorable both for the prolific sea life I saw and the clarity of the water. The advantage of a large island is that a lee shore can be found; thus, theoretically, it should be possible to find a diving site even in bad conditions. So I telephoned Maura Mitchell to see if a last ditch operation could be mounted to save our holiday and get Luciano wet— in the sea. She reported that conditions were far from good; nonetheless, we decided to risk making the Isle of Man the base for our mini-holiday. Maura quietly and efficiently organized accommodation for us. It was then only up to us to get there.

We arrived at Douglas after a hair-raising journey by car ferry in a force eight gale. Luciano, as he struggled to open the door against the pressure of the fierce wind, said he had never encountered such conditions before. Tongue in cheek, I told him the conditions were quite normal and would not deter us from diving. Poor Luciano was not sure whether to take my remark seriously. I told him that we British regard the Mediterranean (the only sea in which he had dived) as no more than a large warm swimming pool. I pressed the point further, telling him that his introduction to real diving—diving off the British Coast—would be a baptism by fire, as the conditions would undoubtedly deteriorate even further.

As it turned out the converse was true. It would be more accurate to describe Luciano's introduction to British diving as a baptism by cold for the water temperature on our first dive was 58 degrees F and the sea was flat and calm.

---

1. **To prove a point, the opening paragraph makes reference to—**

   A. mythology.
   B. the Bible.
   C. a short story.
   D. a novel.

Telemachos and Ulysses (which is the Latin name for Odysseus) are characters from mythology. They were made famous by the Greek poet Homer in the epic poems the *Iliad* and the *Odyssey*. If you haven't studied Greek mythology, this may be a tough question to answer and while both the *Iliad* and the *Odyssey* are long pieces of fiction, they are poems, not novels; so this could be tricky.

If all else fails, use a process of elimination. Chances are a short story will not be the right answer because authors choose their references based on their belief that most people will have heard of the reference and not many short stories are "famous"; eliminate **C**. Telemachos and Ulysses are not names from the Bible, so you can eliminate Choice **B**. That leaves you with a 50/50 shot and based on the names of the characters, Greek mythology makes the most sense. The correct answer is **A. (Literary Response and Analysis)**

---

2. **What does *prolific* mean in the sentence below taken from the passage?**

   > Two members of the club, Mike and Maura, had met my plane on arrival and the few dives I had there were memorable both for the prolific sea life I saw and the clarity of the water.

   A. fascinating
   B. ostentatious
   C. abundant
   D. eager

If you don't know what *prolific* means, try substituting in the answers for the word. For example, "fascinating sea life I saw," "ostentatious sea life I saw," "abundant sea life I saw," and "eager sea life I saw." Through process of elimination, choices **B** (if you know what *ostentatious* means) and **D** make no sense. *Fascinating* could be correct, but earlier in the paragraph, the narrator makes reference to trying to find a "wealth of underwater life"; therefore, Choice **C** makes the most sense. The correct answer is **C. (Word Analysis)**

---

3. **Read this sentence from the passage.**

> Tongue in cheek, I told him the conditions were quite normal and would not deter us from diving.

When discussing the dive with Luciano, the narrator uses the phrase *tongue in cheek* to mean—

A. seriously.
B. jokingly.
C. sarcastically.
D. calmly.

Tongue in cheek is an old saying that means you are joking about what you say. If you don't recognize the phrase, use the phrase in context by looking at the preceding and following sentences. In the preceding sentence the narrator makes reference to the "fierce winds" that make it hard to open a door. In the following sentence he says, "Poor Luciano was not sure whether to take my remark seriously," which connotes the idea that he *shouldn't* be taken seriously. He also goes on to refer to the Mediterranean as a "large warm swimming pool" which is obviously a humorous remark. The correct answer is **B. (Literary Response and Analysis)**

Read the following poem and answer questions 4 through 6.

Those Winter Sundays

by Robert Hayden

Sundays too my father got up early

and put his clothes on in the blueblack cold,

then with cracked hands that ached

from labor in the weekday weather made

(5)   banked fires blaze. No one ever thanked him.

I'd wake and hear the cold splintering, breaking.

When the rooms were warm, he'd call,

and slowly I would rise and dress,

fearing the chronic angers of that house,

(10)   speaking indifferently to him,

who had driven out the cold

and polished my good shoes as well.

What did I know, what did I know

of love's austere and lonely offices?

---

4. The term *blueblack cold* is an example of—

   A.   imagery.
   B.   simile.
   C.   personification.
   D.   alliteration.

The term *blueblack cold* makes it very clear to the reader that it is early and very cold. You should be able to eliminate Choice **B** immediately since a *simile* is where one thing is likened to another by using *like* or *as*. Choice **D** would work only if following the term *blueblack* another "b" word was used. Choice **C** cannot be correct because *blueblack* is not a human trait; therefore, you are left with imagery (a description that appeals to the five senses) as your answer. This problem is not difficult if you review basic literary terms before the test. The correct answer is **A. (Literary Response and Analysis)**

5. Read these last two lines from the poem.

> What did I know,
> what did I know of love's austere and lonely offices?

What device does the author use to express his relationship with his father?

A. allegory
B. figurative language
C. foreshadowing
D. recall

The last two lines make clear that the speaker looks back on his childhood and now understands that his father did love him. The speaker remembers that as a child he was angry and spoke indifferently to his father. As an adult, the speaker realizes that his father warmed the house before everyone else got up, shined his son's shoes, worked long hours, and did it all without a thank you. The recall of his childhood shows his understanding of his dad's love. Once again, a review of literary terms before the test will make this question an easy one. The correct answer is **D. (Literary Response and Analysis)**

6. **What is the tone of the poem?**

A. angry
B. regretful
C. happy
D. ambiguous

Based on lines such as, "No one ever thanked him," "speaking indifferently to him," and "what did I know of love's austere and lonely offices," it is clear that the speaker looks back and regrets his actions or lack of actions toward his father. Don't just focus on only one or two lines out of context. Make sure you read the whole poem twice and that you take it as a whole. For example, if you were to read only the line, "fearing the chronic angers of that house," you might think that the speaker is angry with his father. But the list of nice things the father did with no recognition shows how sorry the speaker is for his behavior. The correct answer is **B. (Literary Response and Analysis)**

Read the following selection and answer questions 7 through 9.

Eleven

by Sandra Cisneros

Sandra Cisneros is a Mexican-American who writes about her years growing up.

What they don't understand about birthdays and what they never tell you is that when you're eleven, you're also ten, and nine, and eight, and seven, and six, and five, and four, and three, and two, and one. And when you wake up on your eleventh birthday you expect to feel eleven, but you don't. You open your eyes and everything's just like yesterday, only it's today. And you don't feel eleven at all. You feel like you're still ten. And you are — underneath the year that makes you eleven.

Like some days you might say something stupid, and that's the part of you that's still ten. Or maybe some days you might need to sit on your mama's lap because you're scared, and that's the part of you that's five. And maybe one day when you're all grown up maybe you will need to cry like if you're three, and that's okay. That's what I tell Mama when she's sad and needs to cry. Maybe she's feeling three.

Because the way you grow old is kind of like an onion or like the rings inside a tree trunk or like my little wooden dolls that fit one inside the other, each year inside the next one. That's how being eleven years old is.

You don't feel eleven. Not right away. It takes a few days, weeks even, sometimes even months before you say

Eleven when they ask you. And you don't feel smart eleven, not until you're almost twelve. That's the way it is.

Only today I wish I didn't have only eleven years rattling inside me like pennies in a tin Band-Aid box. Today I wish I was one hundred and two instead of eleven because if I was one hundred and two I'd have known what to say when Mrs. Price put the red sweater on my desk. I would've known how to tell her it wasn't mine instead of just sitting there with that look on my face and nothing coming out of my mouth.

"Whose is this?" Mrs. Price says, and she holds the red sweater up in the air for all the class to see. "Whose? It's been sitting in the coatroom for a month."

"Not mine," says everybody. "Not me."

"It has to belong to somebody," Mrs. Price keeps saying, but nobody can remember. It's an ugly sweater with red plastic buttons and a collar and sleeves all stretched out like you could use it for a jump rope. It's maybe a thousand years old and even if it belonged to me I wouldn't say so.

Maybe because I'm skinny, maybe because she doesn't like me, that stupid Sylvia Saldivar says, "I think it belongs to Rachel." An ugly sweater like that, all raggedy and old, but Mrs. Price believes her. Mrs. Price takes the sweater and puts it right on my desk, but when I open my mouth nothing comes out. "That's not, I don't, you're not . . . Not mine," I finally say in a little voice that was maybe me when I was four.

"Of course it's yours," Mrs. Price says. "I remember you wearing it once." Because she's older and the teacher, she's right and I'm not.

Not mine, not mine, not mine, but Mrs. Price is already turning to page thirty-two, and math problem number four. I don't know why but all of a sudden I'm felling sick inside, like the part of me that's three wants to come out of my eyes, only I squeeze them shut tight and bite down on my teeth real hard and try to remember today I am eleven, eleven. Mama is making a cake for me for tonight, and when Papa comes home everybody will sing Happy birthday, happy birthday to you.

But when the sick feeling goes away and I open my eyes, the red sweater's still sitting there like a big red mountain. I move the red sweater to the corner of my desk with my ruler. I move my pencil and books and eraser as far from it as possible. I even move my chair a little to the right. Not mine, not mine, not mine.

In my head I'm thinking how long till lunchtime, how long till I can take the red sweater and throw it over the schoolyard fence, or leave it hanging on a parking meter, or bunch it up into a little ball and toss it in the alley. Except when math period ends Mrs. Price says loud and in front of everybody, "Now, Rachel, that's enough," because she sees I've shoved the red sweater to the tippy-tip corner of my desk and it's hanging all over the edge like a waterfall, but I don't care.

"Rachel," Mrs. Price says. She says it like she's getting mad. "You put that sweater on right now and no more nonsense."

"But it's not –"

"Now!" Mrs. Price says.

This is when I wish I wasn't eleven, because all the years inside of me — ten, nine, eight, seven, six, five, four, three, two, and one — are pushing at the back of my eyes when I put one arm through one sleeve of the sweater that smells like cottage cheese, and then the other arm through the other and stand there with my arms apart like if the sweater hurts me and it does, all itchy and full of germs that aren't even mine.

That's when everything I've been holding in since this morning, since when Mrs. Price put the sweater on my desk, finally lets go, and all of a sudden I'm crying in front of everybody. I wish I was invisible but I'm not. I'm eleven and it's my birthday today and I'm crying like I'm three in front of everybody. I put my head down on the desk and bury my face in my stupid clown-sweater arms. My face all hot and spit coming out of my mouth because I can't stop the little animal noises from coming out of me, until there aren't any more tears left in my eyes, and it's just my body shaking like when you have the hiccups, and my whole head hurts like when you drink milk too fast.

But the worst part is right before the bell rings for lunch. That stupid Phyllis Lopez, who is even dumber than Sylvia Saldivar, says she remembers the red sweater is hers! I take it off right away and give it to her, only Mrs. Price pretends like everything's okay.

Today I'm eleven. There's a cake Mama's making for tonight, and when Papa comes home from work we'll eat it. There'll be candles and presents and everybody will sing Happy birthday, happy birthday to you, Rachel, only it's too late.

I'm eleven today. I'm eleven, ten, nine, eight, seven, six, five, four, three, two, and one, but I wish I was one hundred and two. I wish I was anything but eleven, because I want today to be far away already, far away like a runaway balloon, like a tiny *o* in the sky, so tiny-tiny you have to close your eyes to see it.

---

7. How does Rachel feel about her teacher during this incident?

- **A.** She thinks her teacher is very wise.
- **B.** She thinks her teacher is funny.
- **C.** She thinks her teacher is weak.
- **D.** She thinks her teacher is mean.

Rachel says, "Because she's older and the teacher, she's right and I'm not" and "Mrs. Price pretends like everything's okay." She clearly feels betrayed by her teacher and upset that the teacher doesn't seem to see what the problem is. You could quickly eliminate choices **A** and **B** because you know she has a negative feeling. You could eliminate Choice **C** because the quotes point out that her teacher is not weak. The best answer is **D. (Literary Response and Analysis)**

---

8. What purpose does the repetition of a countdown serve?

- **A.** It heightens the excitement of the piece.
- **B.** It serves to keep readers focused on what they are reading.
- **C.** It serves to express all the years that go into making up eleven.
- **D.** It demonstrates the speaker's intelligence.

The entire passage serves as a discussion of all of the years that go into making a person a certain age. By using a countdown, the author is emphasizing the idea that turning a certain age means nothing without all of the other years behind it. The best answer is **C. (Literary Response and Analysis)**

---

9. Which statement from the passage is an example of a simile?

- **A.** "the way you grow old is kind of like an onion"
- **B.** "you might need to sit on your mama's lap"
- **C.** "Maybe because I'm skinny"
- **D.** "you don't feel smart eleven"

Keep in mind that a simile uses *like* or *as* as a comparison. The correct answer is **A. (Literary Response and Analysis)**

For more than two hundred years, adults and children alike have marveled at the picture created in the following lines by Gulliver, in *Gulliver's Travels*. Read the selection and answer questions 10 through 12.

Gulliver's Travels

By Jonathan Swift

On the fifth of November, which was the beginning of summer in those parts, the weather being very hazy, the seamen spyed a rock, within half a cable's length of the ship; but the wind was so strong, that we were driven directly upon it, and immediately split. . . . What became of my companions in the boat, as well as of those who escaped on the rock, or were left in the vessel, I cannot tell; but conclude they were all lost. For my own part, I swam as fortune directed me, and was pushed forward by wind and tide. . . . When I awaked, it was just daylight. I attempted to rise, but was not able to stir: for as I happened to lie on my back, I found my arms and legs were strongly fastened on each side to the ground; and my hair, which was long and thick, tied down in the same manner.

I likewise felt several slender ligatures across my body, from my armpits to my thighs. I could only look upwards. . . . In a little time I felt something alive moving on my left leg, which advancing gently forward over my breast, came almost up to my chin; when bending my eyes downwards as much as I could, I perceived it to be a human creature not six inches high, with a bow and arrow in his hands, and a quiver at his back. In the mean time, I felt at least forty more of the same kind . . . following the first. I was in the utmost astonishment, and roared so loud, that they all ran back in a fright; and some of them, as I was afterwards told, were hurt with the falls they got by leaping from my sides upon the ground.

---

10. **Which words from the selection suggest something about the character of the small people?**
   A. hazy and lost
   B. long and slender
   C. alive and bending
   D. fright and leaping

The six-inch-high people are said to run back "in a fright" and possibly hurt themselves by "leaping" from Gulliver's sides to the ground. Of the choices given, these are the only words that apply to the small people, and they suggest that these people are intimidated by and frightened of Gulliver, undoubtedly because of his size and the "roar" he gives out. The best answer is **D. (Literary Response and Analysis)**

11. Read the following from the selection.

> . . . I perceived it to be a human creature not six inches high, with a bow and arrow in his hands, and a quiver at his back.

In this line from the selection, the word *quiver* means—

A. a handful of ligatures.
B. a nervous reaction.
C. a holder for arrows.
D. protective padding.

While the word *quiver* commonly means a shaking or trembling—that is, a nervous reaction, as in Choice **B,** in this case it does not. Immediately before the use of the term, the sentence says "with a bow and arrow in his hands," a phrase that should lead you to Choice **C** as the correct answer. The quiver in question is a holder for arrows. You could eliminate Choice **A,** even if you don't know the meaning of the word *ligature* (something with which tying up is done, such as a rope) because the choice mentions "handful," and this quiver is "at his back." And protective padding (**D**) is not mentioned in the selection (and, in fact, it is more likely they had no padding, since they were hurt in the fall from Gulliver's sides). The best answer is **C. (Word Analysis)**

12. Gulliver's tone in this passage would be BEST suited to which of the following?

A. a travelogue
B. a persuasive essay
C. a critical review
D. a reference book

Although *Gulliver's Travels* is satiric fiction, it is written in the form of a travelogue—that is, an account of a person's travels to various places in the world. A travelogue is usually written from the personal, *I,* point of view, as is this. And as amazing as Gulliver's experiences are, the writing still seems to be a straightforward description of what happened to Gulliver after the shipwreck. Both a persuasive essay (**B**) and a critical review (**C**) would use language that attempts to bring readers to the writer's point of view on an issue, which isn't the case here. A reference book (**D**) wouldn't be written in the first person (*I*), as this piece is. If you didn't know the meaning of the word *travelogue*, you could have eliminated the other choices to get to the right answer. The best answer is **A. (Literary Response and Analysis)**

CAHSEE English-Language Arts: Writing

The Writing questions of the CAHSEE English-Language Arts are composed of Writing Strategies, Writing Conventions, and Writing Applications. The number of questions that actually count in each of these categories is as follows:

Writing Strategies	12 multiple-choice questions
Writing Conventions	15 multiple-choice questions
Writing Applications	1 essay

Remember, these question types are not in any particular order, except the essay. Of the 79 multiple-choice questions on the CAHSEE English-Language Arts, only 72 actually count toward your score. Although there may be more writing questions, 27 writing multiple-choice questions and 1 essay will count toward your score. The essay question will be the last question in Session 1.

A special note: The writing multiple-choice questions are NOT in order of difficulty.

Before you look at the following specific writing strands, keep in mind that there is no substitute for reading and writing regularly. Knowing what to look for in the writing multiple-choice questions and how to analyze a topic and follow the writing process can be invaluable.

The Writing Strategies Strand

There are 12 Writing Strategies multiple-choice questions that count toward your score on the CAHSEE English-Language Arts. These questions will ask you to find and correct errors and to choose better words and phrases. They are based on a rough draft of an essay or article.

In this section you are not required to write any essays, but you will be asked to edit essays or articles. The questions will be based on the Writing Strategies Standards.

The Writing Strategies Standards include:

<u>**Standard Set 1.0 Writing Strategies (Grades 9 and 10)**</u>

Standard Set 1.1—Coherent Thesis

Establish a coherent thesis and consistent tone and focus throughout the writing. Communicate a clear perspective on the subject.

Standard Set 1.2—Precise Language

Make use of precise language, action verbs, sensory details, and appropriate modifiers. Employ active rather than passive voice.

Standard Set 1.4—Main Ideas and Supporting Evidence

Use supporting evidence to develop the main ideas in the essay.

Standard Set 1.5—Multiple Sources

Analyze and combine information from different sources. Identify the discrepancies and different perspectives.

Standard Set 1.9—Audience, Purpose, and Context

Take into consideration the audience, purpose and formality of the writing when revising to improve the logic and coherence of the organization, the word choice, and the tone.

Some General Strategies

❏ Become familiar with some of the common question types and review the elements of an outstanding essay.

❏ The passages are early drafts of student essays. Some parts of them need to be revised.

❏ Read the selections carefully and answer the questions that follow. These questions test your ability to recognize and correct errors and revise paragraphs following the guidelines of standard written English.

❏ Review the rules of correct grammar and usage that have been emphasized in your high school English classes. There will be questions about sentence structure, diction, and usage in individual sentences or parts of sentences.

❏ Practice reviewing and working with the organization, development, and language in a paragraph or complete essay. Some questions will deal with the whole essay or paragraphs and ask you to decide about the organization, development, and appropriate language.

❏ Be prepared for one or two of the questions to ask you to combine one or two sentences.

❏ Choose the answer that follows the requirements of standard written English and most effectively expresses the intended meanings.

Now let's take a closer look at some common Writing Strategies question types.

Typical Writing Strategies Question Types
Which sentence would BEST begin the essay?
Which of the following sentences would make the MOST effective opening sentence?
Which of the following sentences does NOT fit well in the paragraph in which it is found?
To give a better description of the situation, the underlined word labeled (3) should be changed to—
In order to achieve more precise meaning, the underlined word labeled (2) should be changed to—
Which of the following words is the BEST way to express the meaning of the word *hand* in sentence 2?
What is the BEST way to write sentence 9?
What is the BEST way to combine the sentences labeled (3) and (4)?
Which of the following ideas is supported by evidence in the essay?
What is the BEST source for finding information on the topic?
Which is the MOST effective substitution for the underlined part of sentence 8?
Which of the following would be the MOST precise way to state the underlined words in the sentence labeled (5)?
Which change to the underlined clause labeled (5) would make it more consistent with the first part of the sentence?
Which phrase would BEST replace the underlined phrase labeled (4)?

Sample Questions with Strategies

Following are two examples based on two separate passages from student essays. The question types are noted in these samples to help you focus on what to look for. Strategies are included with explanations of questions.

Example 1

The following is a rough draft of an essay on writing a resume. It may contain errors in grammar, punctuation, sentence structure, vocabulary, and organization. Some of the questions may refer to underlined or numbered sentences or phrases within the text. Read the essay and answer questions 1 through 4.

Writing a Resume

(1) When you write a resume, you are really writing an advertisement for yourself. (2) This document is your chance to make a possible employer see what an asset you would be as an employee. (3) A good way to begin to write a resume is to list everything that will show you qualify for the job. (4) Make sure that when you list your bosses, you spell their names correctly.

(5) When you make a list, begin with your work history. (6) Write down the name of your bosses, the dates you worked for them, and write down what you actually did. (7) Next, cover your education, and include any diplomas or degrees that you earned. (8) Finally, write down any special skills, like an ability to use special machinery or experience with a computer. (9) If you have special accomplishments, include them, too.

(10) Don't forget to include any volunteer work you've done.

---

1. Which of the following words is the BEST substitution for the word *bosses* in paragraphs 1 and 2?

   A. higher-ups
   B. administrators
   C. employers
   D. references

In keeping with the language of the essay, *employers* is the best substitution for the less formal word *bosses*. *Higher-ups* (**A**) is even less formal; it is a slang term. *Administrators* (**B**) can mean *bosses* but it is less precise than *employers* and is too formal. Choice **D** is not a synonym for *bosses*. The best answer is **C**.

---

2. Which of the following sentences does NOT fit well in the paragraph in which it is found?

   A. Sentence 9
   B. Sentence 7
   C. Sentence 2
   D. Sentence 4

Sentence 4 (**D**) doesn't fit well in the first paragraph, which is an introduction. It is a detail and would be better following sentence 6 in paragraph 2, which specifically refers to writing down the names of employers. The other sentences (**A, B, C**) are appropriate to the paragraphs where they appear. Words like *too* (**A**) and *next* (**B**) indicate that the sentences logically follow what goes before them. *This document,* (**A**), also refers directly to *resume* in the sentence that precedes it. Look for clues like these *connection* words and phrases when deciding which sentence does or does not fit in its location. The best answer is **D**.

---

3. Which is the MOST effective substitution for the underlined part of sentence 6?

   A. and what you actually did.
   B. and then write about what you actually did.
   C. and also be sure to write down what you actually did.
   D. Leave as is.

Often, the least wordy choice will be the best answer in questions like this one, as long as it makes sense and is grammatically correct, as it is in this case. "What you actually did" is grammatically parallel to "the name of your bosses" and "the dates you worked for them"; all of them function as nouns. Therefore, you don't need to repeat "write down" (**D**). Choices **B** and **C** also include words that add nothing to the meaning. The best answer is **A**.

---

4. What is the BEST placement of sentence 10?

    A. After sentence 6 in paragraph 2

    B. After sentence 7 in paragraph 2

    C. After sentence 3 in paragraph 1

    D. Leave as is

As it is now, the sentence is simply tacked on to the end of the essay, which is poor placement. It fits much better after sentence 6, which concerns employment. Also, since the sentence is about volunteer work, it doesn't fit as well after sentence 7, which is about education (**B**). The second-best choice is **C**, but since paragraph 1 is an introduction, this detail would be better in paragraph 2. The best answer is **A**.

Example 2

The following is a rough draft of a part of an essay on folk heroes. It may contain errors in grammar, punctuation, sentence structure, vocabulary, and organization. Some of the questions may refer to underlined or numbered sentences or phrases within the text. Read the essay and answer questions 5 through 7.

Folk Heroes

(1) Paul Bunyan is a famous backwoods American hero who never really existed. (2) The giant lumberjack is well-known by most schoolchildren, and stories of him and his giant blue ox Babe are part of American folklore. (3) Many folklorists, however, call the Paul Bunyan tales "faketales" instead of "folk tales" because they didn't come from the "folk." (4) But instead they came from newspapermen, chambers of commerce, and lumber companies.

(5) Some people think that the Bunyan of legends was actually based on a French Canadian logger of the same name. (6) Pictures of the legendary Paul Bunyan are on signs of all kinds, in advertisements for different companies, and even on a United States postage stamp. (7) In the stories about him he does gigantic tasks, such as forming the Grand Canyon by dragging his pick along the ground, and building the top stories on a high-rise hotel on hinges so they could be swung back "to let the moon go by." (8) Like Bunyan, the legendary Pecos Bill is well-known too, even though he didn't really exist, and he too has his face on a postage stamp.

5. Which of the following points is supported by details in the essay?

    A. Pecos Bill is the hero of many tall tales.

    B. Paul Bunyan is known for his strength while Pecos Bill is known for his humor.

    C. Tales about Paul Bunyan are based on his superhuman size and strength.

    D. Although neither Paul Bunyan nor Pecos Bill existed, many people think they did.

Of the possible answers listed, only Choice **C** is supported by details. See the examples in sentence 7. The other choices include Pecos Bill, who is only mentioned in the paragraph, with no details included. The best choice is **C.**

6. Which of the following would probably be the BEST source of information about the Pecos Bill legends?

    A. an encyclopedia

    B. magazine articles about American cowboys

    C. a history of the American West

    D. a book about American folklore

This type of question requires that you understand what sources of information to consult. In this case, probably the best source about Pecos Bill would be **D,** a book about American folklore. Choice **A** might list Pecos Bill, but it is unlikely there would be much information about the legends in which he figures. Both choices **B** and **C** are also doubtful sources of information about a cowboy who is legendary rather than real. The best choice is **D.**

7. Which is the BEST way to combine sentences 3 and 4 in the first paragraph?

    A. Many folklorists, however, call the Paul Bunyan tales "faketales" instead of "folk tales" because they didn't come from the "folk" but from newspapermen, chambers of commerce, and lumber companies.

    B. The Paul Bunyan tales are called "faketales" instead of "folk tales" by many folklorists because they were made up by newspapermen, chambers of commerce, and lumber companies who are really not "folk."

    C. The reason that many folklorists call Paul Bunyan "faketales" instead of "folktales" is because the tales were made up by newspapermen, chambers of commerce and lumber companies, and were not made up by "folk."

    D. Many folklorists, however, call the Paul Bunyan tales "faketales" instead of "folk tales" because they didn't come from the "folk" and they got made up by newspapermen, chambers of commerce, and lumber companies.

Choice **A** is the most efficient and grammatically correct way to combine these two sentences. Choice **B** uses the passive voice rather than the active voice of the verb (*many folklorists call*...rather than *Paul Bunyan tales are called... by folklorists*) and, in addition, is unnecessarily wordy. In Choice **C,** the construction *The reason...is because* is used, which is grammatically incorrect. Choice **D** makes a less precise connection by using *and* rather than *because* to connect the two sentences. In addition, "they got made up" is an awkward, passive construction. The best answer is **A.**

The Writing Conventions Strand

There are 15 Writing Convention multiple-choice questions that count toward your score on the CAHSEE English-Language Arts. These questions will ask you to find and correct errors and to choose the best word or phrase to complete a sentence.

In this section you are not required to write any essays, but you will be asked to edit and complete sentences. The questions will focus on the grammar and mechanics of writing and will be based on the Writing Convention Standards.

The Writing Convention Standards include:

> **Standard Set 1.0 Writing and Oral Language Conventions**
>
> **Standard Set 1.1—Clauses, Phrases, and Punctuation**
>
> Identify and use clauses, phrases, and punctuation correctly. This includes: main and subordinate clauses; gerund, infinitive, and participial phrases; and commas, semicolons, colons, quotation marks, ellipses, and hyphens.
>
> **Standard Set 1.2—Sentence Construction and Usage**
>
> Understand sentence construction and proper English usage. Parallel structure, subordination, and modifier placement, are examples of sentence construction. English usage includes verb tenses, word choice, and comparatives and superlatives.
>
> **Standard Set 1.3—English Grammar, Usage, Sentence Structure, and Diction**
>
> Demonstrate a knowledge of English grammar, usage, sentence structure, and diction.

There are basically two types of question structures—sentence correction and sentence fill-ins. Standards 1.1 and 1.2 are usually covered in the sentence correction format, while Standard 1.3 is usually covered in the sentence fill-in structure.

Now, let's take a closer look at the two types of writing convention question types and directions.

Typical Writing Convention Question Types

- **Sentence correction types:** Select the most effective substitute for each underlined part of the sentence. If no substitution is necessary, choose "Leave as is."

- **Sentence fill-in types:** Choose the word or phrase that best completes the sentence.

Analysis and General Strategies: Sentence Correction Types

The following list analyzes the directions and gives you tips for best approaching a sentence-correction type of question:

- ❏ This question type presents one or two sentences, clauses, or phrases, with all or part underlined.
- ❏ The lettered choices present four possible versions of the underlined part.
- ❏ The rest of the sentence that is not underlined cannot be changed, and must be used to determine which of the four choices is the best.
- ❏ The first three choices change the underline part, while the last choice, (**D**), "Leave as is," should be selected if the original underlined part is the best.
- ❏ Sometimes the original sentence is better than the three proposed alternatives. If you find no error and you feel the original sentence is best, select Choice **D.**
- ❏ Eliminate choices that have errors in them.
- ❏ Note that the correct choice should be clear, unambiguous, and concise.

Sample Questions with Strategies

The following samples cover clauses, phrases, punctuation, sentence construction, and usage.

For questions 1 through 8, choose the answer that is the most effective substitute for each underlined part of the sentence. If no substitution is necessary, choose "Leave as is."

---

1. Bobcats in Southern California weigh from fifteen to twenty-five **pounds. Although they are smaller in desert areas.**

   A. pounds ; although they are smaller in desert areas.
   B. pounds although they are smaller in desert areas.
   C. pounds. Although smaller in desert areas.
   D. Leave as is.

Although they are smaller in desert areas is a subordinate or dependent clause. It shouldn't be separated from the main clause with either a semicolon or a period (**D** or **A**). These punctuation marks make this clause a sentence fragment. Omitting *they are,* as in Choice **C,** doesn't help; the clause is still a fragment. The best choice is **B.** No punctuation is necessary when a subordinate clause like this one follows the main clause.

---

2. Hoping against hope for **good news. We** were all waiting for the phone to ring.

   A. good news ; we
   B. good news : we
   C. good news, we
   D. Leave as is.

Hoping...for good news is a participial phrase, not a sentence. It describes *we* and should be followed by a comma (**C**), not a semicolon (**A**), a colon (**B**), or a period (**D**). Participial phrases are sentence fragments when they are punctuated as if they were sentences.

---

3. He had trained the dog to bring in the **newspaper, however,** the dog usually tore the paper to shreds first.

   A. newspaper. However,
   B. newspaper, however;
   C. newspaper however,
   D. Leave as is.

The original sentence is a run-on—that is, two sentences run together as one. When *however* is used as it is here, it introduces an independent clause that could stand alone as a sentence. That means it should follow a semicolon or period, not a comma. Choice **A** is the best answer.

---

4. The movie had everything the audience **liked, a good story**, action sequences, and plenty of suspense.

   A. liked. A good story
   B. liked; a good story
   C. liked: a good story
   D. Leave as is.

A colon (Choice **C**) is the best punctuation mark for introducing a list. After the colon, use a lower-case letter unless the items in the list are complete statements. A comma is too weak a punctuation mark here (**D**), and a period or semicolon (**A, B**) creates a fragment.

5. **"Mr. Reyes," the professor said, "are you ready to give your presentation?"**

    A. "Mr. Reyes." The professor said, "are you ready to give your presentation."

    B. "Mr. Reyes, the professor said. Are you ready to give your presentation?"

    C. "Mr. Reyes," the professor said: "Are you ready to give your presentation"?

    D. Leave as is.

Punctuation marks (the comma after *Mr. Reyes* and the question mark after *presentation*) are correctly placed within the quotation marks. *Are* shouldn't be capitalized because it is part of the sentence beginning *Mr. Reyes*.: "Mr. Reyes, are you ready to give your presentation?" *The professor said* identifies the speaker and interrupts the sentence, and therefore it is set off by commas and *the* is not capitalized. The sentence is correct as it is (**D**).

6. **The horses need exercise and feed them in the evenings.**

    A. horses need exercising and to be fed in the evenings.

    B. horses need to be exercised and to be fed in the evenings.

    C. horses need both to be exercised and feeding them in the evenings.

    D. Leave as is.

The elements (*to be exercised* and *to be fed*) are in the same form in Choice **B.** Notice that this isn't true of the other choices: *exercising and to be fed* (**A**), *to be exercised and feeding them* (**C**), and *need exercise and feed them* (**D**). When the parts of a sentence serve the same function or express similar ideas, they should match grammatically. When they don't, the error is called faulty parallelism. The best answer is Choice **B.**

7. **Traffic noise has grown sharply in our community caused mostly by heavy big rigs and faster speeds.**

    A. Traffic noise, caused mostly by heavy big rigs and faster speeds, has grown sharply in our community.

    B. Caused mostly by heavy big rigs and faster speeds, our community has seen a sharp rise in traffic noise.

    C. Growing sharply, big rigs and high speeds cause traffic noise.

    D. Leave as is.

The phrase *caused mostly by heavy big rigs and faster speeds* refers to the traffic noise, not the community. This is a case of a misplaced modifier. In the original sentence (Choice **D**) and in Choice **B** the modifier appears to refer to the community. In Choice **C**, *growing sharply* refers to big rigs and high speeds, not traffic noise. The best placement of the modifier is Choice **A.**

8. **He seen his grandparents at graduation after he hadnt seen them in five years.**

    A. seen his grandparents at graduation after he had'nt saw

    B. saw his grandparents at graduation after he had'nt seen

    C. saw his grandparents at graduation after he hadn't seen

    D. Leave as is.

There are two problems in the original sentence. First, *he seen* is ungrammatical. *Seen* must be accompanied by a helping verb, such as *have, has,* or *had.* The simple past tense (*saw*) is correct. The second problem is *hadnt seen*. The tense is right (past participle), but *hadnt* is a contraction of *had not* and requires an apostrophe in place of the missing letter (the *o* in *not*) and should be hadn't (*not hadnt*). Therefore, the correct answer is Choice **C.**

Analysis and General Strategies: Sentence Fill-in Types

The following list analyzes the directions and gives you tips for best approaching a sentence fill-in type of question:

❑ This question type asks you to select from four choices to fill in the blank space or spaces in the sentence given.

❑ The parts of the sentence that are given are correct, cannot be changed or replaced, and must be used to determine which of the four choices is the best.

❑ Eliminate choices that have errors in them. You know that an answer that contains the word *beautifulest* is incorrect, since there is no such word.

❑ Don't get stuck on any one question. If necessary, take a guess and come back to the question later.

❑ Read the word or phrase you selected into the sentence. Note that the correct choice should be clear, unambiguous, and concise.

Sample Questions with Strategies

The following samples cover grammar, usage, sentence structure, and diction.

For questions 9 through 16, choose the word or phrase that best completes the sentence.

---

9. The headwaiter led _____ to a corner table.

   A. him and I
   B. he and I
   C. he and myself
   D. him and me

Both the pronouns in this sentence should be in the objective case (Choice **D**). They are objects of the verb *led*. Sometimes people use the subjective case (Choice **B**) because it sounds more proper to them, but it's wrong. Use the subjective case when the pronoun is the subject of the verb, not the object (*He and I led...*). In Choice **C**, the pronoun *myself* is called reflexive and shouldn't be used in place of *me*. Use *myself* in sentences such as *I hurt myself* or *I myself believe him*. The best choice is **D**.

---

10. What _____ left the keys out on the counter?

    A. kinda person would have
    B. kind of person would have
    C. kind of person would of
    D. kinda person would've

There is no such word as *kinda,* and *would of* is a careless (and incorrect) version of *would have,* so you can eliminate choices **A, C,** and **D**. Both of these errors are probably the result of re-creating in writing what is heard in speech, where letters and words are sometimes slurred. The best choice is **B**.

---

11. _____ going to miss the party if you don't leave soon.

    A. Your
    B. You're
    C. You'll
    D. You

The word *Your* is possessive and you are not looking for a possessive. Eliminate Choice **A.** The best fill in is *You're,* Choice **B,** which is the contraction for *You are.* Choice **C,** *You'll* is the contraction for *you will,* which makes no sense here. Choice **D** might be used as a slang expression, but is not standard written English. The best choice is **B**.

12. Tom scored the highest on his tests and is considered the _____ in the group.

    A. smarter
    B. most smart
    C. smartest
    D. more smart

You could immediately eliminate Choice **B** (*most smart*) and Choice **D** (*more smart*) because they are grammatically incorrect. Since Tom is being compared to more than one person, he would be the smartest in the group. The best choice is **C**.

13. He wanted to ask _____ to dance.

    A. I
    B. me
    C. myself
    D. mine

The pronoun required here must be in the objective case, eliminating Choice **A**. *Me* is correct. Reading the choices into the sentence would help you eliminate most of them. The best choice is **B**.

14. We walked three blocks to the new building _____.

    A. cite
    B. sight
    C. site
    D. scenery

This question deals with diction. Although the words *cite, sight*, and *site,* sound alike, they have different meanings. You are looking for the word that means location or scene – *site,* Choice **C**. Choice **D,** *scenery*, doesn't make sense in this sentence. The best choice is **C**.

15. Unlike many exciting major league baseball _____ was slow and boring.

    A. games: this one
    B. games, this one
    C. games; this one
    D. games this one

If an introductory phrase has more than a few words, you should follow it with a comma. The best choice is **B**.

16. The teacher expected _____ students in her classroom.

    A. less
    B. least
    C. fewest
    D. fewer

The words *less* and *fewer* are often confused. Use *less* for bulk or quantity (things that can't be counted, such as *less* snow or *less* flour) and use *fewer* for individual countable items or people (*fewer* snakes, *fewer* cups of flour). The best choice is **D**.

The Writing Application Strand

You will be expected to write one essay on the CAHSEE English-Language Arts. Your essay must be written in No. 2 pencil on the designated pages of your answer booklet. Any pre-writing must be written in the test booklet or on designated scratch pages. No separate sheets of scratch paper can be used. You may print or use cursive handwriting when writing your essay. The writing prompt for the essay will appear in Session 1, following multiple-choice question 21. The essay will be taken from one of the following writing standards:

> **Standard Set 2.0 Writing Applications (Genres and Their Characteristics)**
>
> **Standard Set 2.1—Write Biographical Narratives**
>
> **Standard Set 2.2—Write Responses to Literature**
>
> **Standard Set 2.3—Write Expository Essays (including research and analytical essays)**
>
> **Standard Set 2.4—Write Persuasive Essays**
>
> **Standard Set 2.5—Write Business Letters**

Scoring the Essay or Response

Your essay, composition, or response will be scored by teachers or trained college graduates. Two readers will score your essay on a 1–4 scale (4 is the highest score). The two readers will not know each other's scores. Their scores will be averaged to arrive at your score. Your score on the writing task is "weighted" to account for 20% of the English-Language Arts scaled score. The remaining 80% of the scaled score is composed of the multiple-choice reading and writing questions.

Analyzing the Scores

Notice that two guides are given to analyze your scores—Response to a Writing Prompt and Response to Literary or Informational Text.

Guide for a Response to a Writing Prompt

Score of 4

The essay . . .

- ❏ Provides a thoughtful, well-written composition that addresses the writing task.

- ❏ Uses specific supporting details and examples.

- ❏ Demonstrates a clear focus and tone.

- ❏ Shows coherent, logical, purposeful organization.

- ❏ Clearly addresses the intended audience.

- ❏ Uses precise, descriptive language.

- ❏ Uses a variety of sentence types.

- ❏ Contains almost no errors in grammar, punctuation, spelling, capitalization, and usage.

A persuasive essay also . . .

- ❏ Clearly states a position and makes a case for that position.

- ❏ Defends the position with specific relevant evidence.

- ❏ Addresses the reader's potential misunderstandings, biases, and expectations.

Score of 3

The essay . . .

- ❏ Provides a composition that addresses the writing task.
- ❏ Uses supporting details and examples.
- ❏ Demonstrates a clear focus and tone.
- ❏ Shows coherent, logical organization.
- ❏ Addresses the intended audience.
- ❏ Uses some descriptive language.
- ❏ Uses a variety of sentence types.
- ❏ Contains some errors in grammar, punctuation, spelling, capitalization, and usage. (These errors do not interfere with the reading and understanding of the essay.)

A persuasive essay also . . .

- ❏ States a position and makes a case for that position.
- ❏ Generally defends the position with specific relevant evidence.
- ❏ Addresses the reader's potential misunderstandings, biases, and expectations.

Score of 2

The essay . . .

- ❏ Provides a composition that is related to the writing task.
- ❏ Uses limited supporting details and examples.
- ❏ Demonstrates an inconsistent focus and tone.
- ❏ Shows little organization.
- ❏ Occasionally addresses the intended audience.
- ❏ Uses simple, predictable language.
- ❏ Uses similar types of sentences (unvaried).
- ❏ Contains several errors in grammar, punctuation, spelling, capitalization, and usage. (These errors may interfere with the reading and understanding of the essay.)

A persuasive essay also . . .

- ❏ Defends a position with little relevant evidence.
- ❏ May address the reader's potential misunderstandings, biases, and expectations.

Score of 1

The essay . . .

- ❏ May provide a weak composition that is related to the writing task.
- ❏ Fails to use supporting details or examples.
- ❏ Demonstrates a lack of focus and tone.
- ❏ Shows no organization.

❑ Rarely addresses the intended audience.

❑ Uses a limited vocabulary.

❑ Provides no sentence variety.

❑ Contains serious errors in grammar, punctuation, spelling, capitalization, and usage. (These errors interfere with the reading and understanding of the essay.)

A persuasive essay also . . .

❑ Fails to defend a position with evidence.

❑ Fails to address the reader's potential misunderstandings, biases, and expectations.

Non-Scorable (NS) Essays

Essays that are written in another language, are off-topic, illegible, incomprehensible, or do not relate to the writing task will be considered non-scorable and will show the code "NS".

Guide for a Response to a Literary or Informational Text

Score of 4

The response . . .

❑ Demonstrates a carefully thought out, comprehensive understanding of the text.

❑ Supports the thesis with accurate and coherent specific textual details and examples.

❑ Shows a clear understanding of any other meanings or complexities within the text.

❑ Uses precise, descriptive language.

❑ Uses a variety of sentence types.

❑ Contains almost no errors in grammar, punctuation, spelling, capitalization, and usage.

A literary text also . . .

❑ Clearly demonstrates a knowledge and understanding of the author's style and use of literary devices.

An informational text also . . .

❑ Carefully addresses the reader's potential misunderstandings, biases, and expectations.

Score of 3

The response . . .

❑ Demonstrates a comprehensive understanding of the text.

❑ Supports the thesis with accurate and coherent general textual details and examples.

❑ Shows a general understanding of any other meanings or complexities within the text.

❑ Uses some descriptive language.

❑ Uses a variety of sentence types.

❑ Contains some errors in grammar, punctuation, spelling, capitalization, and usage. (These errors do not interfere with the reading and understanding of the response.)

A literary text also . . .

❑ Demonstrates a knowledge and understanding of the author's style and use of literary devices.

An informational text also . . .

❑ Addresses the reader's potential misunderstandings, biases, and expectations.

Score of 2

The response . . .

❑ Demonstrates a limited understanding of the text.

❑ Supports the thesis with few general textual details or examples.

❑ Shows a very limited understanding of any other meanings or complexities within the text.

❑ Uses simple, predictable language.

❑ Uses similar types of sentences (unvaried).

❑ Contains several errors in grammar, punctuation, spelling, capitalization, and usage. (These errors may interfere with the reading and understanding of the response.)

A literary text also . . .

❑ May demonstrate a knowledge and understanding of the author's style and use of literary devices.

An informational text also . . .

❑ May address the reader's potential misunderstandings, biases, and expectations.

Score of 1

The response . . .

❑ Demonstrates a minimal understanding of the text.

❑ Fails to use textual details or examples for support.

❑ Shows no understanding of any other meanings or complexities within the text.

❑ Uses a limited vocabulary.

❑ Provides no sentence variety.

❑ Contains serious errors in grammar, punctuation, spelling, capitalization, and usage. (These errors interfere with the reading and understanding of the response.)

A literary text also . . .

❑ Does not demonstrate a knowledge and understanding of the author's style and use of literary devices.

An informational text also . . .

❑ Does not address the reader's potential misunderstandings, biases, and expectations.

Non-Scorable (NS) Responses

Responses that are written in another language, are off-topic, illegible, incomprehensible, or do not relate to the writing task will be considered non-scorable and will show the code "NS".

There are a number of ways to approach writing an in-class type essay. If you've been practicing for this part of the exam in your English class, and you and your teacher are satisfied with the way you handle these types of essays, you can skim this section focusing on the types of writing tasks and continue to write your essays your way. If you aren't confident with your technique or wish to review the process with a few successful techniques, then read this section carefully.

Reviewing the Writing Process

For any writing task, you should envision three steps leading to the finished product:

1. **Preparing to write (Pre-writing)**
2. **Writing**
3. **Proofreading (Editing)**

A Biographical Narrative Topic

Let's use a biographical narrative topic to help us follow the process. The biographical narrative is an essay about a real person who is important to you.

Writing Task:

Students can look back on their years in school and pinpoint one particular course or one particular teacher most instrumental in shaping their lives.

Write a composition reflecting on your own school years and focusing on one such instructor or course. Describe the conditions or qualities that made that particular experience or teacher special. Use specific details or examples.

Checklist for Your Writing

The following checklist will help you. Always make sure that you:

❑ Read the task or tasks carefully.
❑ Organize your writing by including a strong introduction, body, and conclusion.
❑ Always support your ideas with specific details and examples.
❑ Write to your audience by using appropriate words.
❑ Use words that are appropriate for your purpose.
❑ Make your writing interesting to read by varying your sentences.
❑ Check carefully for mistakes in grammar, usage, spelling, punctuation, capitalization, and sentence structure.

Preparing to Write (Pre-writing)

Read the topic and the assignment carefully. Circle or underline key words to help you focus on the assigned task. Reread the assignment. If there are several tasks given, number them and write them down. Let the nature of the assignment determine the structure of your essay.

Recalling, inventing, and organizing information on short notice, given only a few minutes, can be difficult unless you are ready with an effective technique. Take time to organize your thoughts on paper before writing. The three basic techniques are brainstorming, clustering, and outlining.

Brainstorming

The process of creating and accumulating ideas and examples is called "brainstorming." Brainstorming is simply jotting down in the scratch area provided as many thoughts, ideas, and possibilities as you can remember, invent, or otherwise bring to mind to address the topic. Neatness, order, and spelling do not matter at this point.

Writing Simple Notes
Mr. Tyson
Great teacher
Positive
Fair
Organized
Encouraging
Sensitive
Good person

or

Making a Simple Chart	
Person/Class	*Characteristics*
Mr. Tyson	great teacher
word processing	organized
teacher	fair
	encouraging
	sensitive
	positive
	good person

After generating as many ideas or examples as you can within a few minutes, assess and organize your notes. Remember that development relies on specific examples: Decide which examples best enable you to support your points. Eliminate (cross out) those you don't wish to use, and number those you'll want to address in your response. Add any notes regarding more specific details or new thoughts that come to mind. However, don't worry about developing everything completely, because only you use these planning notes. Your time will be better spent developing these points in your writing and not in your notes.

Clustering

Another technique well suited to the timed essay is called *clustering*. Use clustering as a way of organizing your thoughts before you write. Clustering provides a way to put all of your thoughts down on paper before you write so that you can quickly see the structure of the whole paper.

After you choose a topic, write it down in the prewriting area (given under the actual topic question) and draw a circle around that topic:

For a few moments, think of all the elements you might use and connect them to the central topic cluster:

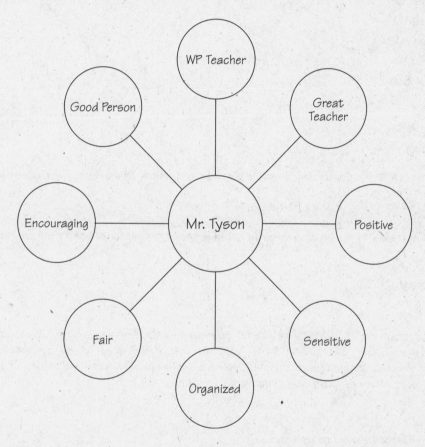

You can then number the parts of the cluster to give an order to your thoughts. You don't have to use all the elements of your cluster.

<u>Outlining</u>

The last technique given here is the well-known outlining. Keeping your outline simple will make it easier to use. The basic structure of this outline is **Introduction, Discussion, Conclusion.** Using this structure will help you build an organized essay.

Introduction

    Mr. Tyson—great teacher

    Organized, positive, sensitive, fair, encouraging

Body or Discussion

    First day

        Organized

        Great teacher

    A few weeks in

        Positive

        Sensitive

    End of semester

        Fair

        Consistent

Conclusion

    Encouraging

    Good person

Again, notice that this outline is informal, but the basic parts, **Introduction, Discussion,** and **Conclusion,** help you focus and organize your response.

> Remember, spend at least 4 or 5 minutes pre-writing and organizing your ideas before you start writing.

Writing the Essay

Opening Paragraph

A strong opening paragraph is essential for a well-developed response. One easy-to-master, yet extremely effective, type of introduction is a GENERALIZE-FOCUS-SURVEY structure. In this three- to four-sentence paragraph, the first sentence *generalizes* about the given topic, the second sentence *focuses* on what you have chosen to discuss, and the last one or two sentences *survey the particulars* you intend to present.

Remember:

- **Generalize**—address the question or topic
- **Focus**—state your position
- **Survey**—mention the points you will discuss (in order)

An effective first paragraph tells your reader what to expect in the body of the response. The GENERALIZE-FOCUS-SURVEY paragraph points toward the specifics you will discuss and suggests the order in which you will discuss them.

Body or Discussion

Writing the body of the response involves presenting specific details and examples that relate to the aspects you introduced in the first paragraph. The body may consist of one long paragraph or several short paragraphs. If you choose to break your discussion into several paragraphs, make sure that each paragraph consists of at least three sentences. Very short paragraphs may make your response appear insubstantial and scattered.

Be realistic about how much you can write. Although the readers want you to support your points adequately, they understand that you must write concisely to finish in time. Providing at least one substantial example, or "for instance," is important for each aspect you discuss in the body of your response.

<u>Conclusion</u>

As you prepare to write the conclusion, you should pay special attention to time. Having a formal conclusion to your response is unnecessary, but a conclusion should function to (1) complete your response to the question, (2) add information that you failed to introduce earlier, or (3) point toward the future.

Proofreading

Always allow a few minutes to proofread your essay for errors in grammar, usage, and spelling. If you detect an error, either erase it cleanly or simply line it out carefully and insert the correction neatly. Keep in mind, both while you are writing and while you are correcting, that your handwriting should be legible. Even though readers are instructed to ignore the quality of handwriting, if the paper is too difficult to read, they may get a negative impression of the essay.

A Specific Approach: The Story Formula

One good way to approach a question that asks you to describe one experience is through the use of the *story formula*. The story formula consists of

- **Setting:** The location of the story
- **Main characters:** The people in the story
- **Plot:** The problem in the story, the crisis or situation to be overcome
- **Climax:** The turning point in the story, when things changed
- **Resolution:** The ending or how you are now as a result of the experience

So, although the number of paragraphs may vary, generally this essay is structured as follows:

- **Paragraph 1:** Introduces the setting and the main characters in the story
- **Paragraph 2:** Introduces the plot
- **Paragraph 3:** Introduces the climax
- **Final paragraph:** Introduces the resolution

The story formula allows you to describe one experience in detail, using clear transitions, while keeping a unifying theme throughout your essay.

Another Specific Approach: The "Why Essay"

One good way to approach a question that asks you to describe, explain, analyze, or evaluate is to use a "why essay" format. A "why essay" is built around a thesis sentence. The thesis sentence begins with your opinion, followed by the word "because," and a list of the most important reasons "why" the opinion is valid, reasonable, or well-founded.

For example, using the previous topic, a thesis statement could be:

Mr. Tyson was an outstanding teacher because he was organized, positive, sensitive, fair, and encouraging.

The thesis statement would come at the end of the introductory paragraph followed by paragraphs that explain each supporting point. The paper ends with a summary of the reasons and a restatement of the thesis sentence. Each paragraph should contain approximately three to five sentences.

The introduction invites the reader to read on. The following reasons (three are usually sufficient) should give supporting examples or evidence. Your concluding paragraph can summarize your reasons, complete your response to the question, add information that you failed to introduce earlier, or point toward the future. You may wish to tie in a restatement of your thesis sentence.

The "why essay" format looks like the following table in outline form:

"Why Essay" Format		
Paragraph Number	*Why Essay Format*	*Examples by Paragraph*
1	Introduction—Thesis Sentence	Paragraph 1
2	Reason 1	Paragraph 2
3	Reason 2	Paragraph 3
4	Reason 3	Paragraph 4
5	Conclusion	Paragraph 5

Types of Writing Tasks with Examples

The Biographical Narrative

Your writing task could be a *biographical narrative*. The biographical narrative asks you to write about a person who is important to you. The biographical narrative writing task requires you to:

- Explain why this person is important to you.
- Use specific details to describe this person and his or her characteristics.
- Relate a sequence of events in specific places.
- Decide how much time you wish to use on each part of the essay.
- Make sure that the reader can "visualize" this person.

Make sure that your response:

- Clearly states who this person is.
- Gives the *reasons* you selected this particular person.
- Addresses all parts of the writing task.
- Is well organized with smooth transitions.
- Provides specific supporting examples or details.
- Uses language correctly (grammar, usage, punctuation).
- Has an introduction, discussion, and conclusion.

Let's take a look at the complete directions, a sample topic, and a completed biographical narrative essay with comments.

Sample Biographical Narrative Essay Topic

Directions

Write your essay on the pages provided in your answer document. You may only use a No. 2 pencil. Do not use pen. You may use the blank space in your test booklet to make notes before you begin writing. Any notes you make in the test booklet will NOT be considered when your essay is scored.

Remember

- Be sure to write your response to the writing prompt given below.
- You may place a title on your essay if you would like, but it is not necessary.
- No dictionary may be used. If you have trouble spelling a word, sound the word out and do the best you can.
- You may write in cursive or print.
- Write clearly! Any changes, erasures, or strike-throughs should be made as neatly as possible.

Writing Task:

Students can look back on their years in school and pinpoint one particular course or one particular teacher most instrumental in shaping their lives.

Write a composition reflecting on your own school years and focusing on one such instructor or course. Describe the conditions or qualities that made that particular experience or teacher special. Use specific details or examples.

Checklist for Your Writing

The following checklist will help you. Always make sure that you:

- ❑ Read the task or tasks carefully.
- ❑ Organize your writing by including a strong introduction, body, and conclusion.
- ❑ Always support your ideas with specific details and examples.
- ❑ Write to your audience by using appropriate words.
- ❑ Use words that are appropriate for your purpose.
- ❑ Make your writing interesting to read by varying your sentences.
- ❑ Check carefully for mistakes in grammar, usage, spelling, punctuation, capitalization, and sentence structure.

Sample Essay

Intro points toward body and discussion points

There were many teachers that were helpful to me in my first year in high school, but if I have to select one that was most instrumental in my development, it would be my word processing teacher, Mr. Tyson. Mr. Tyson was not only an outstanding, organized teacher, but he was also positive, sensitive, fair and encouraging.

Clear introduction addresses topic

Specific examples

When I entered Mr. Tyson's class as a freshman on the first day of school, it was obvious that he was organized. Each of the students had name cards by their computers and the assignment for the week was on the blackboard. He introduced himself, the course requirements and the classroom rules. He discussed extra help sessions, extra credit projects, and his method of teaching. I had a sense that he was an outstanding teacher and that I was going to learn a lot.

Well organized

Specific examples

A few weeks into the semester I could see that I was learning quickly. His approach was tremendously positive. Mr. Tyson would often say, "Feel good about what you do well and work hard on improving your weak areas." When I hit a rough spot or plateau in my typing speed later in the semester, he was immediately sensitive to the problem and gave me specific practice techniques to improve my speed.

Logically arranged
First day
A few weeks into the semester
As first semester comes to a close

Specific examples

As the first semester came to a close, many of us in the class were concerned about how a typing class would be graded. Would the teacher grade on speed, accuracy, or both? Mr. Tyson had laid out his grading system in the first week, but I've had many teachers that just didn't stick with their system. Some teachers seem to bend the rules for their favorite students and not for others. The system Mr. Tyson laid out at the beginning of the year seemed fair and he was consistent. He gave credit just as he said he would, for speed, accuracy, completion of assignments, and extra credit projects. His rules were the same for everyone, he played no favorites and his grades were fair. As he once said, "teachers don't give grades, students earn them."

A few minor errors

Good use of quotes

Nice ending ties essay together

Mr. Tyson was not only a great teacher, but also a good person. He encouraged all of us to work hard in all of our classes. He let us know that he was available to discuss problems we might be having in any of our classes. Mr. Tyson taught me a lot more than just how to type.

Now write your own essay on the biographical narrative writing task given above. Have an English teacher, tutor, or someone else with good writing skills read and evaluate your essay using the checklist below.

Checklist for Response to Writing Prompt

Does your essay . . .

- ❏ Provide a thoughtful, well-written composition that addresses the writing task?
- ❏ Use specific supporting details and examples?
- ❏ Demonstrate a clear focus and tone?
- ❏ Show coherent, logical organization?
- ❏ Clearly address the intended audience?
- ❏ Use precise, descriptive language?
- ❏ Use a variety of sentence types?
- ❏ Contain almost no errors in grammar, punctuation, spelling, capitalization, and usage?

The Persuasive Essay

Your writing task could be a *persuasive essay*. The persuasive essay asks you to defend a position or issue. The issue you will be given is something about which people disagree and you will need to take a stand—agree or disagree. The persuasive writing task requires you to:

- Structure your ideas and arguments logically.
- Support your argument through reasoning or appealing to emotions.
- Relate a personal experience or someone else's experience.
- Clarify your positions using facts, expert opinions, studies and logical reasoning.
- Address the reader's concerns, arguments, biases, counterclaims, and expectations.
- Use technical and subject-specific terms accurately.

Make sure that your response:

- Clearly states your position or opinion in the first paragraph.
- Places your most powerful arguments first and last.
- Addresses all parts of the writing task.
- Is well organized with smooth transitions.
- Gives the *reasons* you selected your position.
- Provides specific supporting examples or details.
- Uses language correctly (grammar, usage, punctuation).
- Has an introduction, discussion, and conclusion.

Remember to follow the writing process

1. **Preparing to write (Pre-writing)**
2. **Writing**
3. **Proofreading (Editing)**

Sample Persuasive Essay Topic

Now let's take a close look at the process using a persuasive essay.

Writing Task:

> Some parents encourage their high school students to get an after-school or weekend job. Other parents cite the importance of getting good grades to discourage their high school students from getting an after-school or weekend job.
>
> Which parents do you agree with? Using an example or examples from your reading, personal experiences or observations, write an essay to support your position.

Preparing to Write (Pre-writing)

Remember to read the topic and the assignment carefully. Circle or underline key words to help you focus on the assigned task. Reread the assignment. If there are several tasks given, number them and write them down.

You should use only one of the four prewriting techniques that follow. See which one you are most comfortable with.

Brainstorming

Simply jot down in the scratch area provided as many thoughts, ideas, and possibilities as you can remember, invent, or otherwise bring to mind to address the topic. Neatness, order, and spelling do not matter at this point.

Writing Simple Notes

Learn skills

Time management

Enhance education

Develop good work ethic

Valuable experience

or

Making a Simple Chart

List the reasons you support your position.

Advantages	Disadvantages
Learn skills	takes time away
Time management	distracting
Enhance education	
Develop good work ethic	
Valuable experience	

Clustering

For a few moments, think of all the elements of that side of the issue and connect them to the central topic cluster:

You can then number the parts of the cluster to give an order to your thoughts. You don't have to use all the elements of your cluster.

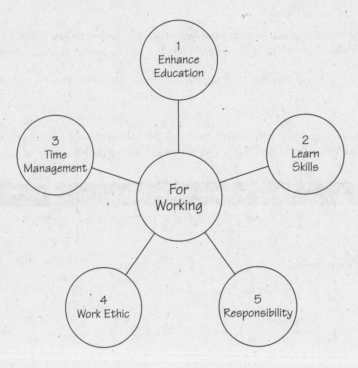

Outlining

Introduction

Working Benefits

Learn skills

Enhance education

Discussion or Body

Learning skills—time management

Enhance education—develop good work ethic

Conclusion or Summary

Working depends on student

Students can gain a lot

Notice that this outline is informal, but the basic parts, **Introduction, Discussion,** and **Conclusion,** help you focus and organize your response.

> **Remember, spend about 4 or 5 minutes pre-writing and organizing your ideas before you start writing.**

Now let's take a look at a persuasive essay writing task and a response.

Writing Task:

Some parents encourage their high school students to get an after-school or weekend job. Other parents cite the importance of getting good grades to discourage their high school students from getting an after-school or weekend job.

Which parents do you agree with? Using an example or examples from your reading, personal experiences or observations, write an essay to support your position.

Sample Essay

This is a good first paragraph. It clearly states the writer's position, and by suggesting that work can develop nonacademic skills, it prepares for the arguments of the next three paragraphs.

Note how the repetition of the word "skills" links the second paragraph with the first.

Paragraph three moves on to another advantage (development of a work ethic). The second sentence explains fully what the writer understands a "work ethic" to be.

The last paragraph is the weakest paragraph of this essay. The writer has argued forcefully in favor of after-school work. There is no reason to weaken the argument with the trite suggestion that it will depend on the individual. What doesn't? In an argument essay like this, it is not necessary (and is usually a waste of time) to pay lip service to the opposing point of view.

There is a great deal of controversy among parents as to whether or not their children should hold a paying job while in high school. Some parents believe that working while in school is a valuable experience; others believe that the importance of good grades **superceeds** any value that a job might offer. **I think that working while in school can be very beneficial to students and provide them with skills that might enhance their "formal" education.**

One of the **skills** is time management. Learning how to balance your activities and obligations is essential as an adult. It is invaluable to know what you can handle and when you are taking on too much. **When I got a job in high school, I began to realize the importance of using my time wisely since I had less of it to throw around.** I think that I gained a lot from having to make those decisions as well as earning my own money.

Another benefit is that students can **develop a work ethic** which can be applied to their academic schooling or any task that they choose to take on. **Understanding the importance of working hard, doing a good job and being responsible are skills that are assets to any endeavor.** Students often develop **confidence** from being counted on to get something done and then rising to that challenge. **Additionally, learning to take pride in your work is really important.** When you care about something your performance often reflects that. Academic success largely depends upon this same kind of pride and confidence.

Ultimately, I believe that whether a child should work while in school **depends on the child.** Some children feel that they can't handle the responsibility while others are willing to try. I think **that students stand to gain a lot from working,** but should be able to **make that choice for themselves** in the end.

A well-chosen word, but misspelled. It should be "supersede."

The writer supports her argument (that part-time work develops the ability to manage time efficiently) by referring to personal experience.

The move to a second point in this paragraph (increased confidence) would be clearer with the addition of a transitional word or phrase (such as "Further" or "Also") to begin the sentence. But, the writer rightly does include a transitional word ("Additionally") at the beginning of the next sentence.

Aside from the last paragraph, this is a very good essay, well-organized, well-supported, and specific. Its word choice, syntax, and mechanics are all competent.

Now write your own essay on the persuasive writing task given above. Have an English teacher, tutor, or someone else with good writing skills read and evaluate your essay using the checklist below.

Checklist for Response to Writing Prompt

Does your essay . . .

- ❏ Provide a thoughtful, well-written composition that addresses the writing task?
- ❏ Use specific supporting details and examples?
- ❏ Demonstrate a clear focus and tone?
- ❏ Show coherent, logical organization?
- ❏ Clearly address the intended audience?
- ❏ Use precise, descriptive language?
- ❏ Use a variety of sentence types?
- ❏ Contain almost no errors in grammar, punctuation, spelling, capitalization, and usage?

(If a persuasive essay include:)

- ❏ Clearly state a position and make a case for that position?
- ❏ Defend the position with specific relevant evidence?
- ❏ Address the reader's potential misunderstandings, biases, and expectations?

The Expository Essay

Your writing task could be an expository essay. The expository essay asks you to explain, give information, or clarify an idea. The expository essay topic usually asks you to write about real people, events, things, and places. The expository writing task may require you to:

- Put together evidence to support your subject.
- Use primary and secondary sources accurately.
- Make distinctions between the information and the importance of facts, data, and ideas.
- Address the reader's potential misunderstandings, biases, and expectations.
- Use technical and subject-specific terms accurately.

Make sure that your response:

- Has a strong beginning.
- Addresses all parts of the writing task.
- Is well organized with smooth transitions.
- Provides specific supporting examples or details.
- Uses language correctly (grammar, usage, punctuation).

Remember to follow the writing process

1. **Preparing to write (Pre-writing)**
2. **Writing**
3. **Proofreading (Editing)**

A Sample Expository Essay Topic

Let's take a look at an expository writing task and a sample response.

Remember

- Be sure to write your response to the writing prompt given below.
- You may place a title on your essay if you would like, but it is not necessary.
- No dictionary may be used. If you have trouble spelling a word, sound the word out and do the best you can.
- You may write in cursive or print.
- Write clearly! Any changes, erasures, or strike-throughs should be made as neatly as possible.

Writing Task:

Think about a major historical event that occurred within the past 15 years. Why was this event important? What effect did it have on the people involved?

Write an essay in which you discuss this historical event. Explain why this event was and is important. Use details and examples to support the importance of the event you have selected.

Checklist for Your Writing

The following checklist will help you. Always make sure that you:

- ❏ Read the task or tasks carefully.
- ❏ Organize your writing by including a strong introduction, body, and conclusion.
- ❏ Always support your ideas with specific details and examples.
- ❏ Write to your audience by using appropriate words.
- ❏ Use words that are appropriate for your purpose.
- ❏ Make your writing interesting to read by varying your sentences.
- ❏ Check carefully for mistakes in grammar, usage, spelling, punctuation, capitalization, and sentence structure.

Sample Essay

First half of sentence is too obvious to be effective.	There are many major historical events that have occured recently, but the one that I can relate to the most is the tragedy of the 9/11 attacks on the United States. This terrible event affected many families, made us realize terror could strike here, and changed our daily lives.	A spelling error or two will not greatly affect your score, but do all you can to avoid or correct them.
Good, specific points in this paragraph.	When the two planes struck the twin towers in New York and the one plane struck the Pentagon on September 11, over 3000 people were killed. The video replays of the planes crashing into the twin towers and then watching them collapse was terrifying. Of the 3000 people killed, many had husbands, wives, and children. There families will never be the same.	Awkward sentence with grammar problems. Be sure to proofread and correct your grammar when necessary.
Directly addresses the importance of the event, although the discussion would be stronger with more detail about this point.	The 9/11 attacks were the first major foreign terrorist attacks on U.S. soil. The freedom that we have actually opened the doors to these terrorists who received flight training in the United States. Our country will never be the same now that we know that terror could strike here at any time.	Good transition to next paragraph, which deals with how the event affected everyone.
Excellent detail about the effects of the event on all in the country, not only those directly involved.	Our daily lives have also changed. We are more cautious of strangers. The TV continually informs us of the terror alert level. And security at airports has increased tremendously forcing us to stand in long lines and arrive at the airport hours early. We watch and hear about the extra precautions at major events like the Super Bowl or the Emmys and hope nothing happens.	
	There is no question that 9/11 attacks were a terrible tragedy that affected all of us in many ways, but these attacks did bring out the strength of character of Americans. Many newspaper articles and tv programs focused on the courage of so many people. Seeing the pictures of this tragic event, the aftermath, and the many scenes of people helping other people will make this recent historic event something that I will never forget.	Adequate closing, which could be strengthened by tightening the sentence. For example: "I will never forget the compelling scenes of this tragic event, its aftermath, and the many people helping one another.

Now write your own essay on the expository essay writing task given above. Have an English teacher, tutor, or someone else with good writing skills read and evaluate your essay using the checklist below.

Checklist for Response to Writing Prompt

Does your essay . . .

- ❑ Provide a thoughtful, well-written composition that addresses the writing task?
- ❑ Use specific supporting details and examples?
- ❑ Demonstrate a clear focus and tone?
- ❑ Show coherent, logical organization?
- ❑ Clearly address the intended audience?
- ❑ Use precise, descriptive language?
- ❑ Use a variety of sentence types?
- ❑ Contain almost no errors in grammar, punctuation, spelling, capitalization, and usage?

The Response to Literature

Your writing task could be a response to literature. The response to literature requires you to read a short literary or possibly informational work and write an essay that responds to tasks given. The tasks may require you to:

- Demonstrate an understanding of the main ideas of the work
- Refer back to the text to support viewpoints or ideas accurately
- Support viewpoints by referring to other works of literature
- Recognize the stylistic techniques used by the author
- Identify other meanings or complexities within the work

Make sure that your response:

- Mentions the title of the story or work
- Has a strong beginning
- Addresses all parts of the writing task
- Is well organized with smooth transitions
- Provides specific supporting examples or details
- Uses language correctly (grammar, usage, punctuation)

Remember to follow the writing process

1. **Preparing to write (Pre-writing)**
2. **Writing**
3. **Proofreading (Editing)**

Writing the Response to Literature

Let's take a look at a short story, a writing task, and a sample response.

One Foot on the Ground

by Glen F. Stillwell

WHEN I looked over our neighbor's fence, I saw Rush Turner lying on his back in the shade of an apple tree. He was whistling "Ole Man River."

"What are you doing?" I asked.

Rush didn't bother to turn his head. "Hoeing tomatoes."

Since there is nothing I like better than hoeing in the shade of a tree, I quickly joined Rush. I had dropped to the ground beside him when his older sister called from the house, "Rush, how about those tomatoes?"

"Listen to that!" Rush grumbled, sitting up slowly. "If it isn't one thing it's another. I'm just not cut out to be a farmer! I like excitement, and nothing ever happens around here but work."

"How about the time you sprained your ankle falling off the spray rig?" I asked. "And the day you were going to town in the back of the truck, and the rear wheel came off, and you tumbled into a crate of strawberries? And then there was the time—"

"None of that was exciting or dangerous," Rush interrupted. He picked up the hoe. "I'm saving my money to take flying lessons. That's the life for me, Kip."

Sprawled out and completely relaxed, I didn't bother to answer him. I was thinking of how nice the sky looks when you don't have to strain your neck to see it, and that it was about time for Steve Barrett, the older brother of Dale, our schoolmate, to come along in his small transport plane. Then dimly I heard it, the roar of the engine growing louder.

As the plane neared us, Rush pointed his hoe skyward and went, "*Ah-ah-ah-ah-ah-ah,*" like a machine gun. Then a surprising thing happened. The airplane began to sputter and cough. As I jumped to my feet, Rush exclaimed, "Hey! I got him! I always thought that a hoe was a deadly weapon." A slow smile crossed his freckle-plastered face.

"Steve's in trouble!" I yelled. "Listen to that engine."

Apparently I was right. The airplane was spiraling around as though it was about to make a forced landing in Turner's pasture. With one accord, Rush and I legged it for the fence back of the garden plot. The plane swooped down over our heads, leveled off, hit the ground sharply and taxied across the field. I drew a deep breath.

A moment later I was running across the pasture, with Rush tagging my heels. We were fifty yards from the ship when Rush yelled a warning. Looking over my shoulder, I saw Turner's young bull, Hugo.

As I glanced again at Hugo I saw that he was in motion, headed for our nearest shelter, the plane. We were right in the line of action, and Hugo was gaining speed with every step. While this was happening, Steve was tinkering with the engine. It was still turning over slowly.

Steve happened to look up, and saw Hugo. He made a dive for the cabin. Since it was nearer than the fence, Rush and I must have set an unofficial world's record for a fifty-yard dash in getting to it. Luckily Steve saw us coming and kept the cabin door open. I'm sure his ship was never boarded faster than we piled in.

Rush and I sagged down on boxes inside the cabin. We were so winded we couldn't speak. While we were sitting there, puffing and blowing, Steve started to laugh.

"Looks like I picked up a couple of hitchhikers," he said, "but I'd like to know what you expect to do with that hoe? Are you going to cultivate a cloud?"

Rush realized he still had his hoe. I suppose it did look sort of funny inside an airplane. "We'll leave when Hugo does," Rush said.

"There's no hurry," Steve answered, grinning. "I guess I owe you fellows something for the use of your field.

How about my giving you a free ride over to Porterville? That's where I'm headed. It's only seven miles and you can probably get a lift back in a truck."

Having never taken a ride in an airplane, I liked the idea. But then I happened to think of that sputtering engine. Rush must have had the same thought because he began to choke and stammer. "No-no, thank you," he said. "Some other time, maybe."

Steve hunched his shoulders. "Okay," he said, "but that bull you call Hugo looks kind of unsociable." His eyes narrowed. "You needn't worry about this engine," he added. "There's nothing wrong with it now. The trouble was just a sticking throttle rod. I fixed it."

"In that case," I said, "what are we waiting for? And thanks, very much."

Rush dove for the door. "I've got hoeing to do," he said. Then he caught my eye and resumed his seat. "Oh, all right. What are we waiting for?"

Steve nodded and gunned the engine.

"Ha! Ha! Ha!" laughed Rush weakly. Turning to Steve, he yelled, "Say, how high are we now?"

"About a thousand feet," Steve answered. "Want to go higher?"

It seemed to me that Rush's freckles were beginning to turn green, but I paid little attention to him. I was looking around the cabin, getting acquainted and trying to keep from thinking how high we were. Then I saw something that made me gulp. Printed in big red letters on the boxes we were seated on was the word, D-Y-N-A-M-I-T-E. I spelled the letters aloud just to make sure I wasn't seeing double.

Rush heard me and I thought his eyes were going to pop out of his head. He hugged the hoe handle and made a little bleating noise.

Steve must have heard us because he turned and looked at us, puzzled. Then he grinned when he saw us staring at the boxes. "Don't worry about that dynamite, fellows," he said. "It probably wouldn't explode if you'd dropped it a thousand feet. I haul a lot of it for the mine near Porterville. It's safer than custard pies."

Steve went on yelling to us above the roar of the engine. "This is often a tiresome job, like running a streetcar. Someday I hope to quit, and take up cattle raising. I've got an idea that would be much more interesting and profitable. Hugo's a Hereford, isn't he?"

Rush nodded with his eyes. You couldn't have moved his head with a crowbar. He sat stiffly erect until we neared Porterville. Then Steve called out, "Hold on to your hats, we're coming down."

I think Rush and I were out of the ship almost before it landed. However, we paused long enough to thank Steve--then we charged across the airport. I started breathing freely when we reached the highway.

We got a lift home in a neighbor's truck. As soon as I arrived, I began catching up on my work. After chopping wood and watering the chickens, I looked over the fence to see what Rush was up to. I first heard his voice, then I saw him hoeing the tomatoes. "Come here," I called. "I want to talk to you."

"I've got no time," he answered. "Soon's I finish weeding these tomatoes, I've got to start on the beans." He paused momentarily to grin at me. "Kind of nice to feel the ground under your feet. You know, I might buy a cow pony instead of taking flying lessons. After all, an airplane costs a lot of money."

"Neither one for me," I said, shaking my head. "I'm going to learn office work, so I can always have at least one foot on the ground."

Rush got a fresh grip on the hoe. As he turned his back, he began singing, "Home on the Range." It was kind of sad, the way he sang it.

Remember

- Be sure to write your response to the writing prompt given below.
- You may place a title on your essay if you would like, but it is not necessary.
- No dictionary may be used. If you have trouble spelling a word, sound the word out and do the best you can.
- You may write in cursive or print.
- Write clearly! Any changes, erasures, or strike-throughs should be made as neatly as possible.

Writing Task:

> In the story "One Foot on the Ground," the reader learns about the three main characters—Kip, the storyteller, and Rush. Their actions and dialogue in the story reveal their personalities and emotions.
>
> Write an essay in which you briefly describe the personality and emotions of Kip, the storyteller. What events in the story give insight into Kip's personality? What literary techniques does the author use? Use details and examples from the story to support your ideas.

Checklist for Your Writing

The following checklist will help you. Always make sure that you:

- ❑ Read the task or tasks carefully.
- ❑ Organize your writing by including a strong introduction, body, and conclusion.
- ❑ Always support your ideas with specific details and examples.
- ❑ Write to your audience by using appropriate words.
- ❑ Use words that are appropriate for your purpose.
- ❑ Make your writing interesting to read by varying your sentences.
- ❑ Check carefully for mistakes in grammar, usage, spelling, punctuation, capitalization, and sentence structure.

A Sample Response for the Literary Writing Task

> Although this is an adequate opening paragraph, it isn't ideal. The writing task is specifically about Kip, and although the action of the story can itself be informative about a character, the writer here doesn't connect the fact that the "adventure starts on the ground, goes into the air and ends on the ground" to Kip's personality or emotions

In the story *"One Foot on the Ground,"* Kip, the storyteller, and his neighbor, Rush, have an exciting adventure that starts on the ground, goes into the air and ends on the ground. Kip's descriptive language in telling the story not only shows his emotions during the action, but also gives insight into his character.

> This point—that Kip's language is what tells the reader about both his emotions and his character—is a good one and an effective introduction to the rest of the essay, which makes good use of direct quotations from the story.

As Kip starts the story, you can tell that he has a sense of humor. When Rush says "I like excitement and nothing ever happens around here but work," Kips replies "How about the time you sprained your angle falling of the spray rig?" He continues with more humorous comments.

> The spelling lapse here is not enough to reduce the score on the essay. Overall, the writer's spelling is very good.

> The writer's point about Kip's sense of humor is right on topic, but this overly general final sentence is weak.

> The fact that Kip is perceptive is also on topic. The writer's point here, realizing the plane is in trouble and the bull is ready to charge, indicates perceptiveness, but is perhaps stretching it a bit. It would be difficult for anyone *not* to notice those things.

It becomes evident that Kip is very perceptive when he notices that his friend's small airplane is in trouble. "Steve's in trouble," Kip yelled. "Listen to that engine." This is reinforced when Kip notices that the Turner's young bull, Hugo, was about to charge Kip and Rush as they went to help the pilot Steve.

> An interesting point that Kip is both adventurous and cautious at the same time.

After Kip and Rush quickly boarded the small plane to avoid the onrushing Hugo, you learn that Kip is adventurous, cautious, and reasonable. When Steve offers Kip and Rush a free ride over the town Kip reasons "Having never taken a ride in an airplane, I like the idea. But then I happened to think of that sputtering engine." When Kip decides to leave the plane, Steve reminds Kip about the young bull, so Kip opts for the plane ride only after he's assured that the plane's problem has been fixed.

> This paragraph and others make good use of appropriate direct quotations from the story to illustrate each of the writer's points.

> Another excellent, specific point, followed by a supporting example from the dialogue. It would be even better, however, if it directly mentioned the "controlled fear" as an example of *emotions.*

As the flight progressed, Kip showed signs of "controlled fear" as he noticed something interesting. "Then I saw something that made me gulp. Printed on the boxes we were seated on was the word, D-Y-N-A-M-I-T-E. I spelled the letters aloud just to make sure I wasn't seeing double." Another example of this fear is when Kip explains, "I think Rush and I were out of the ship almost before it landed. However, we paused long enough to thank Steve ..."

The author uses some interesting literary techniques in his story. He uses a narrative technique with well-placed dialogue between the characters. He lets his storyteller use simple, hometown language to make the story entertaining and humorous.

> While this part of the writing task, dealing with literary techniques, here is dealt with sketchily, the writer at least tries to address it and makes an effective point about the dialogue. The paragraph would be better without the vague first sentence, however.

Now write your own essay on the response to the literary text writing task given above. Have an English teacher, tutor, or someone else with good writing skills read and evaluate your essay using the checklist below.

CAHSEE English-Language Arts: Writing

Checklist for Response to Literary or Informational Text

Does the response . . .

- ❏ Demonstrate a carefully thought out, comprehensive understanding of the text?
- ❏ Support the thesis with accurate and coherent specific textual details and examples?
- ❏ Show a clear understanding of any other meanings or complexities within the text?
- ❏ Use precise, descriptive language?
- ❏ Use a variety of sentence types?
- ❏ Contain almost no errors in grammar, punctuation, spelling, capitalization, and usage?

(For literary text also:)

- ❏ Clearly demonstrate a knowledge and understanding of the author's style and use of literary devices?

(For informational text also:)

- ❏ Carefully address the reader's potential misunderstandings, biases, and expectations?

The Business Letter

Your writing task could be to write a business letter. A business letter may be written for many purposes: to complain, to request, to suggest, to argue, to recommend, to inform, or to comment.

Remember, in a business letter you should:

- Use the proper format.
- Begin with a salutation followed by a colon: Dear Sir or Madam: To Whom It May Concern: Dear Mr. Brown: Dear General Foods: (addressing a company for which you have no specific name) etc.
- Use language appropriate to your audience. Keep in mind the person, company, or group you are writing to.
- Keep the letter short and to the point.
- Make sure that your letter addresses your purpose clearly.
- Pay special attention to spelling, grammar, and punctuation.

Writing the Business Letter

The format of your letter should be something like this:

Return address: your address
Date

Inside address: name and address of the person, company, or group you are writing to

Salutation: Dear Mrs. _____: To Whom It May Concern: Dear Editor:

Body of Letter
Introduction to the point of your letter.
Discussion or particulars of the letter.

Closing: Sincerely, Yours truly,

Your signature
Your typed or printed name

A Business Letter Sample Topic

Writing Task:

All of us have purchased or been given a product that broke easily, was defective, didn't work at all, or didn't meet our expectations. In some cases we tried to fix the product, but in many cases we checked the warranty, returned the product, and asked for a replacement or our money back.

Write a business letter to a manufacturer regarding a product that you would like replaced and explain the reason. Describe the problem and support your request using specific details or examples.

Checklist for Your Writing

The following checklist will help you. Always make sure that you:

- ❑ Read the task or tasks carefully.
- ❑ Organize your writing by including a strong introduction, body, and conclusion.
- ❑ Always support your ideas with specific details and examples.
- ❑ Write to your audience by using appropriate words.
- ❑ Use words that are appropriate for your purpose.
- ❑ Make your writing interesting to read by varying your sentences.
- ❑ Check carefully for mistakes in grammar, usage, spelling, punctuation, capitalization, and sentence structure.

Now let's take a careful look at a sample business letter.

A Sample Letter

22122 Ventura Blvd.
Woodland Hills, CA 91364
July 17, 2005

Wilson Sporting Goods Company
Attention: Returns Department
Freeport Center Bldg. F 13
Clearfield, Utah 84016

Dear Wilson Sporting Goods Company:

My Wilson 2.0 HyperCarbon Racket was given to me as a birthday gift in December 2004 (actually I got two of them) and I must tell you that they are wonderful rackets. Yesterday, when I took my racket in for re-stringing, the tennis shop owner noticed a crack in the throat of the frame and would not restring the racket. He said the racket would break in half. As you can see, the racket is like new (except for the crack) since I only play about twice a month and have two rackets.

I checked on-line for warranty information and called your Consumer Relations Department and understand that this racket is still under warranty. I am returning the racket and hope that you will be able to send me a replacement. Unfortunately, since the racket was a gift, I don't have the receipt or a place of purchase.

Please send my replacement racket to:

    Arnold Agassi
    22122 Ventura Blvd.
    Woodland Hills, CA 91364

Thank you for your assistance.

Sincerely,

Arnold Agassi

Arnold Agassi

Now write your own business letter on the writing task given above. Have an English teacher, tutor, or someone else with good writing skills read and evaluate your letter using the checklist below.

Checklist for Response to Writing Prompt

Does your letter . . .

- ❑ Provide a thoughtful, well-written letter that addresses the writing task?
- ❑ Use specific supporting details and examples?
- ❑ Demonstrate a clear focus and tone?
- ❑ Show coherent, logical organization?
- ❑ Clearly address the intended audience?
- ❑ Use precise, descriptive language?
- ❑ Use a variety of sentence types?
- ❑ Contain almost no errors in grammar, punctuation, spelling, capitalization and usage?
- ❑ Use the proper letter format and spacing?

(For a persuasive letter also:)

- ❑ Clearly state a position and make a case for that position?
- ❑ Defend the position with specific relevant evidence?
- ❑ Address the reader's potential misunderstandings, biases, and expectations?

PART II

REVIEWS

Punctuation and Grammar Review

Punctuation

Many of the rules for punctuation are changing—flexibility in the use of the comma, for example. Some basic principles remain, however, and questions on the exam may involve recognizing incorrect or poor use of various punctuation marks.

Periods

Use periods to end complete sentences that are statements, commands, and requests, or mild exclamations.

> *He spends winters in Florida and summers in Maine.*
> *Please don't feed the bears.*
> *How strange to see a clown driving a van.*

Don't use periods at the end of groups of words that are **not** complete sentences (phrases or dependent clauses). These errors are called *sentence fragments*.

> *When the boy threw open the door and ran into the yard.* (**incorrect:** sentence fragment)
> *Running up and down the stairs ten times during the day.* (**incorrect:** sentence fragment)

Always keep periods within quotation marks whether or not they are part of the quotation.

> *Katie said, "Let's go to the movies."*
> *He referred to his friend as "the cheapskate."*

Question Marks

Question marks end sentences that are questions. They follow the question immediately, even when the question interrupts or comes after a statement.

> *Who knows where Joe is?*
> *You should have discussed this with me first, but can't we work it out between us?*

An exception to this rule occurs when the question is followed by a phrase or clause that modifies it. Then put the question mark at the end of the statement: *How can we be mad at him, considering all the trouble he went through to get here?*

After a question mark, don't use a period or a comma, even if the sentence would normally call for one: *Later I understood what Jason meant when he said, "Why me?"*

In quotations, if the material being quoted is a question, put the mark within the quotation marks. If not, put the question mark outside the quotation marks.

> *The councilman looked around and asked, "Can we count on your help?"*
> *Who was it that said, "All that glitters is not gold"?*

For indirect questions (that is, questions that are being reported rather than directly asked), use a period rather than a question mark.

> *Ethan asked what made the sky so bright.*
> *The manager of the store asked us what we would accept as a settlement.*

Exclamation Points

Exclamation points follow words, phrases, or clauses that express a burst of emotion.

> *Oh, no! Bravo! Hey!*
>
> *What a terrible mess!*
>
> *Fantastic job, Carol!*

Exclamation points may also be used to lend force to a command: *Leave that thermostat alone!*

Omit commas and periods after exclamation points: *"You adorable thing!" he gushed.*

The biggest problem with exclamation points is that they tend to be overused, which dulls their effect and also indicates an immature writing style.

> *The film's last scene was touching*—**not**—*The film's last scene was touching!*

Commas

Commas present a special problem because the rules for them are changing and are often flexible. Don't overuse commas. The best guideline is to consider the meaning of the sentence and decide whether a pause is necessary or desirable.

Generally, when you join *independent clauses* with a *coordinating conjunction,* use a comma before the coordinating conjunction. (The coordinating conjunctions are *and, but, for, nor, or, so,* and *yet.* An independent clause is one that can stand alone as a sentence.)

> *Miguel won the prize, but he gave it to his friend.*
>
> *We wanted to go to the party, and Sam wanted to go with us.*

If the independent clauses being joined are very short, you may omit the comma.

> *He ate fish and he drank wine.*
>
> *We laughed and we cried.*
>
> *He's a pest but we like him.*

Remember that if you use a comma between independent clauses **without** the conjunction, you create a *run-on sentence* (also known as a *comma splice*). A run-on sentence is an error.

> *Wolves are basically social animals, they travel in packs.* (**incorrect:** run-on sentence)
>
> *Wolves are basically social animals, <u>and</u> they travel in packs.* (**correct**)

Use a comma after an introductory *adverbial clause.* Adverbial clauses begin with words like *because, unless, if, when,* and *although.*

> *Because the hurricane had diminished in force, the town was spared.*
>
> *If you decide to fly next week, you will be able to buy a cheaper ticket.*

If clauses like these don't **introduce** the sentence, don't use a comma.

> *The town was spared because the hurricane had diminished in force.*
>
> *You will be able to buy a cheaper ticket if you decide to fly next week.*

Use commas with *participial phrases.* A participial phrase begins with an *-ing* or *-ed* verb.

> *Smiling and shaking hands, the senator made her way to the podium.*
>
> *Trapped by the storm, the passengers decided to play cards.*

Use a comma after any introductory phrase if there is a possibility of misunderstanding a sentence without one, or if the phase is long and complex.

> *Before eating, Jack always runs on the beach.*
>
> *At the beginning of the year before the first game of the season and after practice, you can feel the excitement in the air.*

Use commas to set off interrupting elements in a sentence.

> *As you get towards the end of the novel, of course, you will guess who the masked man is.*
>
> *Don't expect, for example, that the product will remove all stains.*

Use commas with *nonrestrictive elements*. A nonrestrictive element is one that doesn't restrict or limit the subject but instead adds information. It isn't essential to the reader's understanding.

> *My brother, who is thirteen, watches television every night.*
>
> *The television show, which is in its fifth season, is my father's favorite.*

Do **not** use commas with *restrictive elements*. A restrictive element is one that limits the subject and is therefore essential to the reader's understanding.

> *People, who are over 65, are entitled to Medicare.* (**incorrect**)
> *People who are over 65 are entitled to Medicare.* (**correct**)
>
> *The man, who robbed the bank, was spotted on Main Street.* (**incorrect**)
> *The man who robbed the bank was spotted on Main Street.* (**correct**)

Use commas between items in a series: *He ordered five strips of bacon, three eggs scrambled, two pieces of wheat toast, and a large glass of orange juice.* The comma before *and* is optional, but it is usually safer to include it if there is any possibility of confusion.

Some other uses of the comma are as follows:

- in dialogue with *he said, she muttered*, etc.: *She said, "Let's go to the early show." ; "Let's go to the early show," she said.*
- between items in dates and addresses (except between state and zip code): *December 14, 2004; 1328 Say Road, Santa Paula, CA 90266*
- between cities and counties, cities and states, states and countries: *Boise, Idaho; Madrid, Spain*
- after salutations and closings in letters: *Dear Maria,*
- to enclose a title or degree: *Jeff Nelson, M.D., is a renowned doctor of gerontology.*

Semicolons

Semicolons are like periods in that they divide independent clauses when the clauses aren't joined by *and, but, or, nor, for,* and *yet.*

You can prevent run-on sentences by using a semicolon instead of a comma.

> *I expect you to finish the work by three, however, if it takes longer, call me.* (**incorrect**)
> *I expect you to finish the work by three; however, if it takes longer, call me.* (**correct**)
>
> *We discussed the upcoming elections, therefore, the discussion was heated.* (**incorrect**)
> *We discussed the upcoming elections; therefore, the discussion was heated.* (**correct**)

> *They never expected to be invited, they plan to be out of town.* (**incorrect**)
>
> *They never expected to be invited; they plan to be out of town.* (**correct**)

When deciding whether to use a semicolon or a period to divide independent clauses, you should choose a semicolon only when the clauses are closely related.

> *Don't forget to bring a jacket; the weather is cold at this time of year.* (**correct**)
>
> *Don't forget to bring a jacket; Mary is also coming with us.* (**poor use of semicolon**)

Semicolons, instead of commas, can be used in a series, especially when the series items themselves contain commas.

> *Mr. Parker arrived with a basket of apples, all of them ripe and ready to eat; a bag of freshly picked corn; three loaves of French bread; and two pies, both baked by his wife.*

Don't create sentence fragments by using semicolons. Remember: they are more like periods than commas.

> *The judge decided to postpone the trial; because the defendant was ill.* (**incorrect**)
>
> *The judge decided to postpone the trial because the defendant was ill.* (**correct**)

> *My friend insisted on talking during the movie; making everyone mad.* (**incorrect**)
>
> *My friend insisted on talking during the movie, making everyone mad.* (**correct**)

Semicolons go outside quotation marks:

> *He asked me to correct my "atrocious manners"; I told him I'd behave any way I chose.*

Colons

Use a colon after the words *following* or *as follows* when these words introduce a list.

> *The titles chosen are as follows: <u>Moby Dick,</u> <u>The Great Gatsby,</u> and <u>The Old Man and the Sea.</u>*
>
> *Some items are not allowed in carry-on baggage, including the following: knives, scissors, screwdrivers, fireworks.*
>
> *You will probably be expected to answer the following questions: Where were you born? Where do you currently live? Have you left the country in the last six months?*

Don't use a colon when the listed items immediately follow the verb:

> *Our service club sent food, clothing, and gifts for the children.*

You may use a colon to introduce a formal statement or quotation. An independent clause should precede the colon. After the colon, use a capital letter.

> *Remember this: Honesty is always the best policy.*
>
> *This is what he said to us: "You may not turn in your assignments late."*

Other uses of the colon are

- to separate hours and minutes when writing the time: *4:14 p.m.*
- to separate volume and number or volume and page number of a magazine: *Entertainment Weekly VI:4*
- to separate chapter and verse numbers for biblical passages: *Matthew 4:16*
- to introduce a subtitle: *John Wayne: An Actor for the Ages*
- to end the salutation of a business letter: *Dear Dr. Aguinaldo:*

Colons go outside quotation marks: *The article was called "The Last Word": it presented his latest opinion.*

Dashes

A dash or a pair of dashes can be used to interrupt a sentence. Other punctuation marks, such as commas or parentheses, serve the same purpose. Dashes call more attention to the interruption. Commas, on the other hand, are more neutral. Parentheses usually enclose information that is clearly incidental. When using dashes as an interruption, be sure to omit the commas.

> *She was very tall—the tallest woman I had ever seen.* (**correct**)
> *She was very tall, the tallest woman I had ever seen.* (**correct**)

> *The manager of the department—the same man who had hired me—was promoted to vice president.* (**correct**)
> *The manager of the department (the same man who had hired me) was promoted to vice president.* (**correct**)

Like a colon, a dash can be used to introduce an explanation or restatement in place of expressions such as *that is, in other words,* or *namely.* Begin the clause after the dash with a lowercase letter:

> *The reporter pursued the actress—he was determined to get a statement.*

When using dashes instead of commas, be sure to omit the commas.

> *I saw her—the woman who had given us the puppy—when I went to the grocery store.* (**correct**)
> *I saw her, —the woman who had given us the puppy—, when I went to the grocery store.* (**incorrect**)

Don't use dashes too often. They are more noticeable than commas and should be reserved for specific effects.

Parentheses

Parentheses may be used to set off incidental information, such as a passing comment, a minor example or addition, or a brief explanation. Whether to use them is a judgment call, and like dashes they shouldn't be overused.

> *Some of the local store owners (Mr. Kwan and Mrs. Lawson, for example) insisted that the street be widened.* (**correct**)
> *Some of the local store owners—Mr. Kwan and Mrs. Lawson, for example—insisted that the street be widened.* (**correct**)
> *Some of the local store owners, Mr. Kwan and Mrs. Lawson, for example, insisted that the street be widened.* (**correct**)

Use parentheses to enclose a date or citation.

> *Thomas Logan (1932–2004) was mayor during our town's longest period of growth.*
> *According to his critics, Roger Bellamp was a mediocre travel writer (Travis, 261–62).*

Don't put any punctuation mark before parentheses, and put a comma after the closing parenthesis only if the sentence would call for the comma anyway.

> *Use a pointed stick (a pencil with the lead point broken off works well) or a similar tool.* (**no comma should be used**)
> *Banging the wall and screaming (unrestrained by his father, I might add), Sam was acting like a spoiled child.* (**comma follows closing parenthesis because the sentence would normally take a comma**)

If parentheses enclose a sentence-within-a-sentence, don't use a period within the parentheses. Do, however, use a question mark or an exclamation point if it is called for.

> *Dr. Benton's anger (it was fierce) frightened the medical students.*
> *He finally asked (why couldn't he have done so earlier?) whether she wanted to go.*
> *The wedding reception (what a fiasco!) ended abruptly.*

If the parentheses enclose a complete sentence that stands alone, keep the period within them: (*Her father was the only person who spoke up about the problem.*)

Quotation Marks

Use quotation marks at the beginning and end of direct quotations.

> *"You are the person we selected," the chairperson said.*

When quoting from another source, use quotation marks.

> *According to Brian Greene in his book* The Elegant Universe, *"Einstein came up with his explanation by puzzling over something known as the photoelectric effect."*

Use single quotation marks within double ones to indicate a quotation within a quotation.

> "My father says 'Jim, you can achieve whatever you want,'" Jimmy told the teacher.

For other purposes, use quotation marks sparingly. However, following are some possible uses:

- to distance yourself from an offensive term: *The body builder blamed the "big oafs" who judged the contest.*
- to refer to a word as a word: *Does anyone know what "inane" means?*
- to indicate a nickname as part of a formal name: *Hubert "Buddy" Wilson was elected chairman.*
- to set off titles of poems, essays, and articles that are part of a longer work. *The poem "Trees" will be included on the exam.*

An *ellipsis* is a mark consisting of spaced periods. It indicates an omission from a quotation.

A three-dot ellipsis is used when you are omitting something from a sentence that continues after the omission:

> *"The wise collector should probably . . . acquire both paintings."*

The phrase *mortgage the house and* has been omitted from this quotation.

A four-dot ellipsis is used when you are omitting the last part of a quoted sentence but what remains is still a complete thought:

> *The author advises, "In analyzing nonverbal signals, look at the total behavior rather than just one symbol. . . ."*

The phrase *before making a decision,* which ended the sentence, has been omitted from the quotation.

Following is a brief review of the general rules regarding punctuation marks with quotation marks:

- Periods and commas belong inside quotation marks whether or not they are part of the quotation.
- Question marks, exclamation points, and dashes belong inside quotation marks if they are part of the quotation, and outside if they are not.
- Colons and semicolons belong outside quotation marks.

Grammar: Parts of Speech

Grammar is a big subject. This review focuses on the issues that might be covered by questions on the exam. Don't be intimidated by the terminology that is used to explain grammar. On the exam, you won't be expected to name the parts of speech, types of phrases and clauses, and so on. You will be expected to use standard English correctly and to recognize errors.

Nouns and Verbs

Nouns and verbs are the basic building blocks of sentences.

Nouns

Nouns name persons, places, and things (concrete things like *dog* and abstract things like *courage*). Singular nouns stand for one person, place, or thing: *dog, child, man, goose.* Plural nouns stand for more than one: *dogs, tables, projects, children, men, geese.* Although most nouns form the plural with an *-s*, there are many exceptions (for example, *children, men,* and *geese*).

One of the most important functions of a noun is to act as the subject of a sentence. Nouns also act as objects of verbs and prepositions.

> The *chair* stood next to the *door.* (*Chair* and d*oor* are nouns. *Chair* acts as the subject and *door* acts as the object of the preposition *to.*)

> *Success* requires hard *work.* (*Success* and *work* are nouns in this sentence. *Success* acts as the subject and *work* is the object of the verb *requires.*)

Notice that the way a word is used determines whether or not it is a noun. For example, in the sentence *Success requires hard work, work* is a noun. But *work* can also be a verb: *I work very hard.*

Proper Nouns and Common Nouns

If a noun names a specific person or place, or a particular event, it is called a **proper noun** and is capitalized: *Harry Truman, Disneyland, the Great Depression.* If a noun isn't specific in this way, it is called a *common noun.*

> *Uncle Robert* drove us to *South Carolina* last summer. (*Uncle Robert* and *South Carolina* are both capitalized because they name a specific person and a specific place.)

> My *uncle* drove us *south* last summer. (Here, because *uncle* and *south* do not specifically name a person or place, they are not capitalized.)

Collective Nouns

A collective noun is a noun that stands for a group of people, places, or things.

> The *group* decided to go to the movies.

> We joined the health *club* because it provided good exercise equipment.

> The *herd* of cattle was spotted on the hill.

> I hear that the *jury* is asking for clarification.

Usually, a collective noun is treated as a singular noun: "The *group remembers* when *it* was much smaller."

Gerunds

A noun that is formed from the *-ing* form of a verb is called a *gerund.* Like other nouns, a gerund can be the subject or object in a sentence,

> *Swimming* strengthens my arms and legs.

> I love *swimming.*

> *Visiting my friends* is something I look forward to. (This is a gerund phrase that acts as a noun and the subject of the sentence.)

Possessive Case of Nouns

When nouns show ownership, they are in the *possessive case: Allan's car, the committee's recommendation, the animals' cages.* What causes problems with possessive nouns is where to put the apostrophe. The easiest rules to follow are:

- For singular nouns add *-'s* to form the possessive even if the noun ends in an *-s* or *-z* sound: *dog's bone, Jess's car.* Make an exception when an added *-s* would lead to three closely bunched *s* or *z* sounds: *Ulysses', Jesus'.* In these cases, add just an apostrophe.
- For plural nouns add an apostrophe alone: several *months'* bills, the *Rolling Stones'* travel plans, the *dogs'* leashes. If the plural doesn't end in *-s*, add *-'s,* as you would with a singular noun: the *children's* toys, *women's* hats.
- When a possessive noun sounds awkward, use an *of* construction: the *top of the page* instead of *the page's top.*
- To indicate joint ownership, give the possessive form only to the final noun: *John and Terry's garage.*

Verbs

Verbs convey the actions performed by persons, places, and things: "The dog *barks.*" Some verbs don't actually express action but complete statements about the subject by describing or identifying it. This type of verb is called a *linking verb.* Some common linking verbs are *appear, be, become, feel, grow, look, remain, seem, smell, sound,* and *taste.*

Action verbs:

Ron *voted* for the first time.

The choir *sings* every Sunday.

Marty *had dreamed* of this day.

Can you *believe* it?

Linking verbs:

Joe *appeared* angry.

The boys *are* late.

He *seems* interesting.

The dog *smells* bad.

The orange *tastes* sour.

Verb Tenses

Tense refers to time. When is the action of the verb taking place? Although there are more, six tenses are commonly used in English.

Present: the action is going on now (*I walk down the street*)

Past: the action is over (*I walked down the street*)

Future: the action has yet to take place (*I will walk down the street*)

Present Perfect: action in past time in relation to present time (*I have walked down the street for years*—and I am still walking down the street)

Past Perfect: action in past time in relation to another past time (*I had walked down the street many times before I noticed the garden*)

Future Perfect: action that will be completed in the future before another future action (*By next year, I will have walked down the street thousands of times*)

The explanation of the tenses can be confusing, but what you need to recognize is that time sequences should be logical. Sometimes the choice of a tense clearly affects meaning:

Esther *worked* at the department store for a year. (The past tense indicates a completed action. Esther no longer works at the store.)

Esther *has worked* at the department store for a year. (Use of the present perfect tense indicates that a past action is continuing in the present. Esther still works at the store.)

Esther *had worked* at the department store for a year. (Use of the past perfect tense indicates that something else happened after Esther's year. For example, Esther had worked at the store for a year when she took over the sporting goods section.)

Esther *will have worked* at the department store for a year by next summer. (Use of the future tense indicates that by next summer—a future time—Esther will have worked at the store for a year. As of today, she hasn't worked there for a year.)

Be consistent in your use of the tenses. Don't switch from past to present, for example, and do use the perfect tenses when appropriate.

I *walk* into the classroom, *take* my seat, and *picked* up my notebook (**incorrect**)

I *walk* into the classroom, take my seat, and *pick* up my notebook (**correct:** verbs are consistent because they are all in the present tense)

I *walked* into the classroom, *took* my seat, and *picked* up my notebook. (**correct:** verbs are consistent because they are all in the past tense)

Everything you *told* me I *had heard* before. (**correct:** use of past perfect with past tense to indicate an action taking place in the past before another action in the past)

The car wash *stood* where the library *was*. (**incorrect**)

The car wash *stood* where the library *had been* (**correct:** without using the past perfect tense, it sounds as if the car and the library were in the same spot at the same time)

Contrary-to-Fact or Hypothetical Statements

Usually, the verb is in the *indicative mood,* with the tenses formed as shown above. However, some statements are hypothetical or contrary-to-fact. For these, the verb should be in the *subjunctive mood.* What this means is that the tenses are formed differently. Notice the examples below.

If I were a millionaire, *I would buy* a mansion. (This statement is contrary-to-fact, that is, I am not a millionaire. Therefore the subjunctive mood of the verb is called for, and the present subjunctive of *to be* is *were,* not *was.* **The present subjunctive is the same as the past indicative.**)

If he *had worked,* he *could have earned* high wages. (This statement is also hypothetical, or contrary-to-fact. He didn't work. **The past subjunctive is the same as the past perfect indicative.**)

You can recognize a hypothetical statement because the first clause usually begins with *If:*

If I were king; If you had called; If the plan had been approved.

Not all *If* clauses are subjunctive, however. The key is whether the statement is contrary-to-fact:

If I *want* the job, I *must submit* my resume. (**indicative:** not contrary-to-fact. I want the job.)

If I *wanted* the job, I *would submit* my resume. (**subjunctive:** contrary-to-fact. I don't want the job.)

For the second (or consequence) clause of the statement, the *conditional* is used. It is formed with *could* or *would.*

If *I had practiced* (past tense of the subjunctive mood), I *could have won* the race (past tense of the conditional)

A common error is to use the conditional (*would have, could have*) in both clauses of a contrary-to-fact statement.

If I *would have wanted to,* I *would have made* cookies. (**incorrect:** the subjunctive, not the conditional, should be used in the *If* clause.)

If I *had wanted to,* I *would have made* cookies. (**correct:** the subjunctive is used in the *If* clause, and the conditional is used in the consequences clause.)

Irregular Verbs

Even when you understand the correct uses of tenses, you can run into trouble with verbs. The major culprit is the large group of irregular verbs, which form the past tense and past participle in a variety of ways, not by adding -d or -ed as regular verbs do. Following is a list of some frequently used irregular verbs. When you aren't sure about the correct past and past participle forms of a verb that isn't on the list, check the dictionary.

Common Irregular Verbs		
Present Tense	*Past Tense*	*Past Participle*
be	was, were	(have) been
beat	beat	(have) beaten, beat
begin	began	(have) begun
blow	blew	(have) blown
break	broke	(have) broken
bring	brought	(have) brought
catch	caught	(have) caught
choose	chose	(have) chosen
come	came	(have) come
dig	dug	(have) dug
dive	dived, dove	(have) dived
do	did	(have) done
draw	drew	(have) drawn
dream	dreamed, dreamt	(have) dreamed, dreamt
drink	drank	(have) drunk
drive	drove	(have) driven
eat	ate	(have) eaten
fly	flew	(have) flown
forget	forgot	(have) forgotten
freeze	froze	(have) frozen
get	got	(have) gotten
go	went	(have) gone
grow	grew	(have) grown
hang (an object)	hung	(have) hung
hang (a person)	hanged	(have) hanged
lay	laid	(have) laid
lead	led	(have) led
lend	lent	(have) lent

Present Tense	Past Tense	Past Participle
lie (recline)	lay	(have) lain
light	lighted, lit	(have) lighted, lit
ride	rode	(have) ridden
ring	rang	(have) rung
run	ran	(have) run
see	saw	(have) seen
set	set	(have) set
shake	shook	(have) shaken
shine (emit light)	shone	(have) shone
shine (make shiny)	shined	(have) shined
sing	sang	(have) sung
sink	sank, sunk	(have) sunk
slay	slew	(have) slain
speed	sped	(have) sped
spring	sprang, sprung	(have) sprung
steal	stole	(have) stolen
swear	swore	(have) sworn
swim	swam	(have) swum
take	took	(have) taken
tear	tore	(have) torn
wake	waked, woke	(have) waked, woke, woken
wear	wore	(have) worn

Active and Passive Voices of the Verb

The term *voice* refers to the form of a verb indicating whether the subject performs an action (*active voice*) or receives the action (*passive voice*).

> Mary *smashed* the ball over the net. (active voice)
>
> The ball *was smashed* over the net by Mary (passive voice)

An important clue to good writing is to use the active voice whenever you can; it conveys more energy than the passive voice and also results in more concise writing.

> The crafts fair *was put on* by the eighth graders. (passive voice)
>
> The eighth graders *put on* the crafts fair. (**better:** active voice)

> The award *had been presented* to the team *by* the city council. (passive voice)
>
> The city council *had presented* the award to the team. (**better:** active voice)

The flat-screen television set *had been delivered by* the store that day, and the football game *was watched by* all the neighbors. (passive voice)

The store *had delivered* the flat-screen television that day, and all the neighbors *watched* the football game. (**better:** active voice)

Use the passive voice, however, when you don't know the actor or when you want to emphasize the person or thing acted upon rather than the actor. Examples of possible uses of the passive voice are as follows:

When we returned, the car had been towed.

Gold was discovered there early in the last century.

A change in structure was found in the experimental group.

Agreement of Nouns and Verbs

In sentences, verbs and nouns must agree, which means that a singular noun requires a singular verb, and a plural noun requires a plural verb.

The *dog jumps* up and down. (singular noun, singular verb)

The *dogs jump* up and down. (plural noun, plural verb)

Agreement can be tricky. Read sentences carefully to see whether the subject of the verb is singular or plural. Note the examples below.

Statistics is the class I like best. (singular)

Statistics are sometimes misleading. (plural)

The *number* of people coming *is* surprising. (singular)

A *number* of people *are* coming. (plural)

Usually, collective nouns are treated as singular:

Congress is in session.

Your furniture fits into the room nicely.

The team is going on the bus.

But for some collective nouns, when you want to emphasize the individual parts of a group, you may use the plural:

The team are arguing among themselves about the game.

Pronouns

Pronouns are words that stand for nouns.

- **Personal pronouns.** The personal pronouns [*I, you, he, she, it, we, you* (plural), *they*] stand for one or more persons or things. They differ in form depending on their case, that is, how they are used in a phrase, clause, or sentence:

  We enjoy going to the games

  The games interest us.

- **Reflexive pronouns.** These words combine some of the personal pronouns with *-self* or *-selves* to reflect nouns or pronouns, as in *He hurt himself,* or to add emphasis, as in *I myself don't believe it.* Don't use reflexive pronouns as subjects or objects.

  Tom and *myself* don't like it. (**incorrect**)

  Tom and *I* don't like it. (**correct**)

  Bob doesn't like Harold or *myself.* (**incorrect**)

  Bob doesn't like Harold or *me.* (**correct**)

- **Demonstrative pronouns.** These pronouns (*this, that, these, those*) single out what you are talking about:

  These are the ones we want, but this is the most economical choice.

- **Relative pronouns.** These pronouns (*who, whom, which, that*) introduce clauses that describe nouns or pronouns:

  The professor who wrote the book is teaching the class.

  The storm that caused the blackout has moved east.

- **Interrogative pronouns.** These pronouns (*who, whom, whose, which, what*) introduce questions:

  Which is the best one to choose?

  To whom does this belong?

- **Indefinite pronouns.** These pronouns don't specify the persons or things they refer to. There are many words used as indefinite pronouns. Among the most frequent are *all, any, anybody, anyone, both, each, either, everybody, everyone, few, many, neither, nobody, none, no one, one, several, some, somebody, someone:*

  Nobody likes a cheater.

  Many are called but few are chosen.

  Either is all right with me.

Pronoun Case

When a pronoun is the subject of a verb, it is in the *subjective case*. When it is an object, it is in the *objective case*. When it possesses something, it is in the *possessive case*.

With nouns, the subjective and objective cases aren't a problem because nouns have the same form whether they are subjects or objects: The *frog* ate the *bee*. The *bee* stung the *frog*. Regardless of what's happening to the frog and the bee, the nouns *frog* and *bee* don't change form.

Some pronouns, however, change depending on whether they are subjects or objects.

Subjective case	Objective case
I	me
he, she	him, her
we	us
they	them
who, whoever	whom, whomever

In the sentence *Tension existed between Franklin and Winston*, there is no confusion about what case to use for Franklin or Winston. But what about this sentence? *Tension existed between Franklin and him.* Is *him* right? Or should it be *he*? Because the pronoun is the object of a preposition (*between*), *him* is correct here.

Use of the Subjective Case

Use the subjective case of the pronoun when it is the subject of a verb.

I drive to work.

He enjoys dancing.

We bought the lodge.

They are fighting over nothing.

The man *who won the game* was the guest of honor.

When there are compound subjects (more than one actor), don't be confused. Pronouns should still be in the subjective case.

> *Janet and he* (**not** *Janet and him*) enjoy dancing.
>
> *The Wilsons and they* (**not** *The Wilsons and them*) are fighting over nothing.

Pronoun case errors are frequent. In sentences with compound subjects, drop the subject that is a noun and read the sentence with the pronoun alone. You would never say *Him enjoy dancing* or *Them are fighting over nothing.* You'll see immediately that the subjective forms *he* and *they* are correct.

You should also use the subjective case of pronouns after forms of the verb *to be.*

> *It is I* who chose the location.
>
> The real criminals *are we ourselves.*
>
> The man who called the police *was he.*

Sometimes using the subjective pronoun after *to be* may sound unnatural or awkward, but it is still correct. In informal speech and writing, modern usage allows *It's me* or *It is me,* but it's best to stay with the established rule in other cases.

Use of the Objective Case

Use the objective case of pronouns when the pronoun is an object of a verb or an object of a preposition.

> Gilbertson *nominated me* for secretary. (direct object of *nominated*)
>
> The news *hit them* hard. (direct object of *hit*)
>
> Jennifer *gave him* the house and car. (indirect object of *gave*)

Watch out for pronoun case when you have a compound object. Remember that when an object is more than one person, it is still an object.

> The award will be given to *Lee, Sandy, and me* (**not** *I*).
>
> Without *Kate and me* (**not** *I*) the party wouldn't have been a success.
>
> The teacher talked to *Nelson, Robert, and me* (**not** *I*).

If you read the sentence with the pronoun alone, you will see the correct case. You wouldn't say *The award will be given to I; Without I the party wouldn't have been a success;* or *The teacher talked to I.*

Between You and Me Versus *Between You and I*

Some people incorrectly believe that subjective pronouns are more correct than objective ones—for example, that *I* is more "refined" than *me.* The phrases *between you and I* and *for you and I* are common mistakes probably due to overrefinement. The pronouns are objects of prepositions here, and therefore *for you and me* and *between you and me* are correct.

> Just *between you and me* (**not** *I*), John is the best choice for captain.
>
> The tour guide promised that *for you and me* (**not** *I*) he'd include the garden tour.
>
> There is tension *between them and us* (**not** *they and we*).
>
> He had a difficult time choosing *between him and me* (**not** *he and I*).

Pronoun Case with Appositives

An *appositive* is a word or group of words that restates or identifies the noun or pronoun it is next to:

> *My sister Debbie*
>
> *John, the gardener*
>
> *Our friend Carlos*

The presence of an appositive doesn't change the rule for pronoun case. Use the subjective case for subjects and the objective case for objects:

> The decision to close the pool was a setback *for us* (**not** *we*) swimmers.

Possessive Case and Problems with *Its, Whose,* and *Their*

Personal pronouns and the pronoun *who* don't form the possessive case by adding *'s,* as nouns do. Instead, they change their forms to indicate possession: *My, mine; your, yours; his; hers; its; our, ours; their, theirs; whose.*

Some possessive pronouns are confused with other words.

- The possessive of *it* is *its,* not *it's. It's* is a contraction of *it is.*

  The dog wagged *its* tail, **not** The dog wagged *it's* tail.

  It's time to leave for school. (*It's = It is*)

- The possessive of *who* is *whose,* not *who's. Who's* is a contraction of *who is.*

  We talked to the man *whose* car it was, **not** We talked to the man *who's* car it was.

  Who's the one that took your photo? (*Who's = Who is*)

- The possessive of *they* is *their,* not *they're* or *there. They're* is a contraction of *they are,* and *there* refers to a place (*We don't go there*).

  They lost *their* dog, **not** They lost *they're* dog or They lost *there* dog.

Pronoun Reference (Antecedents)

Remember that pronouns stand in for nouns, and an *antecedent* is the noun that a pronoun refers to: "Kelly lifted *Mickey* into the air and then set *him* down."

In this sentence, *Mickey* is the antecedent of *him.*

Sometimes the antecedent of a pronoun is unclear. In the following sentences locate the antecedents of the pronouns:

> The counselor was speaking to Dave, and *he* looked unhappy. (Who looked unhappy—the counselor or Dave?)
> After the girls left the hotel rooms, the maids cleaned *them.* (Did the maids clean the rooms or the girls?)

Avoid unclear pronoun references. Rewrite sentences so that the meaning is clear, even if you have to eliminate the use of the pronoun.

> The counselor was speaking to Dave, who looked unhappy.
> After the girls left, the maids cleaned the hotel rooms.

Pronoun Agreement

A pronoun must agree with its antecedent in number (singular or plural) and gender (masculine or feminine).

> *Harold,* after saying good-bye to *his* family, discovered *he'd* lost *his* wallet. (*Harold* is the antecedent of *his, he'd,* and *his.*)
> Until *they* buy the house, the *Garcias* are staying in a hotel. (*Garcias* is the antecedent of *they,* even though it follows the pronoun.)

Indefinite pronouns cause many agreement problems. Some of these pronouns (*several, few, both, many*) are clearly plural and take plural pronouns and verbs: "*Several are* expected to give up *their* rooms"; "*Both tell their* parents the truth." But other indefinite pronouns, though they may "feel" plural, are singular and take singular verbs and pronouns.

Each is responsible for *her* own ticket, **not** *Each is* responsible for *their* own ticket.

Everyone wants to get *his* name in the paper, **not** *Everyone wants* to get *their* name in the paper. (Note: Because *everyone* can include both males and females, the plural is now sometimes acceptable: *Everyone wants to get their name in the paper.* However, it would be best, when in doubt, to stick to the singular. You can take into account both sexes and still use the singular as follows: *Everyone wants to get his or her name in the paper.*)

In addition to *each* and *everyone*, the following pronouns fall into this group: *either, neither, everybody, no one, nobody, anyone, anybody, someone, somebody.* Only when the use of a singular form would lead to a statement that doesn't make sense should you use a plural form: "*Everyone* left the lecture because *they* heard the fire alarm." Here, the singular *he* wouldn't make sense.

A few indefinite pronouns (*none, any, some, all, most*) fall into an "either/or" category, depending on meaning. Sometimes the distinction is subtle.

None of the men was hurt. (*not one* = singular)

None of the men were hurt. (*no men* = plural)

Some is better than none. (*some* = a quantity = singular)

Some are delicious. (*some* = a number of things = plural)

All is well. (*all* = the sum of all things = singular)

All are well. (*all* = a number of people = plural)

Adjectives and Adverbs

Adjectives and adverbs describe or limit other words. An *adjective* modifies a noun or pronoun, and an *adverb* modifies a verb, an adjective, or another adverb.

He has a *sad smile.* (*sad* = adjective modifying *smile*)

He smiles *sadly.* (*sadly* = adverb modifying *smiles*)

It was an *immediate success.* (*Immediate* = adjective modifying *success*)

The success *came immediately.* (*immediately* = adverb modifying *came*)

Adverbs often end in *-ly* (*quickly, happily, slowly, sweetly*) but not always (*fast, late, hard, here, there*). Some adjectives also end in *-ly* (*a lively child, a friendly dog, a hilly area*). The key to whether a word is an adjective or an adverb is the way the word is used in a sentence. If it describes a noun or pronoun, it is an adjective: *This is hard work.* If it answers a question about a verb (such as how, how much, when, where, and why), it is an adverb: *He works hard.*

It's natural to associate adverbs rather than adjectives with all verbs. But linking verbs, such as forms of *to be, become, smell, taste, seem,* and *look,* use adjectives, which are called *predicate adjectives.* With a linking verb, the modifier is actually telling you about the noun or pronoun, not the verb.

The berries *taste sweet,* **not** *sweetly.*

They were *happy,* **not** *happily.*

Notice the use of adjectives or adverbs in the following sentences, depending on whether a verb is functioning as a linking verb or an action verb.

Flowers *grow beautifully* in that climate. (adverb describing how the flowers grow)

Bronze *grows beautiful* as it ages. (adjective describing bronze)

The dog *smells bad.* (adjective describing the dog's odor)

The dog *smells badly.* (adverb indicating that something is wrong with the dog's sense of smell)

Good Versus *Well*

Good is always an adjective (*good bread, good vibrations, dinner was good*). Don't use *good* as an adverb.

> She *sings well,* **not** She *sings good.*
>
> He *tells* a story *well,* **not** He *tells* a story *good.*

While *good* is always an adjective, *well* can be either an adjective or an adverb, depending on how it is used. *Well* as an adjective refers to being in good health.

> After the antibiotic took effect, he *felt well.* (adjective following a linking verb)

To see the distinction between *well* and *good* as adjectives, look at the following sentences:

> Jerome *looked good* at the party tonight. (Jerome looked attractive.)
>
> Jerome *looked well* at the party tonight. (Jerome looked to be in good health.)

Bad Versus *Badly*

Bad is an adjective and *badly* is an adverb. They are often used incorrectly for each other.

> I *feel bad* about losing the election, **not** I *feel badly* about losing the election. (Here *feel* is a linking verb and should be followed by an adjective, **not** an adverb.)
>
> The soccer team *played badly* in the game, **not** The soccer team *played bad* in the game.(*Badly* is an adverb describing how the team played; an adjective would be incorrect.)

Most Versus *Almost*

Most is an adjective meaning *the greatest in number: Most crimes* go unreported. *Almost* is always an adverb meaning *nearly.* It modifies the adjectives *every* and *all.* Don't use *most* for *almost.*

> *Almost everyone* agreed, **not** *Most everyone* agreed.
>
> *Almost all* the people came, **not** *Most all* the people came.

Forming the Comparative and Superlative Degrees of Adjectives and Adverbs

Adjectives and adverbs change to show degree.

Positive Degree	Comparative Degree	Superlative Degree
sweet (adj.)	sweeter	sweetest
sweetly (adv.)	more sweetly	most sweetly

Use the comparative degree when you are comparing two things, the superlative degree when you are comparing more than two.

> The *strawberries are sweeter than the apples,* but the *oranges are sweetest of all.*

Most one-syllable and some two-syllable adjectives form the comparative and superlative by adding *-er* or *-est.* Sometimes the adjective's final consonant is doubled and sometimes a *-y* is changed to *-i.*

> *tall, taller, tallest*
>
> *smart, smarter, smartest*
>
> *dry, drier, driest*
>
> *happy, happier, happiest*

There are a few exceptions, such as *good, better, best* and *bad, worse, worst*.

If an adjective has two or more syllables, the comparative and superlative degrees are usually formed with *more* and *most*.

> *intelligent, more intelligent, most intelligent*
>
> *difficult, more difficult, most difficult*

Most adverbs form the comparative and superlative with *more* and *most*.

> *slowly, more slowly, most slowly*
>
> *gracefully, more gracefully, most gracefully*

There are a few exceptions, such as *hard, harder, hardest; fast, faster, fastest; soon, sooner, soonest*.

Be careful not to double your comparisons when you form degrees of adjectives.

> *Funny, funnier* (**not** *more funnier*), *funniest* (**not** *most funniest*)

To use the *-er, -est* forms with *more* and *most* is incorrect.

Prepositions

Prepositions are words that show the relationship between nouns/pronouns and other nouns/pronouns.

> The cat **under** the *fence*
>
> The cat **between** the *fence* and the *house*
>
> Everyone **except** the *girl* **in** the blue *dress*
>
> A letter **about** *us*

The words in bold type are prepositions. The italicized words are called *objects of the prepositions*. When the object of the preposition is a pronoun, it should be in the objective case.

> **Between** *him and me,* <u>**not**</u> **Between** *he and I*
>
> **For** *Jane and me,* <u>**not**</u> **For** *Jane and I*

Prepositions are not as easy to spot as nouns, verbs, adjectives, and adverbs. Look for a word that establishes a certain kind of relationship between other words. For example, in *the cat under the fence,* how is the cat related to the fence? He is *under* it.

Words Commonly Used as Prepositions				
about	before	down	off	under
above	behind	during	on	underneath
across	below	except	out	until
after	beneath	for	over	unto
against	beside	from	past	up
along	between	in	since	upon
among	beyond	into	through	with
around	by	like	to	within
at	concerning	of	toward	without

Some prepositions, called *compound prepositions,* are made up of more than one word, such as *according to, because of, in front of, instead of,* and *next to.*

Be careful not to use a preposition when it isn't needed:

> Where have you *been?* **not** Where have you *been at?*
>
> I don't know *where he's gone,* **not** I don't know *where he's gone to.*

Also, don't use two prepositions when you only need one.

> Don't go *near the water,* **not** Don't go *near to the water.*
>
> The book *fell off* the table, **not** The book *fell off of* the table.

A traditional rule about prepositions is that you shouldn't end a sentence with one. This is no longer strictly adhered to. (Notice that the last sentence ends with a preposition.) Sometimes it is simply more natural for a preposition to come at the end of a sentence. You may use your own judgment.

> It is a letter *to which I will not respond,* **compared to** It is a letter *I will not respond to.*

Grammar: Sentences, Phrases, and Clauses

Moving from parts of speech to sentences is like moving from building materials to a building. The sentence is the basic structure of English, and while you may forget the difference between an adjective and an adverb, you'll usually recognize a sentence when you see it, just as you recognize a building even if you don't know the names of all its components. But a group of words pretending to be a sentence may occasionally fool you. Understanding how sentences are built will help you avoid errors.

The Sentence

Subject and Predicate

A sentence is a group of words containing a subject and a predicate that expresses a complete thought.

The *simple subject* is the noun or pronoun (what or who the sentence is about). The *complete subject* is this noun or pronoun and the words that modify it: *The angry child in the red-striped pajamas.*

The *simple predicate* is the verb or verb phrase that tells what the subject does or is or what is done to the subject. The *complete predicate* is the verb and the words that complete it: *stood stubbornly on the old porch.*

Putting the subject and predicate together makes a sentence: *The angry child in the red-striped pajamas stood stubbornly on the old porch.*

A Complete Thought

In addition to a subject and predicate, a group of words must express a complete thought to be a sentence. The group of words *The angry child in the red-striped pajamas stood stubbornly on the old porch* expresses a complete thought, and is therefore a sentence.

A sentence can be very short: *He jumped; She cried; The students sat down.*

A sentence can also be very long: *The argument that money is a burden probably originated with a rich man who was trying to counter the envy of a poor man.* Do not use the length of a group of words to determine whether or not it is a complete sentence.

The following groups of words are not complete sentences.

> *When he jumped*
>
> *When he jumped high into the air*
>
> *Because they are older than we are*
>
> *After they returned from the football game at the local high school*

They are not complete sentences because although they all have a subject and a predicate, they do not form a complete thought. We don't know what happened when he jumped. We don't know what it means that they are older than we are. And we don't know what happened after they returned from the football game.

> *When he jumped, he knocked over a lamp.*
>
> *When he jumped high into the air, he broke a school record.*
>
> *Because they are older than we are, they can get into the nightclub.*
>
> *After they returned from the football game at the local high school, they watched television.*

Now, these groups of words have been made into complete thoughts. They are sentences.

The Phrase

A phrase is any group of related words that, unlike a sentence, has no subject-predicate combination.

Types of Phrases

You won't be expected to differentiate between the types of phrases (*prepositional, participial, gerund, infinitive*), but you will be expected to recognize that a phrase is not a complete sentence. When a phrase is treated as if it were a complete sentence, it is a *sentence fragment,* and this is a basic writing error: *Looking at the photos; the photos in the album.*

Also, correct use of phrases can help you turn short, choppy sentences into more mature ones:

> *The boy was thin. He wore old clothes. He sat down. He was hungry. He ate everything. He left a clean plate.* (short, choppy sentences)
>
> *The thin boy, wearing old clothes, sat down at the table and hungrily ate everything on his plate.* (one longer sentence using phrases)

Prepositional Phrases

These are the most common phrases. They include a preposition and a noun or pronoun as the *object of the preposition.* The object of the preposition can have its own modifiers, which are also part of the prepositional phrase. Following are examples of prepositional phrases. Remember not to mistake any prepositional phrase for a complete sentence.

> *in the room; in the smoky, crowded room*
>
> *of the people; of the twenty-five thousand people*
>
> *by the river; by the deep, rushing river*
>
> *from the teacher; from the tired and frustrated teacher*
>
> *for the party; for the midnight victory party*

When a pronoun is the object of a preposition, it should be in the objective case (*between him and me; from them and us*).

Participial Phrases

A participial phrase begins with a past or present participle of the verb and is followed by its object and its modifiers. These phrases are used as adjectives.

> *Sniffing the fresh air,* Jim realized he had found the place he wanted to live.
>
> The soldiers, *trapped by the enemy,* threw down their guns.

Sniffing in the first sentence and *trapped* in the second are both participles. The participial phrase *trapped by the enemy* is actually an example of a phrase within a phrase; *by the enemy* is a prepositional phrase that acts as modifier for *trapped.* Don't worry about being asked to recognize this on the test. The important rule to remember is that participial phrases used alone are sentence fragments, not sentences.

> *Talking and laughing all the way to the dance recital.* (fragment)
>
> *Talking and laughing all the way to the dance recital,* the girls didn't act worried. (complete sentence)

Gerund Phrases

The gerund phrase may look like a participial phrase because it also begins with the *-ing* form of a verb. But a gerund phrase always acts like a noun in a sentence. Like other nouns, it can be a subject of a sentence, the object of a verb or preposition, or the complement of a linking verb.

> *Riding the black stallion* terrified Justin. (acts as subject of the verb *terrified*)
>
> The police reported *seeing the suspect.* (acts as object of the verb *reported*)
>
> He made his reputation by *talking loudly and vigorously.* (object of the preposition *by*)
>
> You are *asking for trouble.* (complement of the linking verb *are*)

Even when a gerund phrase is long, don't mistake it for a complete sentence.

> *Seeing him get off the bus and run into the station.* (sentence fragment)
>
> *Seeing him get off the bus and run into the station* made me nervous. (complete sentence)

Infinitive Phrases

An infinitive phrase contains the infinitive of a verb (for example, *to sleep, to have slept, to eat dinner, to swim, to decide*) and its objects and modifiers. These phrases usually act as nouns, though they can be used as adjectives and adverbs.

> *To sleep all night* was his only wish. (acts as subject of the verb)
>
> The mayor didn't want *to take an unpopular stand.* (acts as object of the verb *want*)
>
> He had plenty of money *to spend foolishly.* (acts as an adjective modifying *money*)
>
> After the meeting, she drove miles *to clear her mind.* (acts as an adverb modifying *drove*)

Don't mistake an infinitive phrase for a complete sentence.

> *To plan a large party for them during Christmas vacation.* (sentence fragment)
>
> *To plan a large party for them during Christmas vacation* is probably a mistake. (complete sentence)

Splitting Infinitives

Breaking up an infinitive with one or more adverbs is called *splitting an infinitive.* Splitting an infinitive isn't the grammatical sin it used to be, but most careful writers don't split infinitives without a good reason.

> They taught her *to spend money wisely,* **not** They taught her *to wisely spend money.*

Sometimes **not** splitting an infinitive is almost impossible: "We expect the population *to more than double* over the next twenty years." Other times, not splitting an infinitive causes ambiguity or sounds unnatural. In these cases, don't worry about the rule. Clarity and smoothness take precedence over the unsplit infinitives.

> We wanted *to discuss further Russian efforts* to modernize.

Not splitting the infinitive *to discuss* causes ambiguity. Does the adverb *further* modify *Russian efforts* or *discuss?* With a split infinitive, the sentence is clearer: We wanted *to further discuss Russian efforts* to modernize.

> He planned *to take quickly* the children to another room.

Not splitting the infinitive makes the sentence stilted and unnatural. Splitting the infinitive improves the sentence: He planned *to quickly take* the children to another room.

The Clause

Like a phrase, a clause is a group of related words, but unlike a phrase, a clause has a subject and predicate. An *independent* (or *main*) *clause*, along with having a subject and predicate, expresses a complete thought and can stand alone as a sentence. A *subordinate* (or *dependent*) *clause* doesn't express a complete thought and is therefore not a sentence. A subordinate clause that stands alone is a sentence fragment.

Independent Clauses

He saw her. The Browns hurried home. Free speech has a price: These are all complete sentences. When they are joined with other groups of words to make longer sentences, they are referred to as independent, or main, clauses.

Two or more independent clauses can be joined by using *and, but, for, nor, or, so,* and *yet.*

> He saw her, *and* he stopped to ask her how her brother was.
> The Browns hurried home, *but* they arrived too late.
> Free speech has a price, *for* nothing that valuable is really free.

Any of these clauses could stand alone as sentences. An old rule says that you shouldn't begin a sentence with *and, but, for, nor, or, so,* or *yet.* But today, doing so is widely accepted.

> The Browns hurried home. *But* they arrived too late.

Independent clauses can also be joined by a semicolon, but they cannot be joined by a comma.

> Free speech has a price; nothing that valuable is really free. (**correct**)
> Free speech has a price, nothing that valuable is really free. (**incorrect:** using a comma here creates a *run-on sentence* or *comma splice*)

Subordinate (Dependent) Clauses

A subordinate clause, like an independent clause, has a subject and predicate, but it cannot stand by itself as a sentence. It *depends* on something else to express a complete thought. Some subordinate clauses are introduced by *relative pronouns:*

who	which
whom	what
that	whose

Some are introduced by *subordinating conjunctions*. Some words that can act as subordinating conjunctions are as follows:

after	before	than	whenever
although	even if	that	where
as	if	though	wherever
as if	in order that	till	while
as long as	provided (that)	unless	
as though	since	until	
because	so (that)	when	

Types of Subordinate Clauses

A relative clause begins with a relative pronoun and acts as an adjective.

The novel *that won the Pulitzer prize* didn't sell well when it was first published.

The ceremony, *which several celebrities attended,* received intense media coverage.

The Rosales went to the airport to meet Janet, *who had flown in from New York.*

A noun clause serves as a noun in a sentence.

What I want for dinner is a big juicy hamburger.

The captain told us *how he survived the shipwreck.*

A vacation is *what I need most.*

Give it to *whoever needs it most.*

Adverbial clauses begin with subordinating conjunctions. What these conjunctions have in common is that they make the clauses that follow them unable to stand alone. The clauses act as adverbs, answering questions like *how, when, where, why, to what extent,* and *under what conditions.*

Because we wanted to arrive before noon, we left at the crack of dawn.

Unless the payment arrives before Friday, we will have to leave.

I can promise you the best seats in the house *if you buy the tickets by Monday.*

You can take the dog out for a walk *when you get home this afternoon.*

They came to the party, *although they had initially refused, because the famous singer had promised to appear.* (one main clause, two subordinate clauses)

What all subordinate clauses have in common is that they cannot stand alone as complete sentences. When they end with periods or question marks, they become sentence fragments. A semicolon is also an incorrect punctuation mark with a subordinate clause.

Although you promised to come and visit me when you came to Los Angeles. (**incorrect**)

Although you promised to come and visit me when you came to Los Angeles, you chose to visit Disneyland instead. (**correct**)

While his father was in Europe; he took a job at the mill. (**incorrect use of semicolon**)

While his father was in Europe, he took a job at the mill. (**correct**)

He chose one of the new hybrid cars. Because he was sure gas prices would continue to rise. (**incorrect**)

He chose one of the new hybrid cars because he was sure gas prices would continue to rise. (**correct**)

Problems with Sentence Construction

On the exam, you may be asked to recognize sentence errors like fragments, run-on sentences, lack of subject-predicate agreement, misplaced modifiers, or faulty parallel structure.

Run-on Sentences (Comma Splice)

When two independent clauses are run together without proper punctuation, the error is called a *run-on sentence* or a *comma splice*. An independent clause standing alone should end in a period, question mark, or exclamation point. If you want to join independent clauses, you should use a semicolon or one of the seven coordinating conjunctions (*and, but, for, nor, or, so, yet*) between them. A comma should precede the conjunction, but a comma without a conjunction isn't sufficient.

> He drove off in the Mercedes, Erica watched him go. (**incorrect**)
>
> He drove off in the Mercedes. Erica watched him go. (**correct**)
>
> He drove off in the Mercedes; Erica watched him go. (**correct**)
>
> He drove off in the Mercedes, and Erica watched him go. (**correct**)

Some words, called *conjunctive adverbs,* look like conjunctions but aren't. These "imposters" account for many run-on sentences. When a clause begins with one of them, it should be treated as an independent clause and should be followed by a period or semicolon, not a comma.

The following words are conjunctive adverbs:

also	*moreover*
besides	*nevertheless*
consequently	*otherwise*
further, furthermore	*similarly*
hence	*then*
however	*therefore*
indeed	*thus*
likewise	

Notice the incorrect and correct uses of the conjunctive adverbs in the following sentences.

> They came from South America, however they spoke English perfectly. (**incorrect:** run-on))
>
> They came from South America; however, they spoke English perfectly. (**correct**)

> Marilyn sold more tickets than anyone else, therefore she wins the prize. (**incorrect:** run-on)
>
> Marilyn sold more tickets than anyone else. Therefore, she wins the prize. (**correct**)

> The committee must decide, otherwise the project won't be completed. (**incorrect:** run-on)
>
> The committee must decide; otherwise the project won't be completed. (**correct**)

Sentence Fragments

Sentence fragments have been described in the sections covering sentences, phrases, and clauses. On the exam, you may be asked to recognize fragments, and at first glance, one may look like a sentence because it begins with a capital letter and ends with a period. Don't be fooled.

> Unless you want to pay for the motorcycle over time. (**incorrect:** fragment)
>
> Unless you want to pay for the motorcycle over time, you can't afford it. (**correct**)

Whoever left the windows open in the new house on Saturday night. (**incorrect:** fragment)

Whoever left the windows open in the new house on Saturday night should pay for the articles that were damaged by the storm. (**correct**)

Giving the set of china to her niece and the tools to her nephew. (**incorrect:** fragment)

Rose left, giving the set of china to her niece and the tools to her nephew. (**correct**)

Subject-Predicate Agreement

Within a sentence, sometimes there are distractions that can make you misidentify subject and predicate, leading to an agreement problem. Remember that a predicate (verb) must agree in person and number with its subject, regardless of other elements in the sentence. First, locate the subject of the sentence—who or what the sentence is about. Then ask yourself, "Is the subject first, second, or third person (*I/we; you; he, she, it/they*)? Is it singular or plural?" When you've answered these questions, you will know which form the verb should take.

Drinking a glass of milk and *soaking* in the tub *help* (**not** *helps*) me fall asleep.

This sentence has a compound subject: *drinking* and *soaking*. Because of the two subjects, a plural verb is used: *help*.

The decision of the judges *was* (**not** *were*) overruled.

The subject of the sentence is *decision,* not *judges*. Therefore, the verb should be singular (*was*).

The following words are usually singular: *anyone, no one, nobody, someone, somebody, each, either, neither, everyone, everybody.*

Each of the girls *has* (**not** *have*) a suitcase.

Each, not *girls,* is the subject of the sentence. Therefore, a singular verb is correct.

Either Mr. Holloway or Mrs. Sandoval *is* (**not** *are*) planning to pick us up.

The subject of the verb is *Either,* and therefore the verb should be singular (*is*).

The pronouns *all, some,* and *most* may be singular or plural, depending on whether they refer to a quantity of something (singular) or a number of things (plural). Also, the words *any* and *none* can take a singular or plural verb, depending on whether the writer is thinking of one thing or several.

Some of the apples *were* rotten.

Some of the money *was* for Barry.

Any of the books *is* appropriate. (*Any one* is appropriate.)

Any of the books *are* appropriate. (*All* are appropriate.)

Some phrases within a sentence suggest that a plural verb is correct, but these phrases do not, as a rule, affect the number of the subject.

The *principal,* as well as the teachers, *believes* (**not** *believe*) the plan is good.

The *cost,* in addition to the time it will take, *makes* (**not** *make*) the project unfeasible.

The *president,* accompanied by the committee head, *visits* (**not** *visit*) the site.

With the constructions *there is* and *there are, there* is never the subject: *There are* (**not** *there is* or *there's*) *millions of people who have second jobs.* The subject of the sentence is *millions.*

With the constructions *either . . . or* and *neither . . . nor,* use the singular if both elements are singular. If one of the elements is singular and one plural, choose the verb to agree with the element closest to it.

> *Either the director or the assistant director is* (**not** *are*) responsible.
>
> *Neither the director nor the actors are* (**not** *is*) coming today.

Misplaced Modifiers

A common mistake in sentence construction is poor placement of modifiers. If it isn't clear what term a modifier applies to, it is misplaced. Any kind of modifier can be misplaced: an adjective or adverb, phrases acting as modifiers, and clauses acting as modifiers.

> He saw a truck in the *driveway that was black and red.* (**incorrect**)

Unless the driveway was black and red, this is a misplaced modifier.

> He saw a *red and black truck* in the driveway. (**correct**)

This is more likely.

> Perhaps anticipating what modern science would discover, Anna Anderson, who claimed to be the missing Anastasia, requested she be cremated *before her death.* (**incorrect**)

It is doubtful that Anna wanted to be cremated before she died, but the placement of the phrase suggests that's just what she wanted.

> Perhaps anticipating what modern science would discover, Anna Anderson, who claimed to be the missing Anastasia, *requested before her death* that she be cremated. (**correct**)

Remember that the placement of even a simple modifier can change the meaning of a sentence.

> *Not all the home-team players* were available.
>
> *All the home-team players were not* available.

In the first sentence, maybe the home team could still limp along through a game. But the second sentence would mean the game would have to be canceled.

Among the most common misplaced modifiers are participial phrases.

> *Advancing across the desolate plains, the hot sun* burned the pioneers. (**incorrect:** the modifier suggests that the sun is advancing across the plain)

You can rewrite the sentence in various ways to ensure that the modifier is properly placed.

> *Advancing across the desolate plains, the pioneers* felt the burning sun. (**correct**)
>
> *The hot sun burned the pioneers as they advanced* across the desolate plains. (**correct**)

Check the following examples of poorly placed modifiers:

> The *buildings on the hillside constructed of wood shingles* burned first. (**poor placement of modifier**)
> On the hillside, the *buildings constructed of wood shingles* burned first. (**better**)

> He wore a wide leather belt around his *waist, which he had bought in New Mexico.* (**incorrect**)
> Around his waist he wore a wide leather *belt, which he had bought in New Mexico.* (**correct**)

> The editor at the newspaper promised to *check the article when I finished it for accuracy.* (**incorrect**)
> The editor at the newspaper promised to *check the article for accuracy when I finished it.* (**correct**)

Dangling modifiers are similar to misplaced modifiers except that the modifier isn't just separated from the word it modifies—the word it modifies is actually missing. When the modifier is a participial phrase, it is often referred to as a *dangling participle*.

> *Having eaten dinner,* the idea of a cheeseburger was unappealing. (**incorrect**)
>
> *Having eaten dinner,* I found the idea of a cheeseburger unappealing. (**correct**)

> *Studying the lecture notes, the ecosystem* became clearer. (**incorrect**)
>
> The ecosystem became clearer to me *when I studied the lecture notes.* (**correct**)

> *To win the election,* money is essential. (**incorrect**)
>
> *To win the election,* a candidate must have money. (**correct**)

Faulty Parallelism

Parallelism in sentences refers to matching grammatical structures. Elements in a sentence that have the same function or express similar ideas should be grammatically parallel, or grammatically matched.

A failure to create parallel structures when they're appropriate is called faulty parallelism. Notice the difference between correct parallel structure and faulty parallelism.

> The President promises to *reform* health care, *preserve* social security, and *a balanced budget.* (**incorrect**)
>
> The President promises to *reform* health care, *preserve* social security, and *balance* the budget. (**correct**)

> He described *skiing* in the Alps, *swimming* in the Adriatic, and *the drive* across the Sahara Desert. (**incorrect**)
>
> He described *skiing* in the Alps, *swimming* in the Adriatic, and *driving* across the Sahara Desert. (**correct**)

> He spoke more *of his term as ambassador* than *of being president.* (**incorrect**)
>
> He spoke more *of being ambassador* than *of being president.* (**correct**)

It doesn't matter what grammatical structure you choose as long as you remain with it consistently.

> What counts is not *how you look* but *your behavior.* (**incorrect**)
>
> What counts is not *how you look but how you behave.* (**correct**)
>
> What counts is not *your looks* but *your behavior.* (**also correct**)

In some constructions, something is true of one thing but not of the other. *But not* and *rather than* are used to set up these constructions. The parts should be parallel.

> The administration approved the student's right *to drop the class but not meeting* with the professor. (**incorrect**)
>
> The administration approved the student's right *to drop the class but not to meet* with the professor. (**correct**)

> The committee chose *to table* the motion rather than *voting* on it. (**incorrect**)
>
> The committee chose *to table* the motion rather than *to vote* on it. (**correct**)

Errors in parallel structure often occur with *either . . . or; neither . . . nor;* and *not only . . . but also.*

> *Either I will* like the job *or not.* (**incorrect**)
>
> *Either I will* like the job or *I won't.* (**correct**)

> *I have neither the patience to finish* the book *nor do I desire to finish it.* (**incorrect**)
>
> *I have neither the patience to finish* the book *nor the desire to finish it.* (**correct**)

> *Not only does he swim* well *but also biking is* one of his strong points. (**incorrect**)
>
> *Not only does he swim* well *but also he bikes* well. (**correct**)

We expected *not only to be late but also we expected* to be tired. (**incorrect**)

We expected *not only to be late but also to be tired*. (**correct**)

Verbs should be parallel, too. When you have more than one verb in your sentence, don't shift tenses unnecessarily. Also, don't shift from an active to a passive voice.

Yesterday he *tells* me I *didn't apply* in time. (**incorrect**)

Yesterday he *told* me I *didn't apply* in time. (**correct**)

Kate *prepared* the speech on the plane, and *it was delivered by her* at the meeting. (**incorrect:** shift from active voice to passive voice)

Kate *prepared* the speech on the plane and *delivered* it at the meeting. (**correct**)

Words

There are words that sound alike but are spelled differently, words that aren't acceptable usage but are mistakenly used for other words, words that should be used in some situations but not in others, and words that are close but not the same in meaning. The list below is a sampling of these troublemakers.

a, an Use the article **a** before words that begin with a consonant sound and words that begin with a "yew" sound: *a bag, a plan, a historic building, a one-armed man,* (*one* is pronounced as if it began with a **w**), *a united group.* Use **an** before words that begin with a vowel sound: *an advertisement, an executive, an hour* (the **h** is silent).

accept, except *Accept* means *to receive or agree with: I accept the gift; I accept your proposal. Except* as a preposition means *leaving out: Everyone except you is invited.*

advice, advise *Advice* is a noun: *His advice was good. Advise* is a verb: *I advise you not to go.*

affect, effect Usually, *affect* is a verb and *effect* is a noun: *Music affects me a lot. The effect of music is to calm me down.*

among, between In general, use *between* for two items or people and *among* for more than two items or people. *The money was divided between John and Jim. The property was divided among John, Jim, and Julie.*

amount, number Use *amount* to refer to a bulk or mass: *No amount of candy would be enough. Number* refers to individual countable items: *He took a large number of pennies.*

beside, besides *Beside* means *next to, at the side of. Besides* means *in addition to. Besides, I don't want to live beside the freeway.*

capital, capitol Use *capital* when referring to the city that is the seat of government. Use *capitol* when referring to the building where a legislature meets. *The capital of California is Sacramento. When we arrived there, we toured the capitol and other government buildings.*

cite, site, sight *Cite* means *to summon before a court of law, to mention by way of example,* or *to officially mention in a positive way: I am citing you for dumping trash on the highway; I cited the first chapter of the book as proof of my argument; The young police officer was cited for bravery. Site* means *location or scene: We drove quickly to the site of the new house. Sight* means *the ability to see* or *something seen: The ocean was a beautiful sight. His sight returned after the operation.*

conscious, conscience *Conscious* means *aware of, able to think and feel: I was conscious of the tension in the room. After the accident, he was shaken up but still conscious. Conscience* is an inner voice, a sense of right and wrong. *It bothered my conscience that I had lied to the teacher.*

disinterested, uninterested *Disinterested* means *impartial, not taking sides. Uninterested* means *lacking interest. A jury that is disinterested can be fair. Jury members that are uninterested aren't desirable because they may fall asleep during the trial.*

fewer, less Use *fewer* for individual countable items or people and *less* for bulk or quantity. *We expected fewer people to come; The children ate less food than she had brought.*

imply, infer *Imply* means *to suggest something indirectly. Infer* means *to conclude from facts or indications. If I imply by yawning that I'm tired, you might infer that I want you to leave.* Think of *implying* as done by the actor, *inferring* as done by the receiver.

irregardless, regardless There is no such word as *irregardless*. The correct word is *regardless*.

its, it's *Its* is the possessive form of *it: The tree lost its leaves. It's* is a contraction of *it is: It's too bad we can't come.*

lay, lie If you mean *repose*, use *lie*. If you mean *to set or put down*, use *lay: I lie down to rest; I lay the book down on the table. Lie* doesn't take an object, while *lay* does.

like, as Both words can be used as prepositions: *He sleeps like a baby; We see this as an alternative.* But only *as* should be used as a subordinating conjunction, so when you are introducing a dependent clause, don't use *like: The storm came in right after lunch just as (*not *like) I said it would.*

loose, lose *Lose* means *to be unable to find. Loose,* an adjective, means *unrestrained, inexact, not close fitting: I lose my keys frequently; This jacket is too loose.*

passed, past *Passed* is a verb: *I passed the test. Past* is either a noun, an adjective, or a preposition, but never a verb: *The past haunts me; His past actions impressed us; The lake lies past the barn.*

peak, peek *Peak* as a noun means *a pointed end* or *top. He climbed to the peak of the roof. Peek* as a verb means *to glance or look quickly.* As a noun, it means *a glance* or *look. She wanted to peek around the corner.*

precede, proceed *Precede* means *to go before in time, place, rank, etc.: The speech preceded the other festivities. Proceed* means *to move forward: You may proceed to the main entrance.*

principal, principle *Principal* as an adjective means *first in importance.* As a noun, it means *the head of a school. The principal reason that Nelson was chosen to be principal of our school was his dedication. Principle* is a noun that means *a fundamental truth or law or a rule of conduct: One of my principles is to withhold judgment until I hear all the evidence.*

sit, set *Sit* doesn't usually take an object: *I sit down. Set* usually does: *I set the book down.*

stationary, stationery *Stationary* means *still, at rest. Stationery* is paper used for writing letters.

than, then Don't use *then* (which means *at that time*) in comparisons. Use *than: He is wiser than (*not *then) his father was then.*

their, there, they're *Their* is the possessive form of *they: That is their boat. There* usually refers to a place or is used in impersonal construction (*there is, there are*): *We went there to see him. They're* is a contraction of *they are: They're ready to leave now.*

themselves, theirselves *Themselves* is correct. *Theirselves* is not a word.

to, too *To* has several meanings, the first being *toward. Too* means *also or more than enough: I walked to the river, which was too wild for me to swim in. My father thought so, too.*

weather, whether *Weather* is the state of the atmosphere. *Whether* is a functional word that introduces an indirect question involving alternatives: *Whether we go or not depends on what the weather is like.*

whose, who's *Whose* is the possessive of *who. Who's* is a contraction of *who is: Who's going to tell me whose jacket this is?*

your, you're *Your* is the possessive form of *you. You're* is a contraction of *you are: You're certain that this is your jacket?*

Errors to Look For

The following errors are common on the CAHSEE English-Language Arts and other multiple-choice grammar and usage exams. Reviewing these sentences will help you spot and correct the common errors.

Punctuation Errors

I left for Japan on Monday; after I graduated from junior college. (**incorrect**)

I left for Japan on Monday after I graduated from junior college. (**correct**)

She asked me "if I wanted to accompany her on the trip." (**incorrect**)

She asked me if I wanted to accompany her on the trip. (**correct**)

She asked me, "Do you want to accompany me on the trip?" (also **correct**)

Women, who are under thirty-five, may not participate. (**incorrect**)

Women who are under thirty-five may not participate. (**correct**)

Problems with Parts of Speech

Nouns

My eighth-grade Teacher was very helpful. (**incorrect**)

My eighth-grade teacher was very helpful. (**correct**)

The legislature are meeting this week. (**incorrect**)

The legislature is meeting this week. (**correct**)

We studied the civil war in my class. (**incorrect**)

We studied the Civil War in my class.(**correct**)

She forgot to return Nancys' book. (**incorrect**)

She forgot to return Nancy's book. (**correct**)

Verbs

He done everything I asked. (**incorrect**)

He did everything I asked. (**correct**)

If I was rich, I would buy a fancy car. (**incorrect**)

If I were rich, I would buy a fancy car. (**correct**)

She bought groceries and pet supplies and carries them inside. (**incorrect**)

She bought groceries and pet supplies and carried them inside. (**correct**)

If I would have thought of it, I would have called you earlier. (**incorrect**)

If I had thought of it, I would have called you earlier. (**correct**)

I drunk three bottles of water after the race. (**incorrect**)

I drank three bottles of water after the race. (**correct**)

The dress had been bought by my sister. (**poor**)

My sister had bought the dress. (**better**)

Pronouns

Everyone was invited except he and I. (**incorrect**)

Everyone was invited except him and me. (**correct**)

Ask Mr. Jones and he to come early. (**incorrect**)

Ask Mr. Jones and him to come early. (**correct**)

Maggie and him are going to the movies. (**incorrect**)

Maggie and he are going to the movies. (**correct**)

Talk to the counselor, whom will advise you what to do. (**incorrect**)

Talk to the counselor, who will advise you what to do. (**correct**)

Us boys decided we'd discuss it with the coach. (**incorrect**)

We boys decided we'd discuss it with the coach. (**correct**)

It is her who wants to take the trip. (**incorrect**)

It is she who wants to take the trip. (**correct**)

Jonathan told Brad that he was too young to see the movie. (**confusing**)

Jonathan told Brad that Brad was too young to see the movie. (**clearer**)

We unpacked our clothes from the suitcases and then stored them in the garage. (**confusing**)

After we unpacked our clothes, we stored the suitcases in the garage. (**clearer**)

Adjectives and Adverbs

The people in the chorus sang real good. (**incorrect**)

The people in the chorus sang well. (**correct**)

After he ate the whole pie, his stomach felt badly. (**incorrect**)

After he ate the whole pie, his stomach felt bad. (**correct**)

Rick is much more funnier than his brother. (**incorrect**)

Rick is much funnier than his brother. (**correct**)

My grandfather moves quick, even though he's over eighty. (**incorrect**)

My grandfather moves quickly, even though he's over eighty. (**correct**)

Problems with Sentences

Fragments

After the game was over. (**incorrect**)

After the game was over, we drove home. (**correct**)

Running down the road as fast as we could. (**incorrect**)

Running down the road as fast as we could, we managed to catch the dog. (**correct**)

Although we had promised to take her to the carnival. (**incorrect**)

Although we had promised to take her to the carnival, she still pouted. (**correct**)

The man who was climbing the tallest building in the city. (**incorrect**)

The man who was climbing the tallest building in the city looked scared. (**correct**)

Run-on Sentences

They found the old wagon, it was behind the barn. (**incorrect**)

They found the old wagon; it was behind the barn. (**correct**)

I liked the movie, however, it was too long. (**incorrect**)

I liked the movie. However, it was too long. (**correct**)

He spoke for an hour, it seemed much longer. (**incorrect**)

He spoke for an hour, but it seemed much longer. (**correct**)

Subject-Predicate Agreement

He don't enjoy sports the way he used to. (**incorrect**)

He doesn't enjoy sports the way he used to. (**correct**)

Where's Robert and Stan? (**incorrect**)

Where are Robert and Stan? (**correct**)

Paul, along with Jane and Miguel, are going to the concert. (**incorrect**)

Paul, along with Jane and Miguel, is going to the concert. (**correct**)

Not one of your plans are acceptable. (**incorrect**)

Not one of your plans is acceptable. (**correct**)

Neither the junior high school nor the high school have a swimming pool. (**incorrect**)

Neither the junior high school nor the high school has a swimming pool. (**correct**)

Misplaced Modifiers

Watching the sunset, the ocean looked red to me. (**incorrect**)

When I was watching the sunset, the ocean looked red to me. (**correct**)

I met my friend who I hadn't seen for five years at the mall. (**incorrect**)

At the mall, I met my friend, whom I hadn't seen for five years. (**correct**)

Being beautiful, people are attracted to my sister right away. (**incorrect**)

Because she is beautiful, my sister attracts people right away. (**correct**)

Faulty Parallelism

He promised to drive to the lake, open the cabin, and he would clean it, too. (**incorrect**)

He promised to drive to the lake, open the cabin, and clean it, too. (**correct**)

A cool day is better for the race than bright sunshine. (**incorrect**)

A cool day is better for the race than a bright sunny one. (**correct**)

My parents came to America with hopes of making a good living and to be free. (**incorrect**)

My parents came to America with hopes of making a good living and being free. (**correct**)

Common Prefixes, Suffixes, and Roots

Charts to Help You Understand Unfamiliar Words

The following charts should help you to arrive at definitions of unfamiliar words on the CAHSEE English-Language Arts. These prefixes, suffixes, and roots apply to thousands of words. Review this list carefully and become familiar with the prefixes, suffixes and roots. A more comprehensive list is included for reference, in the appendix.

Prefixes		
Prefix	*Meaning*	*Example*
ad-	to, toward	advance
anti-	against	antidote
bi-	two	bicycle
com-	together, with	composite
de-	away, from	deter
epi-	upon	epilogue
equi-	equal, equally	equivalent
ex-	out of	expel
homo-	same, equal, like	homogenized
hyper-	over, too much	hyperactive
hypo-	under, too little	hypodermic
in-	not	insufficient
in-	into	instruct
inter-	between	interstate
mal-	bad	malfunction
mis-	wrong	mistake
mono-	alone, one	monolith
non-	not	nonentity
ob-	against	objection
omni-	all, everywhere	omniscient
over-	above	overbearing
poly-	many	polymorphous
pre-	before	precede
pro-	forward	propel

(continued)

Prefixes *(continued)*		
Prefix	*Meaning*	*Example*
re-	back, again	regress
retro-	backward	retrograde
semi-	half, partly	semicircle
sub-	under	submarine
trans-	across, beyond	transcend
un-	not	unneeded

Suffixes		
Suffix	*Meaning*	*Example*
-able, -ible	able to	usable
-er, -or	one who does	competitor
-fy	to make	dignify
-ism	the practice of	rationalism
-ist	one who is occupied with	feminist
-less	without, lacking	meaningless
-logue	a particular kind of speaking or writing	prologue
-ness	the quality of	aggressiveness
-ship	the art or skill of	statesmanship
-tude	the state of	rectitude

Roots		
Root	*Meaning*	*Example*
arch	to rule	monarch
belli	war, warlike	belligerent
bene	good	benevolent
chron	time	chronology
dic	to say	indicative
fac	to make, to do	artifact
graph	writing	telegraph
mort	to die	mortal
port	to carry	deport
vid, vis	to see	invisible

Analyzing Prose and Poetry

The following may help you understand a passage, article, or poem.

Analyzing Prose

You will be asked questions about prose on the CAHSEE English-Language Arts. They might deal with the issues of genre (the kind of work, such as short story or essay), narrator, content or subject, structure, and style.

Genre

From what kind of work is the selection taken? Is it fiction or nonfiction?

If you're dealing with a work of fiction, chances are you'll have to think about the character or characters in the passage, while a work of nonfiction probably focuses on an issue, on an idea, or on the author him- or herself.

Narrator/Author

Whether the passage is from a work of fiction or nonfiction, you must be aware of who is speaking and what his or her attitudes are toward the characters or the subject of the passage. If you can, identify *who* is speaking, *where* and *when, why,* and *to whom.*

Subject

What is the purpose of the passage? Is it to present an argument or to introduce a character? To coax or entertain or to stir to action? If you can define an author's purpose clearly, most of the questions on the interpretation of meaning will fall neatly into place.

Structure

The normal units of prose are the sentence and the paragraph. As with a poem, try to see how each part advances the progress of the whole. How are the sentences and paragraphs related to each other and to the passage as a whole?

Style

The style of prose is determined by language (both literal and figurative), imagery, grammar and sentence structure—all matters you will deal with in the analysis of poetry. In addition, the analysis of prose is certain to raise questions about the rhetoric of a passage, that is, its use of words to persuade or influence a reader.

Analyzing Poetry

To prepare yourself for the kind of questions that may be asked, try going through each poem and asking the following questions in an order similar to this on the following page.

What is the dramatic situation?

To determine the dramatic situation, ask yourself these questions: Who is the speaker? Or who are the speakers? Is the speaker male or female? Where is he or she? When does this poem take place? What are the circumstances?

Sometimes you'll be able to answer all of these questions, sometimes only a few. It doesn't matter. You've already begun to understand the poem.

What is the structure of the poem?

To figure out a poem's structure, ask yourself the following questions: What are the parts of the poem and how are they related to each other? What gives the poem its coherence? What are the structural divisions of the poem?

In analyzing structure, your best aid is the punctuation. Look first for complete sentences indicated by periods, semi-colons, question marks, or exclamation points. Then ask how the poem gets from the first sentence to the second and from the second to the third. Are there repetitions such as parallel syntax or the use of a simile in each sentence? Answer these questions in accordance with the sense of the poem, not by where a line ends or a rhyme falls.

Think about the logic of the poem. Does it ask questions then answer them? Or develop an argument? Or use a series of analogies to prove a point? Understanding the structure isn't just a matter of mechanics. It will help you to understand the meaning of the poem as a whole and to perceive some of the art, the formal skills, that the poet has used.

What is the theme of the poem?

You should now be able to see the point of the poem. Sometimes a poem says something as simple as "I love you"; sometimes the theme or the meaning is much more complex. If possible, define what the poem says and why. A love poem usually praises the loved one in the hope that the speaker's love will be returned. But many poems have meanings too complex to be reduced to single sentences.

Are the grammar and meaning clear?

Make sure you understand the meaning of all the words in the poem, especially words you thought you knew but which don't seem to fit in the context of the poem. Also make sure you understand the grammar of the poem. The word order of poetry is often skewed, and in a poem, a direct object may come before the subject and the verb. ("His sounding lyre the poet struck" can mean the poet was hit by a musical instrument, but as a line of poetry, it probably means the poet played his harp.)

What are the important literal images and figures of speech?

What are the important literal sensory objects—the images, such as a field of poppies or a stench of corruption? What are the similes and metaphors of the poem? In each, exactly what is compared to what? Is there a pattern in the images, such as a series of comparisons in which men are compared to wild animals? The most difficult challenge of reading poetry is discriminating between the *figurative* ("I love a rose"—that is, my love is like a rose, beautiful, sweet, fragile) and the *literal* ("I love a rose"—that is, roses are my favorite flower). The list of literary devices that a writer might use is enormous. Terms you should definitely know include *metaphor, simile,* and *personification.*

What is the tone of the poem?

Tone is a slippery word, and almost everyone has trouble with it. It's sometimes used to mean the mood or atmosphere of a work. Or it can mean a manner of speaking, a tone of voice, as in "The disappointed coach's tone was scornful." Its most common use as a term of literary analysis, however, is to denote the inferred attitude of an author. When the author's attitude is different from that of the speaker—as is usually the case in ironic works—the tone of voice of the speaker, which may be calm, businesslike, even gracious, may be very different from the satiric tone of the work, which reflects the author's disapproval of the speaker.

Literature Key Terms

Following are terms often used in multiple-choice test questions concerning literature. Such questions don't generally ask you to directly define the terms, but you must be familiar with their meaning in order to answer the question that is asked. In addition, understanding and using the terms when appropriate, can strengthen an essay written in response to a literature selection.

Allegory A story in which people, things, and events have another meaning. An example of allegory is Orwell's *Animal Farm.*

Alliteration The repetition of the same sound. This is usually a consonant at the beginning of two or more words immediately succeeding each other or in short intervals. An example is: "Friends feared forever."

Allusion A reference in a work of literature to something outside the work, especially to a well-known historical or literary event, person, or work. In *Hamlet,* when Horatio says, "ere the mightiest Julius fell," the allusion is to the death of Julius Caesar.

Ambiguity Multiple meanings a literary work may communicate, especially two meanings that are incompatible.

Attitude A speaker's, author's, or character's opinion of a subject. For example, Hamlet's attitude toward Gertrude is a mixture of affection and revulsion, changing from one to the other within a single scene.

Autobiography An author's account of his or her own life.

Biography An accurate history of a single person.

Climax Normally the point of highest interest in a novel, short story, or play. As a technical term of dramatic composition, the climax is the place where the action reaches a turning point; where the rising action (the complication of the plot) ends and the following action (the resolution of the plot) begins.

Comedy A dramatic form intended to amuse the audience. Usually, a comedy moves from an unhappy situation to a happy resolution. The word *comedy* is now also applied to genres other than drama, such as the novel, film, or television show.

Connotation The implications of a word or phrase, as opposed to its exact meaning (*denotation*).

Convention A device of style or subject matter so often used that it becomes a recognized means of expression. For example, a lover observing the literary love conventions cannot eat or sleep and grows pale and lean.

Denotation The dictionary meaning of a word, as opposed to *connotation.*

Diction Word choice. Essay questions on a passage of prose or a poem could ask you to talk about diction or about techniques that include diction. Any word that is important to the meaning and the effect of a passage can be used in your essay. These words are also *details.*

Digression The use of material unrelated to the subject of a work. Departing from the subject; going off-topic.

Euphemism A figure of speech that uses indirection to avoid offensive bluntness, such as *deceased* for *dead* or *remains* for *corpse.*

Figurative language Writing that uses figures of speech (as opposed to literal language or that which is actual or specifically denoted) such as metaphor, simile, and irony. Figurative language uses words to mean something other than their literal meaning. "The black bat night has flown" is figurative, with the metaphor comparing night and a bat. "Night is over," says the same thing without figurative language. No real bat is or has been on the scene, but night is like a bat because it is dark.

Genre A literary form, such as essay, novel, or poem. Within genres like the poem, there are also more specific genres based upon content (love poem, nature poem) or form (sonnet, ode).

Grotesque Characterized by distortions or incongruities; misshapen or bizarre. The fiction of Poe is often described as grotesque.

Hyperbole Deliberate exaggeration, overstatement. As a rule, hyperbole is self-conscious, without the intention of being accepted literally. "The strongest man in the world" or "a diamond as big as the Ritz" are examples of hyperbole.

Imagery The images of a literary work; the sensory details of a work; the figurative language of a work. Imagery has several definitions, but the two that are paramount are the visual, auditory, or physical images evoked by the words of a literary work or the images that figurative language evokes.

Irony A figure of speech in which intent and actual meaning differ—characteristically praise for blame or blame for praise; a pattern of words that turns away from direct statement of its own obvious meaning. The term *irony* implies a discrepancy. In *verbal irony* (saying the opposite of what one means), the discrepancy is between statement and meaning. Sometimes, irony may simply understate, as in "Men have died from time to time. . . ."

Jargon The special language of a profession or group. The term *jargon* usually has negative associations, with the implication that jargon is evasive and not understood by outsiders.

Literal Not figurative; accurate to the letter; matter of fact or concrete.

Lyrical Songlike; characterized by emotion, subjectivity, and imagination.

Metaphor A figurative use of language in which a comparison is expressed without the use of a comparative term like *as, like* or *than*. A simile would say, "night is like a black bat"; a metaphor would say, "the black bat night." When Romeo says, "It is the east, and Juliet is the sun," his metaphors compare her window to the east and Juliet to the sun.

Narrative techniques The methods involved in telling a story; the procedures used by a writer of stories or accounts. *Narrative techniques* is a general term that asks you to discuss the procedures used in the telling of a story. Examples of the techniques you might use are point of view, manipulation of time, dialogue, or interior monologue.

Novel A fictional narrative in prose of considerable length. Shorter works are called novellas, and even shorter ones are called short stories.

Omniscient point of view The vantage point of a story in which the narrator can know, see, and report whatever he or she chooses. The narrator is free to describe the thoughts of any of the characters, to skip about in time or place, or to speak directly to the reader.

Oxymoron A combination of opposites; the union of contradictory terms. Romeo's line "feather of lead, bright smoke, cold fire, sick health" contains four examples of the device.

Parable A story designed to suggest a principle, illustrate a moral, or answer a question. Parables are allegorical stories.

Paradox A statement that seems to be self-contradicting but may, in fact, be true.

Parody A composition that imitates the style of another composition normally for comic effect. A contest for parodies of Hemingway draws hundreds of entries each year.

Personification A figurative use of language that gives the nonhuman (ideas, inanimate objects, animals, abstractions) human characteristics.

Plot The interrelated actions of a play or a novel that move to a climax and a final resolution.

Point of view Any of several possible vantage points from which a story is told. The point of view may be omniscient, limited to that of a single character, or limited to that of several characters, as well as other possibilities. The teller may use the first person and/or the third person.

Rhetorical question A question asked for effect, not in expectation of a reply. No reply is expected because the question presupposes only one possible answer.

Satire Writing that seeks to arouse a reader's disapproval of an object by ridicule. Satire is usually comedy that exposes errors.

Setting The background to a story; the physical location of a play, story, or novel. The setting of a narrative will normally involve both time and place.

Simile A directly expressed comparison; a figure of speech comparing two objects usually with *like, as,* or *than.* It is easier to recognize a simile than a metaphor because the comparison is explicit: my love is like a fever; my love is deeper than a well; my love is as dead as a doornail.

Soliloquy A speech in which a character who is alone speaks his or her thoughts aloud. A monologue also has a single speaker, but in a monologue the speaker talks to others who do not interrupt. Hamlet's "To be, or not to be" and "O! what a rogue and peasant slave am I" are soliloquies.

Strategy (or rhetorical strategy) The management of language for a specific effect. The strategy or rhetorical strategy of a poem is the planned placement of elements to achieve an effect. The rhetorical strategy of most love poems, for example, is deployed to convince the loved one to return the speaker's love. By appealing to the loved one's sympathy ("If you don't return my love, my heart will break."), or by flattery ("How could I not love someone as beautiful as you?"), or by threat ("When you're old, you'll be sorry you refused me."), the lover attempts to persuade the loved-one to love in return.

Structure The arrangement of materials within a work; the relationship of the parts of a work to the whole; the logical divisions of a work. The most common principles of structure are series (A, B, C, D, E), contrast (A versus B, C versus D, E versus A), and repetition (AA, BB, AB). The most common units of structure are play (scene, act), novel (chapter), and poem (line, stanza).

Style The mode of expression in language; the characteristic manner of expression of an author. Many elements contribute to style, and if a question calls for a discussion of style or of "stylistic techniques," you can discuss diction, syntax, figurative language, imagery, selection of detail, sound effects, and tone, using the ones that are appropriate.

Syllogism A form of reasoning in which two statements are made and a conclusion is drawn from them. A syllogism begins with a major premise ("All tragedies end unhappily.") followed by a minor premise ("*Hamlet* is a tragedy.") and a conclusion ("Therefore, *Hamlet* ends unhappily.").

Symbol Something that is simultaneously itself and a sign of something else. For example, winter, darkness, and cold are real things, but in literature they are also likely to be used as symbols of death.

Theme The main thought expressed by a work.

Thesis The theme, meaning, or position that a writer undertakes to prove or support.

Tone The manner in which an author expresses his or her attitude; the intonation of the voice that expresses meaning. Tone is described by adjectives, and the possibilities are nearly endless. Often a single adjective will not be enough, and tone may change from chapter to chapter or even line to line. Tone may be the result of allusion, diction, figurative language, imagery, irony, symbol, syntax, and style.

Tragedy Now defined as a play with a serious content and an unhappy ending. Shakespeare's *Hamlet* or Miller's *Death of a Salesman* are examples.

PART III

PRACTICE TESTS

The actual CAHSEE English-Language Arts has 79 multiple-choice questions and 1 essay. Only 72 of the 79 multiple-choice questions and the essay actually count toward your score. The 7 additional multiple-choice questions, which can be scattered throughout the exam, are being tested for future exams. Each practice test in this section is followed by complete explanations.

The test is given in two sessions and is broken down as follows:

Session 1	21 Multiple-choice questions	1 essay	recommended time: 2 hours
Session 2	58 Multiple-choice questions		recommended time: 1½ hours

Remember there is no time limit on CAHSEE English-Language Arts. If you need additional time, ask the proctor. You should be able to finish the test within the school day. Try to work at a steady pace, skipping problems that give you difficulty, taking a guess answer, and coming back to them later.

The questions in these simulated practice exams follow the California standards and are similar in style and difficulty to the problems on the actual exam. The actual CAHSEE English-Language Arts is copyrighted and may not be duplicated. These questions are not taken from the actual tests.

Answer Sheets for Practice Test 1

(Remove This Sheet and Use It to Mark Your Answers)

Session 1

1 Ⓐ Ⓑ Ⓒ Ⓓ
2 Ⓐ Ⓑ Ⓒ Ⓓ
3 Ⓐ Ⓑ Ⓒ Ⓓ
4 Ⓐ Ⓑ Ⓒ Ⓓ
5 Ⓐ Ⓑ Ⓒ Ⓓ
6 Ⓐ Ⓑ Ⓒ Ⓓ
7 Ⓐ Ⓑ Ⓒ Ⓓ
8 Ⓐ Ⓑ Ⓒ Ⓓ
9 Ⓐ Ⓑ Ⓒ Ⓓ
10 Ⓐ Ⓑ Ⓒ Ⓓ
11 Ⓐ Ⓑ Ⓒ Ⓓ
12 Ⓐ Ⓑ Ⓒ Ⓓ
13 Ⓐ Ⓑ Ⓒ Ⓓ
14 Ⓐ Ⓑ Ⓒ Ⓓ
15 Ⓐ Ⓑ Ⓒ Ⓓ
16 Ⓐ Ⓑ Ⓒ Ⓓ
17 Ⓐ Ⓑ Ⓒ Ⓓ
18 Ⓐ Ⓑ Ⓒ Ⓓ
19 Ⓐ Ⓑ Ⓒ Ⓓ
20 Ⓐ Ⓑ Ⓒ Ⓓ
21 Ⓐ Ⓑ Ⓒ Ⓓ

Session 2

22 Ⓐ Ⓑ Ⓒ Ⓓ
23 Ⓐ Ⓑ Ⓒ Ⓓ
24 Ⓐ Ⓑ Ⓒ Ⓓ
25 Ⓐ Ⓑ Ⓒ Ⓓ
26 Ⓐ Ⓑ Ⓒ Ⓓ
27 Ⓐ Ⓑ Ⓒ Ⓓ
28 Ⓐ Ⓑ Ⓒ Ⓓ
29 Ⓐ Ⓑ Ⓒ Ⓓ
30 Ⓐ Ⓑ Ⓒ Ⓓ
31 Ⓐ Ⓑ Ⓒ Ⓓ
32 Ⓐ Ⓑ Ⓒ Ⓓ
33 Ⓐ Ⓑ Ⓒ Ⓓ
34 Ⓐ Ⓑ Ⓒ Ⓓ
35 Ⓐ Ⓑ Ⓒ Ⓓ
36 Ⓐ Ⓑ Ⓒ Ⓓ
37 Ⓐ Ⓑ Ⓒ Ⓓ
38 Ⓐ Ⓑ Ⓒ Ⓓ
39 Ⓐ Ⓑ Ⓒ Ⓓ
40 Ⓐ Ⓑ Ⓒ Ⓓ
41 Ⓐ Ⓑ Ⓒ Ⓓ
42 Ⓐ Ⓑ Ⓒ Ⓓ
43 Ⓐ Ⓑ Ⓒ Ⓓ
44 Ⓐ Ⓑ Ⓒ Ⓓ
45 Ⓐ Ⓑ Ⓒ Ⓓ
46 Ⓐ Ⓑ Ⓒ Ⓓ
47 Ⓐ Ⓑ Ⓒ Ⓓ
48 Ⓐ Ⓑ Ⓒ Ⓓ
49 Ⓐ Ⓑ Ⓒ Ⓓ
50 Ⓐ Ⓑ Ⓒ Ⓓ

51 Ⓐ Ⓑ Ⓒ Ⓓ
52 Ⓐ Ⓑ Ⓒ Ⓓ
53 Ⓐ Ⓑ Ⓒ Ⓓ
54 Ⓐ Ⓑ Ⓒ Ⓓ
55 Ⓐ Ⓑ Ⓒ Ⓓ
56 Ⓐ Ⓑ Ⓒ Ⓓ
57 Ⓐ Ⓑ Ⓒ Ⓓ
58 Ⓐ Ⓑ Ⓒ Ⓓ
59 Ⓐ Ⓑ Ⓒ Ⓓ
60 Ⓐ Ⓑ Ⓒ Ⓓ
61 Ⓐ Ⓑ Ⓒ Ⓓ
62 Ⓐ Ⓑ Ⓒ Ⓓ
63 Ⓐ Ⓑ Ⓒ Ⓓ
64 Ⓐ Ⓑ Ⓒ Ⓓ
65 Ⓐ Ⓑ Ⓒ Ⓓ
66 Ⓐ Ⓑ Ⓒ Ⓓ
67 Ⓐ Ⓑ Ⓒ Ⓓ
68 Ⓐ Ⓑ Ⓒ Ⓓ
69 Ⓐ Ⓑ Ⓒ Ⓓ
70 Ⓐ Ⓑ Ⓒ Ⓓ
71 Ⓐ Ⓑ Ⓒ Ⓓ
72 Ⓐ Ⓑ Ⓒ Ⓓ
73 Ⓐ Ⓑ Ⓒ Ⓓ
74 Ⓐ Ⓑ Ⓒ Ⓓ
75 Ⓐ Ⓑ Ⓒ Ⓓ
76 Ⓐ Ⓑ Ⓒ Ⓓ
77 Ⓐ Ⓑ Ⓒ Ⓓ
78 Ⓐ Ⓑ Ⓒ Ⓓ
79 Ⓐ Ⓑ Ⓒ Ⓓ

CUT HERE

Essay

On the actual exam you will have **over two pages to write your essay.** Use another sheet of lined paper to complete your essay for this practice test.

_____

_____

_____

_____

_____

_____

_____

_____

_____

_____

_____

_____

_____

_____

_____

_____

_____

_____

_____

_____

_____

_____

CUT HERE

Practice Test 1

Session 1

Read the following article and answer questions 1 through 7.

Gaining on the Men

by Martin Miller
Times Staff Writer

Women's marathon speeds are improving at a record pace. Citing physical advantages, some predict they may soon beat men on their own terms, without a head start.

The Los Angeles Marathon's 20-minute head start for elite female runners helped a woman cross the finish line first this year, possibly setting a precedent for other major races to follow suit.

But eventually, some experts say, the practice may become unnecessary. Women may start winning the 26.2-mile races outright.

Their marathon times have grown shorter and shorter over the years as a flood of participants has deepened the talent pool. And quite simply, when it comes to their biological makeup, woman may be better suited for long distances than men.

"If all else is equal, the longer the race, the more it favors the woman," said Dr. Robert Girandola, an associate

professor of kinesiology at USC who has studied the performance of elite track athletes.

The real question, however, is whether the marathon is a long enough race for a woman's biological advantages to trump a man's. The short answer is exercise physiologists don't know, but they see strong points on both sides.

As Girandola points out, "These runners are hitting 5-minute miles, so even in a marathon you still need power and speed, and that favors a man."

GO ON TO THE NEXT PAGE

Only a couple of generations ago, top race organizers widely believed that women didn't have the physiological wherewithal to complete a marathon. That belief delayed the women's marathon from becoming an Olympic event until 1984.

Over the past couple of decades, men have shaved seconds off their finish times; women have chopped minutes. Meanwhile, the gender gap in marathon times used to be a half-hour, but now that margin has routinely been narrowed to 20 minutes, sometimes less. (Race organizers in Los Angeles created the head start for women by averaging the finish times over the marathon's 19-year history.)

A strength for women runners is that they seem to be able to process heat better than men do, said Greg Crowther, a research associate at the University of Washington. He has studied male-female differences in long-distance running and says this ability would make it less likely for a woman to be overcome by heat.

"Take an elephant and a mouse," said Crowther, a chemical engineer whose doctoral work was in human physiology. "The elephant has a huge internal reserve of heat, but the mouse loses it very quickly. Heat just flies off the mouse."

Also, women metabolize more fat and fewer carbohydrates than men, said Tracy Horton, an assistant professor of nutrition at the University of Colorado Health Sciences Center who has studied the way athletes process food. This is a critical benefit over longer distances because the fuel supplied by carbohydrates is usually exhausted. Thus, a woman can convert fat reserves to energy more efficiently than a man, Horton said.

Larger fat reserves, however, also can hold a woman back in shorter distances, because extra weight slows the runner down. Again, at what point the fat reserves become an asset is unclear, experts say.

Women, too, may bear pain better than men. Although they have been shown to experience pain more quickly than men, women are less likely to become disabled by it, according to researchers at a 1998 gender and pain conference at the National Institutes of Health in Bethesda, Md. A combination of physiological and psychological tools—helps women overcome pain more effectively than men, the researchers said.

No one would deny that Pam Reed of Tucson, Ariz., can overcome pain. She's the two-time champion of the extreme endurance event known as the Badwater Ultramarathon, a 135-mile run from Death Valley halfway up Mt. Whitney. Her closest competitor in last year's race, a man, finished 24 minutes behind her.

Still, the men have much on their side to maintain their dominance of the marathon, say exercise physiologists. They have a higher oxygen-carrying capacity, and so can supply muscles with explosive power and speed. Also, testosterone means less fat and more muscle.

"In general, I'm pessimistic about women overtaking the men in the marathon anyway," said Crowther. "I think it may still be too short a distance to take away the natural advantages men have."

But sometime in the not-too-distant future, Los Angeles Marathon organizers are confident they will see a woman crowned champion with no head start. "At some point, a woman is going to win a marathon on her own merits," said Dr. William Burke, president of the Los Angeles Marathon. "It's a matter of time."

1. **This article provides the MOST information on—**

    A. the manner in which elephants rid themselves of excess heat.

    B. competitors in the Ultramarathon held in Death Valley.

    C. the links between child bearing and women's increased ability to endure pain.

    D. physical advantages that may someday, enable women to beat men in endurance events like the marathon.

2. **A person interested in the ideas discussed in this article would MOST likely find additional articles in which of the following magazines?**

    A. a fashion magazine

    B. a magazine that features stories about athletes

    C. a textbook on anatomy

    D. a general news magazine

3. **According to the passage, the men might retain their dominance in the marathon because—**

    A. extra testosterone means more muscle and men have greater oxygen-bearing capacity than women.

    B. men can endure more pain longer than their female counterparts.

    C. men's larger surface area allows them to rid themselves of excess heat quicker.

    D. more men participate in distance events; hence the talent pool is deeper.

4. **According to the passage, the 20-minute head start given to women at this year's Los Angeles Marathon was—**

    A. given to encourage women to enter the event.

    B. given as partial compensation for decades of discrimination against women in long-distance running.

    C. still inadequate to provide women a chance equal to that of men.

    D. arrived at by averaging the finish times of women compared to those of men over the history of the event.

GO ON TO THE NEXT PAGE

5. Which of the following questions could MOST effectively be developed into a research paper?

A. In what year did women first compete in the Los Angeles Marathon?

B. Should women be permitted to enter marathons?

C. Why is the marathon 26.2 miles long?

D. How do women's physical advantages compare to those of men in other events?

6. Read this sentence from the selection.

> The marathon times have grown shorter and shorter over the years as a flood of participants has deepened the talent pool.

The word *flood* in the above sentence means—

A. a large rushing flow of water.

B. a lake.

C. a huge number.

D. water that covers land that was formerly dry.

7. Which of the following MOST accurately illustrates what the article suggests could happen in the future of marathon running?

A. Women marathoners are good and getting better, but they probably will never catch the men.

B. Sometime soon women may win the Los Angeles Marathon without the advantage of a head start.

C. Women can endure pain better than men.

D. Men's power and speed will prove an insurmountable barrier to women in running events.

Read the following excerpt and answer questions 8 through 16.

Susan Allen Toth (1940–)

This excerpt appears in a literature book Susan Allen Toth helped edit. Because she is an author in her own right and her works are included in the literature book, she is given the unenviable task of writing her own biographical sketch. In this excerpt, Toth explains why for the first time in the book a biographical sketch is being written in first person.

As editor of this section of the textbook, I have the odd task of writing about myself. Of course, I could pretend that someone else was doing it, or write an impersonal narrative, as if I were observing my life from afar. But as a writer and a teacher of writing, I have long felt that too many of us are frightened of using the first-person voice. We have been taught that somehow it is wrong to say *I*. Instead, we learn a dull, vague bureaucratese, filled with passive constructions such as "It can be seen by many readers . . . ," "It can easily be understood that . . . ," or "In conclusion, it can be pointed out that. . . ." We are not fooling anyone—the reader knows it is the individual writer's judgment—but we are pretending that we are part of some impressive institution. We think that *I* doesn't sound important enough. It is also rather scary to write *I*: we don't have anyone else to hide behind.

As a memoirist (someone who writes directly about all or part of her personal experience), I have written two books with an *I*. The first, *Blooming: A Small-Town Girlhood* (1981), is about my childhood and adolescence in Ames, Iowa, in the 1940s and 1950s. The second, *Ivy*

Days: Making My Way Out East (1984) (which is excerpted here), is a kind of sequel, describing my experiences as a Midwestern girl at an Eastern Ivy League women's college. In both books, I try to see my life as clearly as I can, remembering both pain and pleasure, which were often mixed. I am glad when readers find my writing humorous; but I am more deeply pleased by those who also sense my disappointments, fears, and continuing uncertainties, experiences and feelings that were part of my (and most people's) growing up.

The biographical facts of my life are short and don't say much about personality, family, fate, or luck, among other determinants of who you are and what you do. I was born in 1940 in Ames, Iowa, where I lived until I went to Smith College in 1957. After graduating from Smith, I traveled west to Berkeley for a master's degree in English. In 1963 I married and began teaching at San Francisco State. A year later, I moved to Minnesota. In 1969 I finished my Ph.D. at the University of Minnesota and joined the faculty of Macalester College in St. Paul, where I am now firmly and fondly attached. In 1971 my

GO ON TO THE NEXT PAGE

daughter Jennifer was born; in 1974 I was divorced; in 1978 I published my first short story in a national magazine and began thinking I might be able to write a book about growing up in a vanished time. In 1985 I married architect James Stageberg and, after twenty years in St. Paul, moved across the Mississippi to Minneapolis, where I now live in a modernist house that overlooks a city lake. How can mere facts convey the deep tremors of any of these events?

I began publishing fiction and essays rather late in life, although I had been writing in one form or another, from journalism to scholarly research, as long as I can remember. Most of my work since 1978 has been nonfiction, from personal essays to reviews, as well as memoir, in such different periodicals as *Harpers', Redbook, McCalls,* and the *New York Times.*

Since I have always been a willing prey to the web and texture of life, I have a passion for detail. Perhaps that is why I so much admire E. B. White. Like Sarah Orne Jewett, the nineteenth-century New England writer who is the other main influence on my style, White has an eye for the small, but crucial detail that conveys atmosphere and feeling. I am sometimes asked if I kept a journal when I was growing up; unlike many writers, I didn't. My mind seems to be like a grandmother's attic; it accumulates scenes and characters, bits of dialogue, and lots of state properties. I write partly to clean out the attic. And also I like to sort through the piles and see what, among the junk and mess, has value.

8. The author feels that by NOT using first person we—

   A. fool our readers into thinking we did not write the piece.

   B. have been taught correctly.

   C. pretend we are more important than we really are.

   D. cheat the readers.

9. Which of the following BEST describes Toth as an author?

   A. one who writes about personal experiences

   B. one who writes to please her readers

   C. one who only writes about the past

   D. one who feels she has little to say about herself, but a lot to say about others

10. Which statement BEST describes the author's writing philosophy?

   A. The more detailed the better.

   B. The more personal the better.

   C. Write what you know.

   D. Keep a journal.

11. As used in the context of this excerpt, which sentence includes an example of figurative language?

   A. "Instead, we learn a dull, vague bureaucratese, filled with passive constructions such as 'It can be seen by many readers. . . .'"

   B. "White has an eye for the small but crucial detail. . . ."

   C. "I like to sort through the piles and see what, among the junk and mess, has value."

   D. ". . . where I now live in a modernist house that overlooks a city lake."

12. Which word BEST describes the tone of this excerpt?

   A. melancholy

   B. discomfort

   C. eagerness

   D. sympathy

13. Why does Toth mention the fact that her work has appeared in many different types of periodicals?

   A. to convince you that her works are worth reading

   B. to show the immense pride she has in her work

   C. to prove what a successful author she is

   D. to show that her topics are as varied as the periodicals in which they appear

14. Why does the author begin the excerpt with a discussion of the use of the first person in writing?

   A. to set the tone

   B. to explain why this piece is written in first person

   C. to persuade people to write in first person

   D. to criticize the use of third person

15. How does Toth feel about biographical information?

   A. It is to some degree uninformative.

   B. It is essential for understanding the author.

   C. It is essential for understanding the author's work.

   D. It is very interesting information to have.

16. Read this sentence from the excerpt.

> The biographical facts of my life are short and don't say much about personality, family, fate or luck, among other determinants of who you are and what you do.

Based on the context in which it is used, what does *determinants* mean?

   A. elements that determine an outcome

   B. people who are determined

   C. decisions to be made

   D. a loss of hope

GO ON TO THE NEXT PAGE

Read the following article and answer questions 17 through 21.

Out Damned Spot! Which Stain-busters Work?

It's easy to find sprays, powders, and handheld appliances that claim to be great at lifting stains from carpet. But our tests show that most of them are not much better than ordinary dish detergent and water or 3 percent hydrogen peroxide.

We tested seven chemicals in all, using them on mud, red wine, French dressing, and coffee stains that we applied to untreated white carpeting and allowed to dry overnight. Columns in the Quick Ratings . . . show which products were excellent or very good on the four specific stains.

Only OxiClean Active could handle more than mud. Even it couldn't remove the oily French dressing stain, however. Capture, the only powder we tested, is also sold as part of a $20 cleaning kit containing a liquid pretreatment. In our tests, the pretreatment improved performance only marginally.

Quick Ratings Carpet Stain Cleaners
Within types, in order of overall cleaning.

Rating key: Excellent, Very Good, Good, Fair, Poor

Product	Price	Size, oz.	Overall	Mud	Wine	Dressing	Coffee
LIQUIDS							
OxiClean Active	$3.00	21.5	◕	●	●		●
Spot Shot	4.00	14	○	●			
Woolite Power Shot	4.00	12	○	●			
Resolve Spot Magic	4.00	14	○	●			
Wal-Mart Great Value Spot & Stain	2.00	22	◑	●			
Carbona Carpet Wizard	4.30	22	◒	●			
POWDER							
Capture Spot & Soil Remover	5.00	8	○				

We also tested four hand-held scrubbers: Bissell Little Green Proheat Turbo, $100; Hoover Steam Vac Jr., $100; Dirt Devil Spot Scrubber, $40; and Bissell Spot Lifter Powerbrush, $40. All were judged poor at lifting dried stains. They are handy for picking up spills. The Bissell Little Green and Hoover have hoses so that you can use them in tight spaces, such as auto interiors.

The bottom line. Most commercial stain removers and scrubbers aren't any better than inexpensive homemade cleaners. You may want to keep some OxiClean Active on hand for non-oily stains.

17. **Based on the chart contained in the article, which cleaner offers the BEST overall value?**

    A. Spot Shot
    B. Wal-Mart Great Value Spot and Stain
    C. OxiClean Active
    D. Carbona Carpet Wizard

18. **What suggestion does the article make regarding the value of commercial cleaners?**

    A. They are a bargain.
    B. Their chemicals provide the only sure way of removing stains from your belongings.
    C. Dish detergent and water or 3 percent hydrogen peroxide are just as effective as commercial cleaners.
    D. Cleaners that can lift stains from a carpet are apt to be very expensive because they are rare.

19. **What tone does the author establish in this article?**

    A. accusatory
    B. astonished
    C. humorous
    D. analytical

20. **Which of the following is NOT discussed in this article?**

    A. Four types of stains
    B. A procedure for testing the various products
    C. The prices of the various products
    D. The reasons why commercial stain removers aren't any better than homemade cleaners

21. **Read this sentence from the article.**

> It's easy to find sprays, powders, and handheld appliances that claim to be great at lifting stains from carpet.

What does the word *lifting* mean in this sentence from the article?

    A. hoisting above one's head.
    B. carrying from one place to another.
    C. removing.
    D. engaging in an Olympic sport.

Essay

Write your essay on the pages provided in your answer document. You may use only a No. 2 pencil. Do not use pen. You may use the blank space in your test booklet to make notes before you begin writing. Any notes you make in the test booklet will NOT be considered when your essay is scored.

Reminder

- Be sure to write your response to the writing prompt given below.
- You may place a title on your essay if you would like, but it is not necessary.
- No dictionary may be used. If you have trouble spelling a word, sound the word out and do the best you can.
- You may write in cursive or print.
- Write clearly! Any changes, erasures, or strike-throughs should be made as neatly as possible.

Writing Task

> Television is a powerful medium in American society. Some people believe that television is a positive force, informing the viewers with news and educational programs, while also entertaining them with movies, sitcoms, and sports. Critics of television claim it plays a negative role with low quality entertainment and poor coverage of the news.
>
> Do you feel that, on the whole, television is a positive or negative force in society? Write an essay in which you state your position and support it with appropriate examples from your experience or observations.

Checklist for Your Writing

The following checklist will help you. Always make sure that you:

- ❏ Read the task or tasks carefully.
- ❏ Organize your writing by including a strong introduction, body, and conclusion.
- ❏ Always support your ideas with specific details and examples.
- ❏ Write to your audience by using appropriate words.
- ❏ Use words that are appropriate for your purpose.
- ❏ Make your writing interesting to read by varying your sentences.
- ❏ Check carefully for mistakes in grammar, usage, spelling, punctuation, capitalization, and sentence structure.

END SESSION 1

Session 2

Read the following excerpt from Emily Dickenson's poem about a train and answer questions 22 through 27.

I Like to See It Lap the Miles

by Emily Dickinson

I like to see it lap the Miles—

And lick the Valleys up—

And stop to feed itself at Tanks—

And then—prodigious step

(5)   Around a Pile of Mountains—

And supercilious peer

In Shanties—by the sides of Roads—

And then a Quarry pare

To fit its Ribs

(10) And crawl between

Complaining all the while

In horrid—hooting stanza—

Then chase itself down Hill—

And neigh like Boanerges—

(15) Then—punctual as a Star

Stop—docile and omnipotent

At its own stable door—

22. While the poem is actually about a train, the train is described in terms of—

   A. a snake.
   B. a cat.
   C. a horse.
   D. a cow.

23. What does the word *prodigious* mean in this line from the poem?

> And then—prodigious step

   A. small
   B. large
   C. of great importance
   D. carefully

24. The speaker views the train—

   A. with interest and admiration.
   B. as an insignificant object rolling along the hillside.
   C. as supercilious.
   D. wistfully.

25. The last stanza of the poem differs from the other stanzas in that—

   A. the last stanza describes the end of the journey, while the others describe the journey.
   B. the first three stanzas contain figurative language, but the last stanza does not.
   C. the last stanza involves a stop, while none of the others do.
   D. the first three stanzas are in terms of the thoughts of the train, while the last is in terms of the poet's thoughts about the train.

GO ON TO THE NEXT PAGE

26. Emily Dickinson uses many dashes in this poem. What are readers supposed to do when they come to a dash?

    A. ignore it

    B. read quickly

    C. pause

    D. stop reading

27. What does Dickinson mean when she says, "Complaining all the while/ In horrid—hooting stanza"?

    A. The train's brakes squeak.

    B. The train is going too fast when going down hill.

    C. The train sounds like a horse.

    D. The train blows its whistle.

The following article is about the dates written on food product containers. Read the article and answer questions 28 through 31.

Food Wise—The Dating Game

It's breakfast time, and you're craving a cheese omelette. Your carton of eggs says, "EXPFEB12"; the cheddar says, "Use by Feb. 23"; the milk says, "Sell by March 1." It's March 4. Can you safely scramble, or should you switch to cereal, which is telling you "Best if used by 3-5"? If you're unsure, you're not alone. The boxes, cans, and cartons in our kitchens are trying to tell us something, but we may not be getting the message.

Except for poultry, infant formula, and some baby food, product dating is not required by the federal government, but more than 20 states mandate dating of some foods. When dates are applied, generally by the manufacturer and occasionally by the store, they're stated in a variety of ways: You might see Nov. 25, 11-25 or 1125. The terms used are somewhat flexible, too, since there's no standard. Here, some words to the wise about the words on foods:

"Use by," "best if used by," or "quality assurance" date: The last date the product is likely to be at peak flavor and quality. One of these dates is often placed on foods such as cereal, which may decline in flavor and quality. It doesn't mean the food is unsafe after that date.

"Sell by" or "pull": An indication, to the retailer, of the last day on which a product should be sold. It takes into account time for the food to be stored and used at home. You should buy it before the date, but don't have to use it by then. You should be able to use milk, say, for up to about seven days after the sell-by date.

Pack or package date: The date the food—fresh meat, for example—was packed or processed. Consumers can tell which package is fresher and choose that one. A pack date isn't an indication of safety.

"Expiration": For most foods, this indicates the last date on which they should be eaten or used. Eggs are an exception: If you buy federally graded eggs before the expiration date (which must be no more than 30 days from when they were put in the carton), you should be able to use them safely for the next 3 to 5 weeks.

"Born on": Initiated by Anheuser-Busch, it's supposed to let buyers choose the freshest beer. According to the company, its beer is freshest and tastes best within 110 days from the born-on date.

GO ON TO THE NEXT PAGE

Coded date: A series of letters or numbers or both used by the manufacturer to track foods across state lines and, if necessary, recall them. The code isn't meant as a use-by date.

Other words to the wise: As a rule, high-acid canned foods such as tomatoes can be stored on the shelf for 12 to 18 months; properly stored low-acid canned foods such as meat, fish, and most vegetables will keep 2 to 5 years. Don't use a can that's bulging. If perishable foods are packaged and frozen properly, they will be safe to eat after the expiration date, although the food may suffer freezer burn if it's stored for a long time. And if a food bears a date without words? Unfortunately, you'll have to guess what it means.

28. **According to the article, the "quality assurance date" informs the consumer—**

   A. the date the product was packaged.
   B. whether the food is likely to be recalled.
   C. the final date the food is likely to be at its peak.
   D. the date that the food becomes dangerous to consume.

29. **What is the purpose of this article?**

   A. to inform the consumer about the dangers lurking on their grocers' shelves
   B. to suggest that the Federal government needs to take an expanded role in the protection of the nation's food
   C. to discuss the creation of a uniform dating code for food products
   D. to inform the public as to the meaning of the various codes present on food packaging

30. **Which of the following questions could MOST effectively be developed as a research paper?**

   A. What would be the advantages of developing a standardized way of dating products?
   B. Why did Anheuser-Busch create the "born-on" dating system?
   C. Should I examine the dates on all the canned goods in my cupboard?
   D. How do manufacturers track foods across state lines?

31. **Read this sentence from the selection.**

   > The boxes, cans and cartons in our kitchens are trying to tell us something, but we may not be getting the message.

   What does the author mean by this sentence?

   A. There are a number of extremely dangerous products on our grocers' shelves, and we had best be prepared to deal with them.
   B. Every product has a story.
   C. Secret messages are often hidden in the text on the backs of cereal boxes.
   D. Packaging contains a lot of valuable information regarding product dating, but many consumers don't know what it means.

The following essay was written by Charles Osgood; a journalist for *CBS News* for twenty years. In this essay he discusses a broadcast that did not go as planned. Read the essay and answer questions 32 through 36.

Our Finest Hour

by Charles Osgood

(1) Only occasionally do most reporters or correspondents get to "anchor" a news broadcast. Anchoring, you understand, means sitting there in the studio and telling some stories into the camera and introducing the reports and pieces that other reporters do. It looks easy enough. It is easy enough, most of the time. . . .

(2) It was back when I was relatively new at *CBS News*. I'd been in the business a while, but only recently had moved over to *CBS News*. I was old, but I was new. It was a Saturday night and I was filling in for Roger Mudd[1] on the *CBS Evening News*. Roger was on vacation. The regular executive producer[2] of the broadcast, Paul Greenberg, was on vacation, too. And so were the regular cameraman and the regular editor and the regular director. Somewhere along the line we had one too many substitutes that night.

(3) I said "Good evening" and introduced the first report and turned to the monitor to watch it. What I saw was myself looking at the monitor. Many seconds passed. Finally there was something on the screen. A reporter was beginning a story. It was not the story I had introduced. Instead, it was a different story by a different reporter. This was supposed to be the second item in the newscast. So I shuffled my script around and made the first piece second and the second piece first. When I came back on camera, I explained what it was we had seen and reintroduced the first piece. Again there was a long awkward pause. I shuffled my papers. I scribbled on the script. I turned to the monitor. Finally, the floor director, who was filling in for the regular floor director, cued me to go on. So I introduced the next report. It didn't come up either, so I said we'd continue in just a moment. Obvious cue for a commercial, I thought, but it took a while to register in the control room. When a commercial did come up, there was a frantic scramble in the studio to reorganize what was left of the broadcast. But by now everything had come undone.

1 **Roger Mudd** was a CBS News reporter from 1961 to 1980. He was a backup anchor person for Walter Cronkite during the time of this story.

2 **Executive producer** Person responsible for the quality of the newscast.

GO ON TO THE NEXT PAGE

(4) When the commercial was over, I introduced a piece from Washington. What came up was a series of pictures of people who seemed to be dead. One man was slumped over a car wheel. Two or three people were lying in the middle of the street. Another man was propped up against the wall of the building, his eyes staring vacantly into space. Then came the voice of Peter Kalisher. "This was the town where everyone died," he said. I knew nothing whatsoever about this piece. It was not scheduled for the broadcast. Peter Kalisher was in Paris as far as I knew. But there had been nothing on the news wires about everybody in Paris having died. In the "fishbowl," the glassed-in office where the executive producer sits, there were at least three people yelling into telephones. Nobody in there knew anything about this piece either. The story was about some little town in France that was demonstrating the evils of cigarette smoking. Seems the population of the town was the same number as smoking-related deaths in France in a given year. It was a nice story well told, but since nobody in authority at CBS News, New York, had seen it or knew what was coming next, they decided to dump out of it and come back to me. I, of course, was sitting there looking at the piece with bewilderment written all over my face, when suddenly, in the midst of all these French people pretending to be dead, I saw myself, bewilderment and all.

(5) All in all, it was not the finest broadcast *CBS News* has ever done. But the worst part came when I introduced the "end piece," a feature story that Hughes Rudd had done about raft racing on the Chatahoochie River.[3] Again, when I finished the introduction, I turned to the monitor and, again, nothing happened. Then, through the glass window of the "fishbowl," I heard a loud and plaintive wail. "What is going on?" screamed the fill-in executive producer. I could hear him perfectly clearly, and so could half of America. The microphone on my tie-clip was open. Standing in the control room watching this, with what I'm sure must have been great interest, was a delegation of visiting journalists from the People's Republic of China.[4] They must have had a really great impression of American electronic journalism. The next Monday morning, sitting back at the radio desk where I belonged, I became aware of a presence standing quietly next to my desk. It was Richard Salant, the wise and gentle man who was then president of *CBS News*. He'd been waiting until I finished typing a sentence before bending over and inquiring softly: "What *was* going on?"

3 **Chatahoochie River** (cha te hü′ chē) River running south through Georgia and forming part of the borders of Georgia, Alabama, and Florida.
4 **People's Republic of China** Official name of China.

32. **The title of the essay is an example of—**

    A. irony.
    B. metaphor.
    C. personification.
    D. figurative language.

33. **Which sentence foreshadows trouble for the news broadcast?**

    A. "Only occasionally do most reporters or correspondents get to 'anchor' a news broadcast."
    B. "It looks easy enough."
    C. "Somewhere along the line we had one too many substitutes that night."
    D. "But by now everything had come undone."

34. **The tone of the essay could BEST be described as—**

    A. angry.
    B. humorous.
    C. frantic.
    D. embarrassed.

35. **Based on Osgood's description of Richard Salant, how did Mr. Salant react to the broadcast?**

    A. He was very angry and took it out on Osgood.
    B. He did not care one way or the other how the broadcast went.
    C. He congratulated Osgood on a job well done.
    D. He understood that mistakes happen, but was still confused about the incident.

36. **Read this sentence from the selection.**

    > Then, through the glass window of the "fishbowl," I heard a loud and plaintive wail.

    Based on the context in which it is used in the story, what does *plaintive* mean?

    A. melancholy
    B. excited
    C. confused
    D. disgruntled

GO ON TO THE NEXT PAGE

The following instructions are given for Requesting Use of Copyrighted Material from Educational Publications Development. Read the instructions and answer questions 37 through 41.

Steps for Requesting Use of Copyrighted Material

1. Please submit all permission requests in writing.

   ❏ Fax to: (818) 225-5555

   ❏ Mail to: Copyrights and Permissions

   Educational Publications Development (EPD)

   22202 N. Ventura Blvd. Suite 445

   Woodforde Hills, CA 91366

   Attn: H. Simpson

   ❏ Email: hsimpson@epd.com

2. Please include the following information:

   ❏ The requester's name

   ❏ The name of the requesting organization or publisher

   ❏ The requester's mailing address, e-mail address, telephone and fax numbers

   ❏ The complete title of the publication from which material is being requested

   ❏ The page numbers of the material being requested for use

   ❏ A photocopy of the material being requested for use

   ❏ The full title and publisher of the work in which the material may be used

   ❏ The purpose and audience of the publication in which the material may be used

   ❏ The number of copies that will be printed containing the copyrighted material

   ❏ The number of complete pages of the work in which the material will be used

   ❏ The specific use of the material being requested

3. EPD cannot grant permission to reprint the following:

   ❏ Publications not published by EPD.

   ❏ Articles, stories, or pages not copyrighted by EPD

   ❏ Entire publications published after 1998

4. Responses will be mailed back to the requester within six weeks. If approved, a contract stating the policies and conditions will be sent and must be signed and returned within six weeks. The contract will not be valid until you receive a countersigned copy of the contract.

37. According to the document, requests can be sent to Educational Publications Development by mail, fax, or email. However, responses will be communicated ONLY by—

A. fax
B. phone
C. mail
D. email

38. What is the purpose of this document?

A. to encourage publication of long neglected works
B. to instruct interested parties how to obtain permission to use copyrighted material
C. to serve as a research aid
D. to document copyright violations and punish wrongdoers

39. Based on information contained in the document, which of the following statements about obtaining copyright permission is accurate?

A. Entire publications published after 1998 are available.
B. The only thing necessary to obtain permission to publish copyrighted material is the payment of the specified fees.
C. All requests have to be made in writing.
D. A contract becomes valid when you, the person requesting the copyrighted material, sign the contract.

40. This document provides the LEAST information on—

A. the cost of the service.
B. contact information.
C. time frames in which you can expect a response.
D. the information necessary to obtain permission to use copyrighted material.

41. The word *valid* in the following sentence means—

> The contract will not be valid until you receive a countersigned copy of the contract.

A. that which is legally in effect.
B. something that is subject to some reservations or doubt.
C. an attempt to prove a scientific hypothesis.
D. intellectually respectable

GO ON TO THE NEXT PAGE

Read the following article about black holes and answer questions 42 through 44.

Black Holes

Black holes are caused when stars collapse from their own gravity. Supposedly, not even light can escape the pull of the gravity in the hole. The physicist Stephen Hawking, in the 1970s, said that once a black hole formed, it lost mass by radiating energy which contained no information about the inside matter. Once the hole had evaporated, all information was lost. However, this theory presented a problem because according to the laws of quantum physics, such information can't be completely wiped out. Hawking contended that the gravitational pull was so strong it unraveled the laws of quantum physics. His position today, however, is that black holes never shut themselves off completely and, as they emit more heat, they eventually open up and release information. This appears to be a solution to the paradox, although as one of his colleagues said, "The jury is still out."

42. **Based on the passage, in the 1970s Hawking explained that no information about the inside of a black hole was possible because—**

   A. a black hole emitted nothing except light.
   B. the mass of a black hole collapsed.
   C. the energy radiating from the black hole contained no information.
   D. the laws of quantum physics made it impossible to detect information.

> This appears to be a solution to the paradox, although as one of his colleagues said, "The jury is still out."

43. **The sentence _The jury is still out_ means that Hawking's new theory is—**

   A. still unproved.
   B. far-fetched.
   C. contradicting the evidence.
   D. not compatible with the laws of quantum physics.

44. **What tone does the author establish in the article?**

   A. disapproving
   B. informative
   C. cheerful
   D. negative

In this excerpt, Bryan Woolley has been asked to place something in a time capsule that will be opened in 2029. He chooses to put in the following essay about his hopes for the future. Read the essay and answer questions 45 through 48.

To the Residents of A.D. 2029

by Bryan Woolley

I wish I could report to the future that our current status is hunky-dory, that we live in the Golden Age of something or other. Until recently it was possible for Americans to believe that. There's no doubt that in the twentieth century, at least, the people of the United States have enjoyed the highest standard of living that the world has known up to this point in history. We've had so much of everything, in fact, that we've thought our supplies of the essentials of life—land, food, air, water, fuel—would last forever, and we've been wasteful. Sometimes we've even been wasteful of human life itself.

Lately, though, a sense of decline has set in. We've begun to realize that we're in trouble. We've poured so much filth into our water that much of it is undrinkable, and no life can live in it. Even the life of the ocean, the great mother of us all, is threatened. Scientists say the last wisp of pure, natural air in the continental United States was absorbed into our generally polluted atmosphere over Flagstaff, Arizona, several years ago. Parts of our land are overcrowded, parts neglected, parts abused, parts destroyed. We continue to depend on unrenewable resources—petroleum, natural gas, and coal—for most of the fuel that heats and cools our homes; runs our industry, agriculture, and business; and propels our transportation. We've suddenly discovered that those resources are disappearing forever. Without usable land, air, water, and fuel, food production would be impossible, of course. In addition, the United States and the Soviet Union are at this moment trying to make treaties that we hope will keep us from destroying all life and the possibility of life if we decide to destroy each other before the fuel runs out.

So I would classify the current status as shaky, which makes the outlook for the future—even so near a future as A.D. 2029—uncertain.

An uncertain future is no new thing, of course. The future has always existed only in the imagination, a realm of hope and dread with which we can do little more than play games. But the games sometimes become serious. The Europeans postulated another land across the ocean for centuries and then came and found it. Jules Verne traveled under the sea and to the moon in his mind many years before we could make the machines to catch up

GO ON TO THE NEXT PAGE

with him. If, as we say, Necessity is the mother of Invention, then Desire is the father of Possibility.

Because of man's amazing record of making his dreams come true, I refuse to be pessimistic about the future, despite the frightening aspects of the present. As long as we—both as a race and as a crowd of individuals—retain our capacity for dreaming, we also keep the possibility of doing. And when doing becomes necessary, we invent a means to do so. Especially when we're in danger, as we are now.

Some of our present dangers surely will be around in 2029, for they're part of being human. We're too far from solving poverty, disease, and probably even war to be done with them in another half-century. Collin County probably will still need its courts and its jail—maybe more courts and a newer, stronger jail.

But if my generation and my sons' generation do what we must to prolong the possibility of survival and the likelihood of this being read, most of the problems about which I'm worrying may seem quaint. If so, they'll be replaced by others that will seem as serious to those who gather to open the time capsule as mine do to me. Golden Ages exist only in retrospect, never for those who are trying to cope with them.

So for the beleaguered residents of 2029 I wish four things:

- A deeper understanding of history, to better avoid repeating the errors of the past, for if each generation keeps on inventing its own mistakes, some of the old ones will have to be thrown out.

- A healing of the schism between man and the rest of nature. Our present disrespect for the natural world is our most serious stupidity to date. We must realize that man can't long outlive the other living creatures.

- A wider and more profound appreciation of beauty. Music, poetry, pictures, and stories feed the soul as surely as wheat and meat and rice feed the body, and the soul of America is malnourished.

- A sense of humor. If man ever stops laughing at himself, he can no longer endure life, nor will he have reason to.

45. What is the author's vision of the future?

    A. pessimistic

    B. uncertain

    C. optimistic

    D. cautious

46. Mr. Woolley's reference to Jules Verne is an example of—

    A. allusion.

    B. personification.

    C. alliteration.

    D. figurative language.

47. By comparing current views of the future with those of early Europeans and Jules Verne, Woolley makes the point that—

    A. humans are dreamers.

    B. humans are doomed.

    C. if humans can imagine it, they can do it.

    D. humans postulate, but do very little.

48. Based on the connotation of the word *golden,* a Golden Age can BEST be described as—

    A. a period of good weather.

    B. a period when gold is very valuable.

    C. a period of beauty.

    D. a period of happiness, peace, and prosperity.

GO ON TO THE NEXT PAGE

Read the excerpt and answer questions 49 through 52.

The Boxer's Heart: How I Fell in Love with the Ring

by Kate Sekules

Kate Sekules grew up in London, moved to New York, and took an aerobics class that involved boxing moves. Sekules loved the boxing so much that she wrote about her thoughts on the topic.

Show me a female boxer who wasn't a tomboy and I'll show you a liar. Not that tomboyhood is restricted to embryo pugilists; far from it. Tomboys are everywhere, and they are normal, and they are expected to grow out of it, though many, like me, never quite do. It is not the same for little boys, for whom displaying feminine behavior is taboo. This contradiction implies that qualities customarily associated with masculinity (aggression, drive, forthrightness, ebullience) are useful, whereas those generally tagged feminine (gentleness, kindness, self-deprecation, concern with appearance) are dispensable, verging on undesirable. But that notion is way outdated. A girl child today has role models—rock chicks, Xena, Oprah, Venus and Serena—who synthesize tomboyhood and femininity. Girlpower wasn't available to my generation. For women my age and a decade on either side, being a tomboy was a rebellion against what seemed the weak position; it was a brand of defiance. Personally, I have not finished kicking against a prescribed female role that restricts us. Doors have opened, sure, but what makes me mad is that it's still okay for girls to grow up believing what they weigh and wear is more important than what they know and read, say and do. Sports can cure that. I am fighting stereotypes.

> Not that tomboyhood is restricted to embryo pugilists; far from it.

49. Based on the context in which it is used in the story, what does *pugilists* mean?

    A. tomboys

    B. girls

    C. boxers

    D. liars

50. According to Sekules, how have people's attitudes about being a tomboy changed over the years?

    A. Tomboys are now considered emotionally weak.

    B. It is now acceptable, even cool, to be a tomboy.

    C. Being a tomboy shows that you are rebellious.

    D. Being a tomboy makes you a role model.

51. Read this sentence from the story.

> Personally, I have not finished kicking against a prescribed female role that restricts us.

This sentence is an example of—

    A. onomatopoeia.

    B. metaphor.

    C. simile.

    D. iambic pentameter.

52. Read this line from the story.

> ... qualities customarily associated with masculinity (aggression, drive, forthrightness, ebullience) are useful ...

Based on the context in which it is used in the story, what does *ebullience* mean?

    A. exuberance

    B. fear

    C. optimism

    D. conceit

GO ON TO THE NEXT PAGE

The following is a draft of an essay explaining some aspects of report writing. It may contain errors in grammar, sentence structure, vocabulary, and organization. Some of the questions may refer to underlined or numbered sentences or phrases within the text. Read the essay and answer questions 53 through 57.

Writing a Report

(1) For a report, select a subject that isn't too broad or too narrow. (2) Choose one you are interested in learning about but also one for which there is information available in libraries or on the Internet. (3) A report, unlike a personal essay, should focus on facts that are accumulated through research. (4) The purpose of footnotes in a report is to give credit to others for words and ideas.

(5) Gather your information from several sources, not just one. (6) Reports that rely on an encyclopedia alone are inadequate. (7) Use magazine and newspaper articles as well as other books. (8) An important place to consult for materials that will be useful is the library card catalog. (9) And for the Internet, make use of a good search engine.

(10) Be sure to write down all the information about the sources you use. (11) Often you will want to quote something, and this is acceptable if you use quotation marks and give proper credit. (12) Give other people's ideas credit, too, even if you phrase them in your own words. (13) Using footnotes is the way most people do it.

53. Which of the following sentences does NOT fit well in the paragraph in which it is found?

A. sentence 4
B. sentence 7
C. sentence 11
D. sentence 12

54. Which of the following is the BEST way to combine and rewrite sentences 8 and 9?

A. An important place to consult for materials that will be useful is the library card catalog, or, for the Internet, a good search engine should be employed.
B. For materials that will be helpful, consult the library card catalog or, for the Internet, use a good search engine.
C. Consulting the library card catalog and using a good search engine for the Internet is a good place to search for materials that will be useful.
D. The library card catalog should be consulted for materials that will be useful and a good search engine on the Internet should be made use of.

55. Which of the following sentences would make the MOST effective opening sentence for the first paragraph?

A. Report writing can be a lot of fun.
B. Personal essays are easier to write than reports.
C. The first step in writing is deciding what to write about.
D. The most difficult part of report-writing is preparing the footnotes.

56. Which of the following would MOST improve the first paragraph of the essay?

A. specific example of topics that are too broad or too narrow
B. an explanation of how to prepare a bibliography
C. guidelines for using the Internet to find materials
D. eliminating the second sentence

57. Which of the following is the BEST rewritten version of sentence 13 in the third paragraph?

A. Most people, when they want to give credit, use footnotes to do so.
B. Cite your sources in footnotes.
C. Sighting sources in your footnotes is a good idea.
D. Customarily, when giving credit to people for their words and ideas, writers use the proven method of footnotes.

GO ON TO THE NEXT PAGE

The following is a draft of a paragraph on the depletion of forests in America. It may contain errors in grammar, sentence structure, vocabulary, and organization. Some of the questions may refer to underlined or numbered sentences or phrases within the text. Read the paragraph and answer questions 58 through 61.

Saving Our Forests

(1) Until the second half of the 20th Century, most Americans weren't very careful about using natural resources. (2) They mined for minerals, changed the course of rivers, and replaced wilderness with cities. (3) In the process they cut down forests that had been in place for thousands of years. (4) Today only ten percent of old-growth forests remain all in one piece, with demand for wood products expected to grow by fifty percent in the next fifty years. (5) Air quality in our cities has gotten bad, although in recent years regulations have helped somewhat. (6) We are in danger of losing our forests altogether unless we try to find solutions, from little things, like not relying on paper stuff so much, to bigger things, like supporting stronger government logging regulations.

58. Which of the following sentences does NOT fit well into this paragraph?

A. sentence 6
B. sentence 5
C. sentence 4
D. sentence 2

59. In this paragraph, what is the BEST position for sentence 1?

A. following sentence 5
B. between sentences 4 and 5
C. following sentence 2
D. Leave as is.

60. The BEST way to express the meaning of the word *stuff* in sentence 6 is—

A. things.
B. products.
C. material.
D. household items.

61. Which of the following would be the BEST source of information about opposition to strict logging regulations?

A. newspaper editorials about logging practices
B. an encyclopedia item about logging
C. a current almanac
D. a history of logging operations

My Summer Experience

(1) When I spent a summer working on my uncle's cattle ranch, I learned some things about myself. (2) First of all, I learned that I hate to get up early. (3) Every morning at 5:00 a.m. Uncle Rick got me out of bed to milk the cow and clean out his horse's stall. (4) Milking wasn't so bad but cleaning up after a horse is definitely not fun, especially at five in the morning. (5) Second, I discovered I'm a faster learner that I thought I was. (6) Within a week I knew how to round up stray cattle and get them into the corral, and after a month I could lasso a horse in only one try. (7) I was helped by the experienced ranch hands to learn about cattle and the ways in which they should be handled. (8) Third, I learned that I am not afraid to stand up for myself, unlike many kids my age. (9) The best thing about working on the ranch was that I made more money than I could have as a box boy at our local grocery store, which was my other choice as a summer job.

The following is a draft of a paragraph on a personal experience. It may contain errors in grammar, sentence structure, vocabulary and organization. Some of the questions may refer to underlined or numbered sentences or phrases within the text. Read the draft and answer questions 62 through 64.

62. Which of the following sentences does NOT fit well into this paragraph?

A. sentence 3
B. sentence 6
C. sentence 8
D. sentence 9

63. Which of the following would be the BEST way to improve this paragraph?

A. Provide an example of the point made in sentence 8.
B. Remove "I" from the essay.
C. Use more formal language.
D. Eliminate the first sentence.

64. Which of the following is the BEST way to rewrite sentence 7?

A. Learning about cattle and the ways in which they should be handled was helped by the experienced ranch hands.
B. To learn about cattle and how to handle them was helped by the experienced ranch hands.
C. The experienced ranch hands helped me learn about cattle and how to handle them.
D. Leave as is.

GO ON TO THE NEXT PAGE

For questions 65 through 74, choose the answer that is the most effective substitute for each underlined part of the sentence. If no substitution is necessary, choose "Leave as is."

65. That night the timber <u>wolf revived; looking fiercer</u> than ever.

   A. wolf revived. Looking fiercer
   B. wolf revived: looking fiercer
   C. wolf revived, looking fiercer
   D. Leave as is.

66. <u>After, everyone left the theater a fire</u> was detected in the balcony.

   A. After everyone left the theater, a fire
   B. After everyone left the theater. A fire
   C. After everyone left the theater; a fire
   D. Leave as is.

67. <u>"When can you meet us for lunch" asked the chairman of the committee as she left the room.</u>

   A. "When can you meet us for lunch" asked the chairman of the committee as she left the room?
   B. "When can you meet us for lunch?" asked the chairman of the committee as she left the room.
   C. "When can you meet us for lunch"? asked the chairman of the committee as she left the room.
   D. Leave as is.

68. Although he enjoyed swimming in the ocean <u>every afternoon after school. If</u> he had too much homework, he couldn't spare the time.

   A. every afternoon after school: If
   B. every afternoon after school; if
   C. every afternoon after school, if
   D. Leave as is.

69. When they <u>returned, the house had been completely demolished, however,</u> the barn was still standing.

   A. returned, the house had been completely demolished; however,
   B. returned; the house had been completely demolished, however
   C. returned the house had been completely demolished however
   D. Leave as is.

70. Robert <u>went to the market, walks over to the produce section, and picked</u> out the biggest eggplant he could find.

   A. went to the market, walked over to the produce section, and picked
   B. has gone to the market, walks over to the produce section, and has picked
   C. goes to the market, walks over to the produce section, and had picked
   D. Leave as is.

71. <u>The teacher took a survey of how many people had been in auto accidents in our class.</u>

   A. How many people had been in auto accidents is the survey the teacher took in our class.
   B. In our class the teacher took a survey of how many people had been in auto accidents.
   C. In our class a survey was taken by the teacher of how many people had been in auto accidents.
   D. Leave as is.

72. <u>Playing softball on Friday, the sun was so hot we didn't do our best.</u>

   A. Playing softball on Friday, the sun kept us from doing our best.
   B. Playing softball on Friday, we didn't do our best because the sun was so hot.
   C. We didn't do our best because the sun was so hot playing softball on Friday.
   D. Leave as is.

73. Jamie had <u>worked at the department store for six months before the manager promoted her.</u>

   A. worked at the department store for six months before the manager promotes her.
   B. works at the department store for six months before she will be promoted by the manager.
   C. worked at the department store for six months before she will have been promoted by the manager.
   D. Leave as is.

74. The president of the club promises <u>a balanced budget, to plan more activities, and improvements to the meeting hall.</u>

   A. a balanced budget, to plan more activities, and improve the meeting hall.

   B. balancing the budget, planning more activities, and to make improvements to the meeting hall.

   C. to balance the budget, plan more activities, and make improvements to the meeting hall.

   D. Leave as is

For questions 75 through 79 choose the word or phrase that best completes the sentence.

75. When the dog ran out to meet _____ owner, it barked and jumped up and down.

   A. its'

   B. it's

   C. its

   D. it

76. The Martinez family_____believe they are going to be on television.

   A. cannot hardly

   B. hardly cannot

   C. can't hardly

   D. can hardly

77. The movie *Batman* was _____ than I expected.

   A. more good

   B. best

   C. more better

   D. better

78. _____decided to travel across the country in the twenty-year-old van.

   A. Him and me

   B. He and I

   C. Him and I

   D. He and her

79. _____willing and able to take on the responsibilities of the job.

   A. They're

   B. They'll

   C. Their

   D. There

END SESSION 2   STOP

Answer Key for Practice Test 1

(WA) Word Analysis   (RC) Reading Comprehension   (LR) Literary Response and Analysis

Session 1

For "Gaining on the Men"

1. D (RC) ❑	**4.** D (RC) ❑	**7.** B (RC) ❑
2. B (RC) ❑	**5.** D (RC) ❑	
3. A (RC) ❑	**6.** C (WA) ❑	

For "Susan Allen Toth"

8. C (LR) ❑	**11.** C (LR) ❑	**14.** B (LR) ❑
9. A (LR) ❑	**12.** B (LR) ❑	**15.** A (LR) ❑
10. A. (LR) ❑	**13.** D (LR) ❑	**16.** A (WA) ❑

For "Out Damned Spot! Which Stain-busters Work?"

17. C (RC) ❑	**19.** D (RC) ❑	**21.** C (WA) ❑
18. C (RC) ❑	**20.** D (RC) ❑	

Session 2

For "I Like to See It Lap the Miles"

22. C (LR) ❑	**24.** A (LR) ❑	**26.** C (LR) ❑
23. B (WA) ❑	**25.** A (LR) ❑	**27.** D (LR) ❑

For "Food Wise"

28. C (RC) ❑	**30.** A (RC) ❑
29. D (RC) ❑	**31.** D (WA) ❑

For "Our Finest Hour"

32. A (LR) ❑	**34.** B (LR) ❑	**36.** A (WA) ❑
33. C (LR) ❑	**35.** D (LR) ❑	

For "Steps for Requesting Use of Copyrighted Material"

37. C (RC) ❑	**39.** C (RC) ❑	**41.** A (WA) ❑
38. B (RC) ❑	**40.** A (RC) ❑	

For "Black Holes"

42. C (RC) ❑	**44.** B (RC) ❑
43. A (RC) ❑	

For "To the Residents of A.D. 2029"

45. B (LR) ❑	**47.** C (LR) ❑
46. A (LR) ❑	**48.** D (WA) ❑

For "The Boxer's Heart: How I Fell in Love with the Ring"

49. C (WA) ❑	**51.** B (LR) ❑
50. B (LR) ❑	**52.** A (WA) ❑

For Writing Strategies

53. A ❑	**57.** B ❑	**61.** A ❑
54. B ❑	**58.** B ❑	**62.** D ❑
55. C ❑	**59.** D ❑	**63.** A ❑
56. A ❑	**60.** B ❑	**64.** C ❑

For Writing Conventions

65. C (WC) ❑	**70.** A (WC) ❑	**75.** C (WC) ❑
66. A (WC) ❑	**71.** B (WC) ❑	**76.** D (WC) ❑
67. B (WC) ❑	**72.** B (WC) ❑	**77.** D (WC) ❑
68. C (WC) ❑	**73.** D (WC) ❑	**78.** B (WC) ❑
69. A (WC) ❑	**74.** C (WC) ❑	**79.** A (WC) ❑

Reviewing Practice Test 1

Review your simulated CAHSEE English-Language Arts Practice Test by following these steps:

1. Check the answers you marked on your answer sheet against the Answer Key. Put a check mark in the box following any wrong answer.
2. Fill out the Review Chart below.
3. Read all the explanations (pp. 165–171). Go back to review any explanations that are not clear to you.
4. Fill out the Reasons for Mistakes chart below.
5. Have your essay evaluated using the checklist that is included.
6. Go back to the review sections and review any materials necessary before taking the next practice test.

Don't leave out any of these steps. They are very important in learning to do your best on the CAHSEE English-Language-Arts.

Review Chart

Use your marked Answer Key to fill in the following Review Chart for the multiple-choice questions.

	Possible	Completed	Right	Wrong
Word Analysis (WA) (7)	10			
Reading Comprehension (RC) (18)	20			
Literary Response and Analysis (LR) (20)	22			
Writing Strategies (WS) (12)	12			
Writing Conventions (WC) (15)	15			
Totals	79			

The numbers in ( ) are the actual number of each type that count toward your score.

Reasons for Mistakes

Fill out the following chart only after you have read all the explanations that follow. This chart will help you spot your strengths and weaknesses and your repeated errors or trends in types of errors.

	Total Missed	Simple Mistake	Misread Problem	Lack of Knowledge
Word Analysis (WA)				
Reading Comprehension (RC)				
Literary Response and Analysis (LR)				
Writing Strategies (WS)				
Writing Conventions (WC)				
Totals				

Examine your results carefully. Reviewing the above information will help you pinpoint your common mistakes. Focus on avoiding your most common mistakes as you practice. The "Lack of Knowledge" column will help you focus your review. If you are missing a lot of questions because of "Lack of Knowledge," you should go back and spend extra time reviewing the basics.

Explanations for Practice Test 1

Session 1

For "Gaining on the Men"

1. **D.** Choices **A, B,** and **C** are clearly details and therefore not suitable as answers. Choice **D** is the main idea of the article. (**Reading Comprehension**)

2. **B.** The article focuses on male and female runners. Choice **A** is unlikely because although a fashion magazine might appeal to women, it would hardly be expected to have an article about women runners written with a detailed look at physiological differences between men and women. Choice **C** would largely feature anatomy unrelated explicitly to sport. Choice **D** might contain such an article, but it is clearly not the best choice. (**Reading Comprehension**)

3. **A.** Choice **A** is mentioned in the article. Research suggests that women actually bear pain better than men ruling out **B.** Choice **C** is not the answer as the analogy of the elephant and the mouse suggests. **D** is not mentioned in the article. (**Reading Comprehension**)

4. **D.** This answer is stated in paragraph 8. Choice **B** is hardly logical and is not mentioned. Choice **A** is not likely because many women enter already. Choice **C** is clearly untrue because with the handicap, a woman finished first. (**Reading Comprehension**)

5. **D.** Choice **A** is too brief to need anything more than a cursory look in an almanac. Choice **B** is a nonissue, since women are already competing. Choice **C** might lead to an interesting anecdote, but like A is not really research-worthy. Choice **D** offers the reader a chance to learn something, would require some relatively lengthy work in secondary sources, and is a logical extension of the article itself. (**Reading Comprehension**)

6. **C.** While **A** and **D** are also meanings of the word *flood,* the context in which the word appears suggests that the author is trying to convey the idea that a sudden large increase of participants is what he's talking about. (**Word Analysis**)

7. **B.** Choice **C** is probably true right now. Choices **A** and **D** do not suggest that women are quickly closing a gap that may well disappear before long. References to the Los Angeles Marathon both open and close the document, suggesting **B** is the answer. (**Reading Comprehension**)

For "Susan Allen Toth"

8. **C.** The author says that not using *I* leads to a "dull, vague bureaucratese," not a writing style you could consider "correct" (Choice **B**). But in the first paragraph, Toth states, "we are pretending that we are part of some impressive institution", that is, more important than we really are; therefore, **C** is correct. Choices **A** and **D** are never stated. (**Literary Response and Analysis**)

9. **A.** In the second paragraph, Toth defines herself as a memoirist. (**Literary Response and Analysis**)

10. **A.** Not only does Toth discuss the type of minute detail she uses in her writing, but in the last paragraph she says, "I have a passion for detail." Choices **C** and **D** are never stated, and while the author does write personal narratives, she doesn't write only those, nor does she suggest the *degree* of personal handling that is best (**B**). (**Literary Response and Analysis**)

11. **C.** Toth compares the details of her life to piles of items that need to be sorted. Metaphors are types of figurative language; so the answer is **C.** (**Literary Response and Analysis**)

12. **B.** Toth opens the piece by discussing the "odd task" of writing about herself and that she struggles with whether she should use first person or be objective and use third person. You could infer that she was uncomfortable with the task. Choices **A, C** and **D** are expressed nowhere in the text.. The best choice is **B.** (**Literary Response and Analysis**)

13. D. In the fourth paragraph, Toth discusses the different types of writing she has done and the different places it has appeared. She says that while she started writing fiction and essays later in life, she has always been writing. Choice **D** is the correct answer because she is expressing the type of author she is. She doesn't need to convince you to read her work, since you already are; the tone of the biography doesn't suggest immense pride, and her success, except perhaps in terms of personal satisfactions, is not discussed. (**Literary Response and Analysis**)

14. B. As the introduction to this piece stated, Toth is both an editor and a contributor in a literature book. Author's biographies are not normally written in first person because the authors themselves are not writing them; the editors or biographers are. Toth explains that since she is both author and editor in this book, she must write her own biography (her autobiography). Although the author is critical of the use of the third person in specific instances, she is not critical of it in general. Choice **D** can be eliminated. Choice **B** is the correct answer since she is explaining why she is the only author in the textbook to use first person in the biography. (**Literary Response and Analysis**)

15. A. Toth explains in the third paragraph that biographical facts cannot express who the author is or how the author has become the person he or she is. (**Literary Response and Analysis**)

16. A. Even if you don't know the definition of *determinants,* you can try the other words as answers. Since Toth is discussing factors that make you who you are, **A** is the best answer. (**Word Analysis**)

For "Out Damned Spot! Which Stain-busters Work?"

17. C. Spot Shot has the second highest price for the second to the least amount of product. Wal-Mart Great Value Spot and Stain is the cheapest per ounce but has only a fair rating. OxiClean Active is the only cleaner with a very good rating. Carbona Carpet Wizard is the most expensive and rates only fair. (**Reading Comprehension**)

18. C. The second sentence of the article states that "most of them [cleaners] are not much better than ordinary dish detergent and water or 3 percent hydrogen peroxide. Choices **A** and **B** are incorrect because there are lower-cost alternatives that have the same cleaning ability. Choice **D** is incorrect because there is no way to know the cost of such a product based on the information in the article. (**Reading Comprehension**)

19. D. The author is analyzing the ability of commercial cleaners and handheld scrubbers to get out stains. The tone is sober and thoughtful. The other terms do not apply. (**Reading Comprehension**)

20. D. The article does say that commercial cleaners aren't much better than homemade ones, but no explanation is given as to *why* it's true. The other three choices are all mentioned in the passage. (**Reading Comprehension**)

21. C. Although **A, B** and **D** are alternative meanings of the word *lifting,* **C** is the only one that fits the context of the sentence. One wants to remove stains, not carry them from one place to another. (**Word Analysis**)

Have an English teacher, tutor, or someone else with good writing skills read and evaluate your essay using the checklist below.

Checklist for Response to Writing Prompt

Does your essay . . .

- ❑ Provide a thoughtful, well-written composition that addresses the writing task?
- ❑ Use specific supporting details and examples?
- ❑ Demonstrate a clear focus and tone?
- ❑ Show coherent, logical organization?
- ❑ Clearly address the intended audience?
- ❑ Use precise, descriptive language?
- ❑ Use a variety of sentence types?
- ❑ Contain almost no errors in grammar, punctuation, spelling, capitalization and usage?
- ❑ Clearly state a position and make a case for that position?
- ❑ Defend the position with specific relevant evidence?
- ❑ Address the reader's potential misunderstandings, biases, and expectations?

Session 2

For "I Like to See It Lap the Miles"

22. C. The poem makes reference to neighing and a stable, which are both associated with a horse. (**Literary Response and Analysis**)

23. B. The definition of *prodigious* is large. If you take the word in context and consider the following line of the poem, you can see that the train takes a large step around a pile of mountains. (**Word Analysis**)

24. A. The speaker says "I like to see it ..." and then shows that the train has much power and yet can be both "docile and omnipotent." She clearly is interested in the train and admires its strength and grace. (**Literary Response and Analysis**)

25. A. Most of the poem describes the journey that the train takes—over miles, through the valley, around the mountains, through the quarry, and down the hill. The last stanza, however, describes the end of the journey, as the train finally stops "at its own stable door." All of the stanzas contain figurative language (**B**). Choice **C** is difficult to rule out in this question because most of the poem is, indeed, about motion, but notice that in the first stanza there is a moment when the train comes to a stop "to feed itself at Tanks." All of the stanzas are in terms of the poet's thoughts and perceptions concerning the train. (**Literary Response and Analysis**)

26. C. A dash tells the reader to slow down or pause at that point of reading. You can't simply stop—the poem isn't over—but you can pause to get the effect that the author wants. (**Literary Response and Analysis**)

27. D. The only thing on a train that hoots is its whistle. If you think about the sound a train whistle makes, it could be thought of as complaining. A horse and brakes don't "hoot," so **D** is the only answer that makes sense. (**Literary Response and Analysis**)

For "Food Wise"

28. C. The third paragraph states that the quality assurance date is "the last date the product is likely to be at peak flavor and quality." (**Reading Comprehension**)

29. D. Choice **A**'s sensational tone does not match the article's. Choice **B** is neither stated nor implied. Choice **C** offers an interesting idea, but it is not advocated anywhere in the article. The article is clearly informational in tone and content, therefore **D** is the answer. (**Reading Comprehension**)

30. A. This choice offers the best example of an answer that can be developed into a research paper. It has sufficient depth and import to warrant research. Choice **B** is trivial by comparison, **C** suggests a certain alarmist tone not justified by the article, and while **D** is interesting, the answer is a simple one and is clearly given in the text. (**Reading Comprehension**)

31. D. Choice **A**'s tone is far too alarming, which doesn't match the tone of the article. **B** may be true but is a little vague. **C** is clearly inappropriate. **D** captures the intent of the article—to inform and instruct. (**Word Analysis**)

For "Our Finest Hour"

32. A. The story is clearly not about CBS's finest hour; therefore, it is ironic. (**Literary Response and Analysis**)

33. C. Osgood implies that had they fewer substitutes, they probably would not have had so many problems. Osgood's statements that "only occasionally do . . . reporters . . . 'anchor' a news broadcast" and that it "looks easy enough" are not examples of foreshadowing. They are statements of fact, or at least his opinion of facts. Choice **D** is an example of the problem having already occurred. (**Literary Response and Analysis**)

34. B. Just as the title is ironic, Osgood tells the story in a humorous manner. While, at the time of the events, people may have been angry, frantic, or embarrassed, Osgood does not repeat the story in those ways. He is now able to look back on the moment as being a funny one. (**Literary Response and Analysis**)

35. D. Based on Osgood's description of Salant being "wise and gentle," and "inquiring softly," it appeared that Salant was not upset about the broadcast. His question, "What *was* going on?" does show his interest; therefore, **D** is the correct answer. (**Literary Response and Analysis**)

36. A. Even if you don't know the meaning of the word *plaintive,* try substituting in the other answers. Since at this point in the story all of the crewmembers are frustrated, a sad or "melancholy" wail is the correct answer. Don't be tricked by **C.** While everyone is confused, the wail itself is not a confusing one. **(Word Analysis)**

For "Steps for Requesting Use of Copyrighted Material"

37. C. EPD lists only mail as a method of receiving your response from the company. The best answer is **C. (Word Analysis)**

38. B. The document serves as a step-by step guide to enable individuals and others to obtain permission to use copyrighted materials. They might be used for research, but that is not the purpose of this document (**C**). The other choices are far beyond the scope of this document. The best choice is **B. (Reading Comprehension)**

39. C. Entire publications published after 1998 are *not* available (**A**). Eleven pieces of information are required, as well as mailing the form and signing the contract, to receive permission, and no fee structure is mentioned (**B**). A contract becomes valid when the person requesting the material receives the *countersigned* copy (**D**). The best answer is **C. (Reading Comprehension)**

40. A. You can contact the company via fax, email, or mail (**B**). Responses will be mailed back to the requesting party within six weeks (**C**). The document lists a number of things one has to do to obtain permission to use copyrighted material (**D**). The best choice is **A. (Reading Comprehension)**

41. A. In this context, *valid* means that which is *legally in effect.* The best answer is **A. (Word Analysis)**

For "Black Holes"

42. C. The energy (or heat) radiating from the black hole gives no clues about the inner mass. Choice **A** is contrary to information in the passage. Stars collapse to form black holes, but the black hole itself evaporates, making Choice **B** incorrect. Choice **D** is not the point that is made about the laws of quantum physics. The best answer is **C. (Reading Comprehension)**

43. A. The courtroom metaphor is used to underline the point that Hawking's new theory is still just a theory: the "verdict" isn't in yet. Choice **B** is wrong; there is no evidence that the new theory is viewed by scientists as "far-fetched." Also, it does not contradict the evidence, Choice **C,** and in fact, contrary to Choice **D,** is more compatible with the laws of quantum physics than the 1970s theory. The best answer is **A. (Reading Comprehension)**

44. B. By carefully considering the words used by the author you can see that the article is neither negative (**D**) nor disapproving (**A**). The subject matter and the language used also eliminate Choice **C,** cheerful. The author's tone is straightforward and informative. The best answer is **B. (Reading Comprehension)**

For "To the Residents of A.D. 2029"

45. B. Woolley states his opinion in paragraph four as uncertain; therefore, **B** is correct. **(Literary Response and Analysis)**

46. A. To *allude* to something means to make reference to something or someone outside of the piece of literature. Jules Verne wrote a book about the future, so **A** is correct. **(Literary Response and Analysis)**

47. C. Woolley states in paragraph five that man has an "amazing record of making his dreams come true." While that does mean that humans are dreamers, it would be incomplete to leave the statement at that. Woolley makes this statement to prove a point. Humans are dreamers, but we seem to dream and then make those dreams come true. **(Literary Response and Analysis)**

48. D. Based on Woolley's discussion of his hopes for the future and his concern for the present, it is evident that Golden Age has a positive connotation. The only choice that encompasses his hopes for the future and his present fears is **D. (Word Analysis)**

For "The Boxer's Heart: How I Fell in Love with the Ring"

49. C. Even if you don't know the definition, use the word in context. Substitute for *pugilists* the words in the other answer choices and you'll find that none of them really make sense. **(Word Analysis)**

50. B. The speaker discusses current role models and the concept of "girlpower." Choices **A** and **D** are never stated, and **C** was only true of her generation. **(Literary Response and Analysis)**

51. B. The speaker uses the idea of figuratively kicking and struggling in daily life and compares it to literally kicking. Since a metaphor is a direct comparison, **B** is the correct answer. **(Literary Response and Analysis)**

52. A. Even if you don't know the definition for *ebullience,* try substituting in the other words. Since *ebullience* is part of a list of words that describe masculine traits, and those traits all seem to share the theme of strength, **A** is the best fit for the answer. **(Word Analysis)**

For Writing Strategies

53. A. Choice **A** is best. The reference to footnotes in the first paragraph does not fit well with the paragraph's main topic. The sentences in the other choices are placed more logically.

54. B. Choice **B** is best. It is direct, not wordy, and grammatically correct. Choice **A** is awkward because the two main clauses are not parallel in structure. Choice **C** is also awkward and includes a grammatical error. The *is* should be *are* because of the compound subject (*consulting . . . and using . . .*). Choice **D** awkwardly uses a passive rather than active construction.

55. C. Choice **C** is best. It directly concerns choosing a subject for a report and therefore leads into sentences 1 and 2. Choice **A,** along with not fitting in the paragraph, is a weak, mechanical opening. Choice **B** is not a topic sentence for this paragraph and, in addition, there is nothing in the paragraph to suggest the statement is true. Choice **D** also doesn't introduce the topic of this paragraph.

56. A. Of the choices here, **A** is best. The first paragraph would benefit from an example or two of good and poor report topics. Examples or details are important in any essay or report. Choices **B** and **C** are beyond the scope of this draft, and **D** is simply incorrect; sentence 2 fits well in the paragraph.

57. B. Choice **B** is best. It conveys the point directly and succinctly. Both **A** and **D** are wordy. Choice **C** is incorrect. The right word here is "cite," not "sight."

58. B. Choice **B** is best. The paragraph is about forests, not air quality. All of the other sentences here support the main topic.

59. D. Choice **D** is the best. This is a good introductory sentence. It leads smoothly into the main topic (sentence 4). None of the other choices are appropriate locations for this general statement.

60. B. Choice **B** is the best. Choice **A,** like the slangier "stuff," is too general. Choices **C** and **D** are better but not as inclusive as **B.**

61. A. Choice **A** is the best here. Pros and cons of an issue are often covered in editorials, which are opinion pieces. Choices **B** and **D** might include some information, but it would be skimpier and less focused than the opinions in relevant editorials.

62. D. Choice **D** is best. The paragraph is about what the writer learned about himself or herself. Sentence 9 introduces a different point and is therefore not a good concluding sentence. Choices **A, B,** and **C** all relate to the main topic.

63. A. Choice **A** is best. The writer gives examples of the other two points he/she makes but gives no example of this point. Choices **B** and **C** aren't good because this is a personal essay, and both the use of *I* and of informal language are appropriate to the author's purpose. Choice **D** is wrong; sentence 1 is the topic sentence of the paragraph.

64. C. Choice **C** is best. It is in the active rather than passive voice, which none of the other choices are, and it is also a smoother, less wordy sentence.

For Writing Conventions

65. C. "Looking fiercer than ever" is a participial phrase that describes the wolf, and it cannot stand alone as a sentence. It should be separated from the main clause ("That night the timber wolf revived") with a comma. The other punctuation marks (a semicolon, a period, and a colon) would make the phrase a sentence fragment. Therefore, the best answer is **C**.

66. A. This sentence consists of a subordinate clause and an independent clause. Which one is subordinate? "After everyone left the theater." This clause can't stand alone. We are left wondering what happened after everyone left the theater. Use a comma to separate a subordinate clause from the main clause. The best answer choice is **A**. In the original sentence, the comma is in the wrong place, and the punctuation marks in choices **B** and **C** make the subordinate clause a sentence fragment.

67. B. is the best answer because a question mark should directly follow the question, and if the question is in quotation marks, the question mark should be in them, too. Therefore, Choice **C** is incorrect. The original sentence doesn't use a question mark at all, and in answer **A,** the mark is in the wrong place.

68. C. "Although he enjoyed swimming in the ocean every afternoon after school" isn't a complete thought. It is a subordinate clause. A colon, semicolon, or period makes it a sentence fragment. A comma (Choice **C**) is the correct punctuation mark.

69. A. Two sentences are run together with a comma here. Instead, a semicolon is needed before "however." Choice **A** is the best answer. (Also acceptable would be a period after "demolished" and a capital H on "however," but this choice isn't offered.) In Choice **B,** not only is a comma separating two complete sentences, but a semicolon is placed after "returned," which makes a fragment ("When they returned"). Remember: semicolons are used between clauses when each clause could be a sentence by itself.

70. A. The problem in this sentence is inconsistent verb tenses. In Choice **A,** all the verbs are in the past tense, making this answer the best. In the other choices, the verb tenses are mixed. Choice **B** has two present-perfect tenses ("has gone" and "has picked") and one present tense ("walks"). Choice **C** has two present tenses ("goes" and "walks") and one past perfect tense ("had picked"). The original sentence uses two past tenses ("went" and "picked") and one present tense ("walks").

71. B. Did the auto accidents happen in the class? That's what the original sentence seems to say. The problem is that the phrase "in our class" is misplaced. Choice **B** makes it clear that "in our class" is the place where the teacher took the survey. Choice **A** is an example of awkward sentence order. Choice **C** uses the passive voice of the verb ("a survey was taken"). It is better to use the active voice ("teacher took") when possible.

72. B. Did the sun play softball? This problem is called a dangling participle. Choices **A** and **C** don't solve the problem. "Playing softball on Friday" is the participial phrase, and it modifies "we," not "sun." The change to the sentence in Choice **B** properly places it.

73. D. The sentence is correct as it is **D**. The first verb is in the past perfect tense and the second verb is in the past tense. These tenses are correct because it is clear that the first action took place before the second action. The other choices use tenses that don't go together, and in addition, choices **B** and **C** use the passive voice of the verb ("will be promoted" and "will have been promoted"), which is less effective than the active voice.

74. C. In this sentence, the problem is called *faulty parallelism*. Simply put, elements in a sentence that have the same function should match grammatically. In this case, these elements are all things that the president promises: to balance the budget, plan more activities, and make improvements to the meeting hall (Choice **C**). In choices **A** and **B,** and in the original sentence, these elements don't match: in **A,** "a balanced budget, to plan more activities, and improve the meeting hall"; in **B,** "balancing . . . , planning . . . , and to make . . ."; in the original sentence, "a balanced . . . , to plan . . . , and . . . improvements. . . ."

75. C. The correct possessive of "it" is "its." Because many possessives are formed with apostrophes ("Bob's car," "Dad's golf clubs"), people often make the mistake of thinking that "it's" is the possessive form of "it." But "it" doesn't follow the rule. "It's" is a contraction of "it is," not a possessive form.

76. D. A double negative is a construction where two negative words are used when one is enough. "Cannot," "can't" and "hardly" are all negative words; therefore, **A, B,** and **C** are all examples of a double negative. **D** is the best answer.

77. D. The correct comparative of "good" is "better" Both **A** and **C** are incorrect comparatives of "good." Choice **B** is called the superlative and doesn't make sense here.

78. B. Pronoun cases are tricky. In this sentence, the subjective case is needed because the pronouns are the subjects of the verb "decided." It is easy to see this when you remove one of the pronouns. For example, you wouldn't say "Me decided to travel"(**A),** "Him decided to travel" (**A, C**), or "Her decided to travel" **D.**

79. A. "They're" (Choice **A**) is a contraction of "they are" and the correct word here. (Notice that the apostrophe takes the place of the omitted letter *a* in "are".) "They'll" is a contraction of "They will" (**B**). "Their" is the possessive form of "they" ("their car"), and "there" is usually an adverb that means "in or at that place": "I found my car there." Confusing "their," "there," and "they're" is a common mistake.

Answer Sheets for Practice Test 2

(Remove This Sheet and Use It to Mark Your Answers)

Session 1

1 Ⓐ Ⓑ Ⓒ Ⓓ
2 Ⓐ Ⓑ Ⓒ Ⓓ
3 Ⓐ Ⓑ Ⓒ Ⓓ
4 Ⓐ Ⓑ Ⓒ Ⓓ
5 Ⓐ Ⓑ Ⓒ Ⓓ
6 Ⓐ Ⓑ Ⓒ Ⓓ
7 Ⓐ Ⓑ Ⓒ Ⓓ
8 Ⓐ Ⓑ Ⓒ Ⓓ
9 Ⓐ Ⓑ Ⓒ Ⓓ
10 Ⓐ Ⓑ Ⓒ Ⓓ
11 Ⓐ Ⓑ Ⓒ Ⓓ
12 Ⓐ Ⓑ Ⓒ Ⓓ
13 Ⓐ Ⓑ Ⓒ Ⓓ
14 Ⓐ Ⓑ Ⓒ Ⓓ
15 Ⓐ Ⓑ Ⓒ Ⓓ
16 Ⓐ Ⓑ Ⓒ Ⓓ
17 Ⓐ Ⓑ Ⓒ Ⓓ
18 Ⓐ Ⓑ Ⓒ Ⓓ
19 Ⓐ Ⓑ Ⓒ Ⓓ
20 Ⓐ Ⓑ Ⓒ Ⓓ
21 Ⓐ Ⓑ Ⓒ Ⓓ

Session 2

22 Ⓐ Ⓑ Ⓒ Ⓓ
23 Ⓐ Ⓑ Ⓒ Ⓓ
24 Ⓐ Ⓑ Ⓒ Ⓓ
25 Ⓐ Ⓑ Ⓒ Ⓓ
26 Ⓐ Ⓑ Ⓒ Ⓓ
27 Ⓐ Ⓑ Ⓒ Ⓓ
28 Ⓐ Ⓑ Ⓒ Ⓓ
29 Ⓐ Ⓑ Ⓒ Ⓓ
30 Ⓐ Ⓑ Ⓒ Ⓓ
31 Ⓐ Ⓑ Ⓒ Ⓓ
32 Ⓐ Ⓑ Ⓒ Ⓓ
33 Ⓐ Ⓑ Ⓒ Ⓓ
34 Ⓐ Ⓑ Ⓒ Ⓓ
35 Ⓐ Ⓑ Ⓒ Ⓓ
36 Ⓐ Ⓑ Ⓒ Ⓓ
37 Ⓐ Ⓑ Ⓒ Ⓓ
38 Ⓐ Ⓑ Ⓒ Ⓓ
39 Ⓐ Ⓑ Ⓒ Ⓓ
40 Ⓐ Ⓑ Ⓒ Ⓓ
41 Ⓐ Ⓑ Ⓒ Ⓓ
42 Ⓐ Ⓑ Ⓒ Ⓓ
43 Ⓐ Ⓑ Ⓒ Ⓓ
44 Ⓐ Ⓑ Ⓒ Ⓓ
45 Ⓐ Ⓑ Ⓒ Ⓓ
46 Ⓐ Ⓑ Ⓒ Ⓓ
47 Ⓐ Ⓑ Ⓒ Ⓓ
48 Ⓐ Ⓑ Ⓒ Ⓓ
49 Ⓐ Ⓑ Ⓒ Ⓓ
50 Ⓐ Ⓑ Ⓒ Ⓓ

51 Ⓐ Ⓑ Ⓒ Ⓓ
52 Ⓐ Ⓑ Ⓒ Ⓓ
53 Ⓐ Ⓑ Ⓒ Ⓓ
54 Ⓐ Ⓑ Ⓒ Ⓓ
55 Ⓐ Ⓑ Ⓒ Ⓓ
56 Ⓐ Ⓑ Ⓒ Ⓓ
57 Ⓐ Ⓑ Ⓒ Ⓓ
58 Ⓐ Ⓑ Ⓒ Ⓓ
59 Ⓐ Ⓑ Ⓒ Ⓓ
60 Ⓐ Ⓑ Ⓒ Ⓓ
61 Ⓐ Ⓑ Ⓒ Ⓓ
62 Ⓐ Ⓑ Ⓒ Ⓓ
63 Ⓐ Ⓑ Ⓒ Ⓓ
64 Ⓐ Ⓑ Ⓒ Ⓓ
65 Ⓐ Ⓑ Ⓒ Ⓓ
66 Ⓐ Ⓑ Ⓒ Ⓓ
67 Ⓐ Ⓑ Ⓒ Ⓓ
68 Ⓐ Ⓑ Ⓒ Ⓓ
69 Ⓐ Ⓑ Ⓒ Ⓓ
70 Ⓐ Ⓑ Ⓒ Ⓓ
71 Ⓐ Ⓑ Ⓒ Ⓓ
72 Ⓐ Ⓑ Ⓒ Ⓓ
73 Ⓐ Ⓑ Ⓒ Ⓓ
74 Ⓐ Ⓑ Ⓒ Ⓓ
75 Ⓐ Ⓑ Ⓒ Ⓓ
76 Ⓐ Ⓑ Ⓒ Ⓓ
77 Ⓐ Ⓑ Ⓒ Ⓓ
78 Ⓐ Ⓑ Ⓒ Ⓓ
79 Ⓐ Ⓑ Ⓒ Ⓓ

CUT HERE

Essay

On the actual exam you will have **over two pages to write your essay.** Use another sheet of lined paper to complete your essay for this practice test.

_____

_____

_____

_____

_____

_____

_____

_____

_____

_____

_____

_____

_____

_____

_____

_____

_____

_____

_____

_____

_____

Session 1

The following article is about becoming a better and safer driver. Read the article and answer questions 1 through 7.

Roadwork Ahead

by John Dinkel

John Dinkel has been actively involved with the automotive industry for more than 25 years. He is the former editor in chief of *Road & Track* and the former publisher of *WESTWAYS*.

Acquiring a few new attitudes, habits and skills can make you a better and safer driver.

Having spent a good chunk of my adult life driving, testing, racing, and writing about cars and proper driving techniques, I've come to realize that most drivers are ill-equipped to cope with even the simplest of emergency situations. And it's really not their fault. Most of the problem lies with a system that emphasizes passing a driving test over becoming a good driver.

What does it mean to "drive better"? It means driving more smoothly and efficiently, which also makes driving more fun. But most important, it means increasing your control of the driving environment and keeping yourself out of bad driving situations, or, if you find yourself in one, improving your chances of emerging unscathed.

It's not difficult to become a better driver, but you'll need to change some of your attitudes and acquire a few new skills and habits. It's really not different from excelling at golf, tennis, or the piano. You have to learn the correct techniques and then practice them.

Pointers from the Pros

Some of the best lessons for improving ordinary street and highway driving come from race-car drivers, who run wheel-to-wheel with other cars, often at speeds well above 100 mph. Driving a race car might seem like a very different experience from commuting, but you and race-car drivers share at least two goals: You both want to get to your destinations as efficiently as possible and in one piece.

GO ON TO THE NEXT PAGE

So here are some tips from racing drivers/instructors Danny McKeever and Bob Bondurant to consider and practice the next time you get behind the wheel.

"Drive the racetrack first and the traffic second."
—*Danny McKeever*

Whether you're on the California speedway or a California freeway, you always need to know where you are on the road. Keep your eyes moving. Look for trouble far ahead and to either side, and check your mirrors frequently. Pay attention to the bigger picture.

Take an active approach to driving. You're not just along for the ride. Make a conscious effort to stay alert. Don't let yourself get distracted by passengers, food, music, or your cell phone, or by thinking about your plans for the day.

Be aware of subtle signs from other drivers. Often, they telegraph their next move before they make it. Learn to watch for telltale signals such as head movements, which will often precede lane changes. And be sure to clearly indicate your intentions to other drivers by using your turn signals.

Also, don't drive directly behind the vehicle in front of you. Move a little to the left or right, staying within your lane, of course. This often lets you see vehicles farther down the road, and if one of those drivers steps on the brakes, you'll have additional time to react.

"Always have an escape route in mind."
—*Bob Bondurant*

Suppose you're driving down the freeway at 65 mph when traffic suddenly slows. You brake to avoid the Ford Expedition in front of you. But what about the guy in that Chevy Suburban behind you? Maybe he's daydreaming or talking on a cell phone. If you're constantly checking your mirrors and the traffic in the lanes to either side of you, you probably have an out.

Always position yourself so you have an escape route. For example, avoid driving in the middle of a pack of cars. Instead, lead or follow the pack from a safe distance.

"Be smooth. Treat the pedals as dimmer switches, not as on-off switches."—*Danny McKeever*

It's best to keep the weight of your car evenly distributed on the tires, because balance increases your control. But if you accelerate hard, the car's weight goes to the rear. Brake hard, and it goes to the front; corner hard, and it goes to the side.

The key is to apply pressure to the throttle (accelerator) and brakes incrementally. Otherwise, the car's responses will be exaggerated, increasing the chances that you'll lose control and wind up in a collision. When accelerating, imagine there's an egg between your foot and the accelerator pedal.

As for braking, try this: The next time you have to stop for a traffic light or a stop sign, apply the brakes with continuous pressure and see how close you can come to the crosswalk without crossing the line. The first few times, you'll probably have to apply either less or more pressure than you think. But soon you'll get the hang of it, and you'll be amazed at how much better you'll be able to read braking distances and the effort required to stop smoothly and effectively.

"Keep a light grip on the steering wheel."
—Bob Bondurant

Lots of people put a death grip on the steering wheel. But when you do this, your muscles become tense, and you're more likely to make jerky, unnecessary adjustments to your steering, which reduces your control of the car.

Instead, maintain a light grip on the wheel, and relax. Then you'll be able to feel how the car is responding through the tires' contact with the road, which lets you drive in a more fluid, intuitive manner and increases your control.

If you're relaxed and trust your instincts, the car will tend to go where you look. This is especially helpful if you get into a bad situation. Let's say, for example, you're skidding out of control toward a light pole. If you look where you want the car to be, 50 feet away from the pole instead of wrapped around it, you're more likely to steer in the direction you want the car to go. Focus on the pole, and chances are that you'll steer into it.

"Few races are won on the first turn of the first lap, but many are lost before the first lap is completed."
—Danny McKeever

Off the racetrack, this translates as: Don't treat street or highway driving as a competition. It's a situation where nobody wins, but somebody can lose.

A lot of collisions happen not just because drivers exceed the speed limit but because they drive too fast for the conditions. So don't just thoughtlessly adhere to the posted speed limit, which indicates a maximum speed, not necessarily what's appropriate. That could depend on the weather, visibility, or traffic density.

Avoiding potential problems is often simply a matter of slowing down and lowering the pulse of things a bit. It's easier to do this if you deliberately leave a little earlier the next time you head for the office, the movies, or the ballgame. You'll enjoy the drive more, you'll arrive more relaxed, and you'll reduce the chances of making a bad driving decision that catches up with you.

GO ON TO THE NEXT PAGE

1. **Which of the following BEST summarizes the main idea of the article?**

   A. Always have an escape route wherever you drive.
   B. Don't drink and drive.
   C. Some of the best tips for better street and highway driving come from racecar drivers.
   D. Never drive slower than the speed limit.

2. **Which of the following is NOT discussed in the article?**

   A. It's wise to keep the weight of the car evenly distributed on all four tires.
   B. Relaxing is a good idea when you're behind the wheel.
   C. Try to avoid distractions when you drive.
   D. Checking your airbag periodically is recommended.

3. **Read this sentence from the article.**

   > Avoiding potential problems is often simply a matter of slowing down and lowering the pulse of things a bit.

   The phrase *lowering the pulse of things a bit* MOST likely means—

   A. driving too fast can literally be dangerous to your health.
   B. slowing down, relaxing, and leaving extra time to get to your destination reduce the chances that you'll have an accident.
   C. driving like a racer is exciting.
   D. people with a history of heart problems would be best advised to leave the driving to others.

4. **The following are references for readers interested in cars. In which of them would you MOST likely find information on safe driving?**

   A. "The Best SUVs of 2004," K. Lewinsky. *The American Motorist*. August 2003.
   B. "Arrive Alive: Avoiding Common Road Hazards," H. Hagopian. *Car and Driver*. Fall 2002.
   C. "From Dirt Track to Indianapolis: One Driver's Story," G. Lewis. *Sport*. 34:17 May 89.
   D. "Diagnosing Transmission Ills," J. K. Lewisohn. *The Journeyman's Guide to Car Repair*, pg.45–50.

5. **The article suggests that driving in the middle of a pack of cars is—**

   A. a bad idea because it does not permit you an escape route if something goes wrong.
   B. a bad idea because you will be slowed down by all that traffic.
   C. a good idea because there is safety in numbers.
   D. a good idea because you are less likely to be singled out by police officers if you are a part of a large group.

   > Be aware of subtle signs from other drivers. Often, they telegraph their next move before they make it.

6. **The word *telegraph* in the above sentence means—**

   A. to send a message by wire.
   B. to transport images by radio waves.
   C. to see at a distance.
   D. to show clearly that they're about to do something.

7. **This article provides the MOST information on—**

   A. learning some new skills and habits that will make you a better driver.
   B. how race drivers drive cars skillfully at high speeds.
   C. why tailgating is dangerous.
   D. learning to relax at the wheel.

The following poem explains the relationship between the shark and the pilot-fish that swim along side. Read the poem and answer questions 8 through 10.

The Maldive Shark

by Herman Melville

About the shark, phlegmatical one,

Pale sot of the Maldive sea,

The sleek little pilot-fish, azure and slim,

How alert in attendance be.

(5)   From his saw-pit of mouth, from his charnel of maw

They have nothing of harm to dread.

But liquidly glide on his ghastly flank

Or before his Gorgonian head;

Or lurk in the port of serrated teeth

(10)   In white triple tiers of glittering gates,

And there find a haven when peril's abroad,

An asylum in jaws of the Fates!

They are friends; and friendly they guide him to prey,

Yet never partake of the treat—

(15)   Eyes and brains to the dotard lethargic and dull,

Pale ravener of horrible meat.

GO ON TO THE NEXT PAGE

8. **Which of the following BEST describes the relationship between the pilot-fish and the shark?**

   A. indifference
   B. fear
   C. misplaced trust
   D. mutual benefit

9. **The phrase *glittering gates* in line 10 is—**

   A. an example of alliteration in a phrase describing teeth.
   B. a description of the glistening scales of the pilot-fish.
   C. an example of figurative language that compares the shark to a gate.
   D. a rhythmic example of a simile.

10. **Which of these lines from the poem MOST directly concerns an ironic situation?**

    A. "The sleek little pilot-fish, azure and slim,"
    B. "And there find a haven when peril's abroad,"
    C. "Eyes and brains to the dotard lethargic and dull,"
    D. "Pale ravener of horrible meat."

Read the following passage and answer questions 11 through 15.

On Summer

by Lorraine Hansberry

> Lorraine Hansberry was a young African-American author who died at a very young age. Her work *To Be Young Gifted and Black* was a collection of her writings published posthumously. "On Summer" is from that collection and is about her childhood memories of summer.

It has taken me a good number of years to come to any measure of respect for summer. I was, being May-born, literally an "infant of the spring" and, during the later childhood years, tended, for some reason or other, to rather worship the cold aloofness of winter. The adolescence, admittedly lingering still, brought the traditional passionate commitment to melancholy autumn—and all that. For the longest kind of time I simply thought that *summer* was a mistake.

In fact, my earliest memory of anything at all is of waking up in a darkened room where I had been put to bed for a nap on a summer's afternoon, and feeling very, very hot. I acutely disliked the feeling then and retained the bias for years. It had originally been a matter of the heat but, over the years, I came actively to associate displeasure with most of the usually celebrated natural features and social by-products of the season: the too-grainy texture of sand; the too-cold coldness of the various waters we constantly try to escape into, and the icky-perspiry feeling of bathing caps.

It also seemed to me, esthetically speaking, that nature had got inexcusably carried away on the summer question and let the whole thing get to be rather much. By duration alone, for instance, a summer's day seemed maddeningly excessive; an utter overstatement. Except for those few hours at either end of it, objects always appeared in too sharp a relief against backgrounds; shadows too pronounced and light too blinding. It always gave me the feeling of walking around in a motion picture which had been too artsily-craftsily exposed. Sound also had a way of coming to the ear without that muting influence, marvelously common to winter, across patios or beaches or through the woods. I suppose I found it too stark and yet too intimate a season.

GO ON TO THE NEXT PAGE

11. **Which statement BEST describes the narrator's opinion of summer?**

    A. The season of summer serves no purpose.
    B. Things associated with summer seem too exaggerated.
    C. Adolescents cannot fully appreciate summer.
    D. Summer is always too hot.

12. **The phrases *too grainy texture*, *icky-perspiry*, and *too artsily-craftsily* are examples of—**

    A. imagery.
    B. metaphors.
    C. similes.
    D. allegory.

13. **The purpose of the narrator's flashback in the second paragraph is to—**

    A. set the tone of the story.
    B. persuade the reader to agree with her.
    C. describe herself to the reader.
    D. explain her bias against summer.

> . . . nature had got inexcusably carried away on the summer question . . .

14. **The line from the selection is an example of—**

    A. personification.
    B. symbolism.
    C. onomatopoeia.
    D. apostrophe.

15. **Read this sentence from the selection.**

> I suppose I found it too stark and yet too intimate a season.

   By using the words *stark* and *intimate*, what does Hansberry mean in the sentence above?

    A. She is confused about her feelings.
    B. The season is too glaring and yet too private at the same time.
    C. The season is too loud and yet too quiet at the same time.
    D. She feels aloof and yet close to the season.

Read the following essay and answer questions 16 through 21.

New Directions

by Maya Angelou

Maya Angelou is a famous African-American author. The essay "New Directions" is about an African-American woman who makes the best of a situation in a time when finding work was very hard for African Americans.

In 1903 the late Mrs. Annie Johnson of Arkansas found herself with two toddling sons, very little money, and a slight ability to read and add simple numbers. To this picture add a disastrous marriage and the burdensome fact that Mrs. Johnson was a Negro.

When she told her husband, Mr. William Johnson, of her dissatisfaction with their marriage, he conceded that he too found it to be less than he expected, and had been secretly hoping to leave and study religion. He added that he thought God was calling him not only to preach but to do so in Enid, Oklahoma. He did not tell her that he knew a minister in Enid with whom he could study and who had a friendly, unmarried daughter. They parted amicably, Annie keeping the one-room house and William taking most of the cash to carry himself to Oklahoma.

Annie, over six feet tall, big-boned, decided that she would not go to work as a domestic and leave her "precious babes" to anyone else's care. There was no possibility of being hired at the town's cotton gin or lumber

mill, but maybe there was a way to make the two factories work for her. In her words, "I looked up the road I was going and back the way I come and since I wasn't satisfied, I decided to step off the road and cut me a new path." She told herself that she wasn't a fancy cook but that she could "mix groceries well enough to scare hungry away and from starving a man."

She made her plans meticulously and in secret. One early evening to see if she was ready, she placed stones in

GO ON TO THE NEXT PAGE

two five-gallon pails and carried them three miles to the cotton gin. She rested a little, and then, discarding some rocks, she walked in the darkness to the saw mill five miles farther along the dirt road. On her way back to her little house and her babies, she dumped the remaining rocks along the path.

That same night she worked into the early hours boiling chicken and frying ham. She made dough and filled the rolled-out pastry with meat. At last she went to sleep.

The next morning she left her house carrying the meat pies, lard, an iron brazier [a portable barbecue], and coals for a fire. Just before lunch she appeared in an empty lot behind the cotton gin. As the dinner noon bell rang, she dropped the savors into boiling fat and the aroma rose and floated over to the workers who spilled out of the gin, covered with white lint, looking like specters.

Most workers had brought their lunches of pinto beans and biscuits or crackers, onions and cans of sardines, but they were tempted by the hot meat pies which Annie ladled out of the fat. She wrapped them in newspapers, which soaked up the grease, and offered them for sale at a nickel each. Although business was slow, those first days Annie was determined. She balanced her appearances between the two hours of activity.

So, on Monday if she offered hot fresh pies at the cotton gin and sold the remaining cooled-down pies at the lumber mill for three cents, then on Tuesday she went first to the lumber mill, presenting fresh, just-cooked pies as the lumbermen covered in sawdust emerged from the mill.

For the next few years, on balmy spring days, blistering summer noons, and cold, wet, and wintry middays, Annie never disappointed her customers who could count on seeing the tall, brown-skin woman bent over her brazier, carefully turning the meat pies. When she felt certain that the workers had become dependent on her, she built a stall between the two hives of industry and let the men run to her for their lunchtime provisions.

She had indeed stepped from the road which seemed to have been chosen for her and cut herself a brand-new path. In years that stall became a store where customers could buy cheese, meal, syrup, cookies, candy, writing tablets, pickles, canned goods, fresh fruit, soft drinks, coal, oil and leather soles for worn-out shoes.

Each of us has the right and the responsibility to assess the roads which lie ahead, and those over which we have traveled, and if the future road looms ominous or unpromising, and the roads back uninviting, then we need to gather our resolve and, carrying only the necessary baggage, step off that road into another direction. If the new choice is also unpalatable, without embarrassment, we must be ready to change that as well.

16. What is the narrator's main purpose in this essay?

   A. to persuade readers to go into business for themselves
   B. to describe to readers what it is like to go through a divorce
   C. to inform readers about what it takes to become successful
   D. to inspire readers to make changes in their lives

17. Read this sentence from the essay.

   > "I looked up the road I was going and back the way I come . . ."

   This sentence is an example of—

   A. metaphor.
   B. simile.
   C. personification.
   D. allegory.

18. Which statement from the essay BEST describes Annie Johnson's motivation for opening a business?

   A. "He did not tell her that he knew a minister in Enid with whom he could study and who had a friendly, unmarried daughter."
   B. "In 1903 the late Mrs. Annie Johnson of Arkansas found herself with two toddling sons, very little money, and a slight ability to read and add simple numbers."
   C. "She would not go to work as a domestic and leave her 'precious babes' to anyone else's care."
   D. ". . . she wasn't a fancy cook but that she could 'mix groceries well enough to scare hungry away and from starving a man.'"

19. Which of the following BEST describes Annie Johnson?

   A. determined
   B. reclusive
   C. meticulous
   D. overbearing

20. Read this sentence from the essay.

   > He did not tell her that he knew a minister in Enid with whom he could study and who had a friendly, unmarried daughter.

   This sentence implies—

   A. Mr. Johnson has a great opportunity if he moves to Enid.
   B. Mr. Johnson is leaving his wife for another woman.
   C. Enid is a pleasant town.
   D. The minister and his daughter are very friendly.

21. By not having Annie Johnson narrate her story, the essay can be viewed as—

   A. objective.
   B. subjective.
   C. fiction.
   D. nonfiction.

Practice Test 2

GO ON TO THE NEXT PAGE

Essay

Write your essay on the pages provided in your answer document. You may only use a No. 2 pencil. Do not use pen. You may use the blank space in your test booklet to make notes before you begin writing. Any notes you make in the test booklet will NOT be considered when your essay is scored.

Reminder

- Be sure to write your response to the writing prompt given below.
- You may place a title on your essay if you would like, but it is not necessary.
- No dictionary may be used. If you have trouble spelling a word, sound the word out and do the best you can.
- You may write in cursive or print.
- Write clearly! Any changes, erasures, or strike-throughs should be made as neatly as possible.

Writing Task

> Some students at your school are concerned about the lack of school spirit because of low attendance at after-school sporting events, plays, and dances.
>
> Write a persuasive letter to the student council at your school, attempting to convince the members to try some new ideas to encourage students to get involved in after-school activities. Convince your audience by explaining the importance of school spirit and giving some specific examples of new ideas.

Checklist for Your Writing

The following checklist will help you. Always make sure that you:

- ❏ Read the task or tasks carefully.
- ❏ Organize your writing by including a strong introduction, body, and conclusion.
- ❏ Always support your ideas with specific details and examples.
- ❏ Write to your audience by using appropriate words.
- ❏ Use words that are appropriate for your purpose.
- ❏ Make you writing interesting to read by varying your sentences.
- ❏ Check carefully for mistakes in grammar, usage, spelling, punctuation, capitalization, and sentence structure.

END SESSION 1

Session 2

Read the following story and answer questions 22 through 27.

Helen Keller and Anne Sullivan

Knowledge is love and light and vision.

by Helen Keller

> Helen Keller became ill at age two and was left blind and deaf. For the next five years she grew up in a world of darkness and emptiness. She was afraid, alone, and without any anchor. This is the story of her meeting the teacher who would change her life

The most important day I remember in all my life is the one on which my teacher, Anne Mansfield Sullivan, came to me. I am filled with wonder when I consider the immeasurable contrasts between the two lives, which it connects. It was the third of March, 1887, three months before I was seven years old.

On the afternoon of that eventful day, I stood on the porch, dumb and expectant. I guessed vaguely from my mother's signs and from the hurrying to and fro in the house that something unusual was about to happen, so I went to the door and waited on the steps. The afternoon sun penetrated the mass of honeysuckle that covered the porch, and fell on my upturned face. My fingers lingered almost unconsciously on the familiar leaves and blossoms, which had just come forth to greet the sweet Southern spring. I did not know what the future held of marvel or surprise for me. Anger and bitterness had preyed upon me continually for weeks and a deep languor had succeeded this passionate struggle.

Have you ever been at sea in a dense fog, when it seemed as if a tangible white darkness shut you in, and the great ship, tense and anxious, groped her way toward the shore with plummet and sounding-line, and you waited with beating heart for something to happen? I was like that ship before my education began, only I was without compass or sounding-line, and had no way of knowing how near the harbor was. "Light! Give me light!" was the wordless cry of my soul, and the light of love shone on me in that very hour.

I felt approaching footsteps. I stretched out my hand as I supposed it was my mother. Someone took it, and I was caught up and held close in the arms of her who had come to reveal all things to me, and, more than all things else, to love me.

GO ON TO THE NEXT PAGE

The morning after my teacher came she led me into her room and gave me a doll. The little blind children at Perkins Institution had sent it and Laura Bridgman had dressed it; but I did not know this until afterward. When I played with it a little while, Miss Sullivan slowly spelled into my hand the word "d-o-l-l." I was at once interested in this finger play and tried to imitate it. When I finally succeeded in making the letters correctly I was flushed with childish pleasure and pride. Running downstairs to my mother I held up my hand and made the letters for doll. I did not know that I was spelling a word or even that words existed; I was simply making my fingers go in monkey-like imitation. In the days that followed I learned to spell in this uncomprehending way a great many words, among them pin, hat, cup, and a few verbs like sit, stand, and walk. But my teacher had been with me several weeks before I understood that everything has a name.

One day, while I was playing with my new doll, Miss Sullivan put my big rag doll into my lap also, spelled "d-o-l-l" and tried to make me understand that "d-o-l-l" applied to both. Earlier in the day we had had a tussle over the words "m-u-g" and "w-a-t-e-r." Miss Sullivan had tried to impress it upon me that "m-u-g" is mug and that "w-a-t-e-r" is water, but I persisted in confounding the two. In despair she had dropped the subject for the time, only to renew it at the first opportunity. I became impatient at her repeated attempts and, seizing the new doll, I dashed it upon the floor. I was keenly delighted when I felt the fragments of the broken doll at my feet. Neither sorrow nor regret followed my passionate outburst. I had not loved the doll. In the still, dark world in which I lived there was no strong sentiment or tenderness. I felt my teacher sweep the fragments to one side of the hearth, and I had a sense of satisfaction that the cause of my discomfort was removed. She brought me my hat, and I knew I was going out into the warm sunshine. This thought, if a wordless sensation may be called a thought, made me hop and skip with pleasure.

We walked down the path to the well house, attracted by the fragrance of the honeysuckle with which it was covered. Someone was drawing water and my teacher placed my hand under the spout. As the cool stream gushed over one hand she spelled into the other the word water, first slowly, then rapidly. I stood still, my whole attention fixed upon the motions of her fingers. Suddenly, I felt a misty consciousness as of something forgotten—a thrill of returning thought; and somehow the mystery of language was revealed to me. I knew then that "w-a-t-e-r" meant the wonderful cool something that was flowing over my hand. That living word awakened my soul, gave it light, hope, joy, set it free! There were barriers still, it is true, but barriers that could in time be swept away.

I left the well-house eager to learn. Everything had a name, and each name gave birth to a new thought. As we returned to the house, every object that I touched seemed to quiver with life. That was because I saw everything with the strange, new sight that had come to me. On entering the door I remembered the doll I had broken. I felt my way to the hearth and picked up the pieces. I tried vainly to put them together. Then my eyes filled with tears; for I realized what I had done, and for the first time I felt repentance and sorrow.

I learned a great many new words that day. I do not remember what they all were; but I do know that mother, father, sister, teacher were among them—words that were to make the world blossom for me, "like Aaron's rod, with flowers." It would have been difficult to find a happier child than I was, as I lay in my crib at the close of that eventful day and lived over the joys it had brought me, and for the first time longed for a new day to come.

22. **What did Helen first think of Miss Sullivan spelling *doll* into her hand?**

   A. She thought it was a game.
   B. She knew it meant *doll*.
   C. She thought she was being punished.
   D. She thought Miss Sullivan had spelled *water*.

23. **What does Helen mean when she compares herself to a ship lost in fog?**

   A. She gets lost easily.
   B. She feels a kinship with the ocean because the fog swallows the ocean like it swallows her.
   C. Because she cannot see or hear, she is unable to find her way in life, just like the ship in the fog.
   D. She enjoys maritime activities.

24. **"My fingers lingered almost unconsciously" is an example of—**

   A. metaphor.
   B. simile.
   C. imagery.
   D. personification.

25. **Why does Helen consider meeting Miss Sullivan the most important day of her life?**

   A. The event gave her a new friend.
   B. It opened up the world of language to her.
   C. It was the day Helen was cured.
   D. It was Helen's birthday.

26. **The story is an example of—**

   A. tragedy.
   B. comedy.
   C. retrospect.
   D. foreshadowing.

GO ON TO THE NEXT PAGE

27. **Read the following sentence from the story.**

> Anger and bitterness had preyed upon me
> continually for weeks and a deep languor had
> succeeded this passionate struggle.

**Based on the context in which it is used in the
story, what does *languor* mean?**

A. listlessness

B. passion

C. melancholy

D. assertiveness

The following article is about the rising rates of cable television. Read the article and answer questions 28 through 33.

Why Are Cable Rates Still Rising?

Cable rates have continued to spiral upward, rising by more than 50 percent in the past eight years.

Cable companies often blame the rapidly rising costs they must pay to the most popular cable net-
(5) works, such as ESPN, to carry their programming. The cable providers say they have no choice but to pay them, since some of the channels have a monopoly on profitable programming such as sports. The cable companies say they're forced to
(10) pass along the higher fees to subscribers.

Further, the cable companies say, they've added channels to their lineup and invested in customer service.

Investigations by the General Accounting Office
(15) and others have confirmed the rise in programming fees. And our survey of some 1,200 cable customers showed an increase in the average number of channels received via digital cable since our last survey, in 2001.

(20) Less generally accepted is whether the cost of added digital channels and 24/7 customer service

justify the rise in rates. Consumers Union, publisher of *Consumer Reports*, in a joint report with the Consumer Federation of America, says the
(25) increases have more to do with a lack of serious competition for most cable companies, in the relatively rare cases where consumers have a choice of cable companies; the GAO report found, cable rates are about 15 percent lower than in noncom-
(30) petitive markets. Further, the CU-CFA report argues, some of the added channels are there mainly because the media conglomerates that own many major cable operators also have substantial stakes in the cable networks.

(35) Since few people regularly watch all the channels they're offered on cable, wouldn't cable subscribers pay less if they could choose channels à la carte? According to the GAO, à la carte pricing would reduce advertising revenue and might
(40) "result in higher per-channel rates and less diversity in program choice." But CU says subscribers who don't watch many channels could come out ahead.

GO ON TO THE NEXT PAGE

For now, to keep a lid on your cable costs, (45) ensure that the tiers and premium channels you've selected are worth it to you. And if you don't want to face more steep rate hikes, consider using a rooftop antenna or switching to satellite. While there's no guarantee of future trends, satellite's rates (50) have risen more moderately than cable's in recent years.

28. **Based on this article, which of the following statements is true?**

    A. Paying for channels " à la carte " will soon be a reality.

    B. Cable companies will often bargain, resulting in lower rates for the knowledgeable customer.

    C. Cable prices have decreased in many locales in recent years.

    D. Switching to a rooftop antenna or satellite may be a good alternative to rising cable prices.

29. **The cable companies state that their prices have risen in direct response to—**

    A. increased competition from video rentals.

    B. more government regulation.

    C. rising costs, more channels, and greater customer service expense.

    D. inflation.

30. **Read the following sentence from the selection.**

> Since few people regularly watch all the channels they're offered on cable, wouldn't cable subscribers pay less if they could choose channels à la carte?

According to the passage, what does the Government Accounting Office (GAO) believe might happen if à la carte pricing were to be instituted?

    A. Advertising revenue would be reduced and per channel rates might increase.

    B. The cable companies would lose hundreds, if not thousands, of customers.

    C. Cable televisions would become available in more remote rural areas.

    D. The American public would petition Congress to take over the cable industry.

31. **What tone does the author create in this article?**

    A. humorous

    B. depressed

    C. mildly critical

    D. angry

32. Consumers who want to *keep a lid on* cable costs, probably want to—

A. keep the prices where they are or maybe even reduce them.

B. switch to satellite dish.

C. lobby Congress to pass à la carte pricing laws.

D. give up cable altogether and read more books.

Further, the . . . report argues, some of the added channels are there mainly because the media conglomerates that own many major cable operators also have substantial stakes in the cable networks.

33. What does the word *stakes* mean in the sentence above?

A. large pieces of meat

B. sharply pointed sticks

C. money at risk in a gambling game

D. an important share in a business

GO ON TO THE NEXT PAGE

Read the following excerpt and answer question 34 through 37.

It's Not About the Bike: My Journey Back to Life

by Lance Armstrong, with Sally Jenkins

Lance Armstrong is a cancer survivor and six-time Tour de France winner. This excerpt is from his first autobiography.

(1) Sydney was everything we'd imagined it would be. The emerald-green bay seemed to lap right at the feet of the skyscrapers, and mangrove trees sheltered the older Victorian buildings. The only disappointment of the Olympics was my actual performance. I finished 13th in the road race, which was won by Jan Ullrich. I could swallow that without too much frustration, because the flat course didn't suit me. My more realistic medal expectations were in the time trial. But then I got out-dueled in that event, too, and took the bronze.

(2) When I set out alone on the three-lap course that snaked from the Sydney Cricket Grounds to the beach and back, I already knew that my Postal teammate Vyacheslav Ekimov, had logged a blisteringly fast time. I started fluidly, and by the first lap I was only a second behind him. But after a lap and a half, I was three seconds down. I couldn't seem to get my body moving any faster. I was going all-out—my heart monitor told me so—and yet I kept losing time. After the second lap I was six seconds down, and on the third and final lap I could feel myself falling farther behind. It wasn't close at the end; there would be no miraculous ride for me in the Olympics. I crossed the finish line in 58 minutes, 14 seconds, a full 34 seconds behind Eki, and 26 seconds behind Ullrich, for the bronze.

(3) I could not have gone any harder. When you prepare for an event, and you do your best and go your hardest, and then you don't get it, you just have to say, "I didn't deserve to win." And I didn't. Eki deserved every ounce of gold in his medal. As upset as I was to lose, I was also that happy for him, because he had put his effort all on the line to help me win the Tour.

(4) After the medal ceremony, I walked past my bike, and cheerfully kissed my wife. Kik was proud of me; she said later that she wished Luke had been old enough to understand what went on that day, because she wanted him to see the kind of man we'd like him to be in the face of a loss. That made me as proud as anything I've ever done in front of her.

(5) Sometimes I think the biggest thing cancer did was knock down a wall in me. Before cancer I defined myself purely in terms of "winner" or "loser," but I don't have that kind of rigid vanity anymore. It's kind of like my hair. I used to care about the way I looked, I worried about my appearance all the time, and I had to make sure my hair was just right before I walked out the door. Now I cut it all off. My wife trims it with a clipper, and it's so easy to take care of that I'll wear it this way for the rest of my life.

(6) Since the illness I just care a lot less if people like me or not. I still care a little, but with the birth of my son, it's diminished even more. My wife likes me, and I hope my son will like me. It's their good opinion that I desire now. We had a party to get to. It was October 1, and the next day, October 2, would mark the four-year anniversary of my cancer diagnosis. In the world of cancer patients it's a very significant date, and for me personally, it was the most important date in my life, more important

than any birthday or any holiday. No victory or loss could compare to it.

(7) Kik calls my anniversary *Carpe Diem* Day, to remind us to always seize the moment. Every year we spend that day celebrating our existence. We remind ourselves that it's a myth to say that I beat cancer. The drugs beat cancer. The doctors beat cancer. I just survived it. We remind ourselves that according to most recent cancer-survival rates, I am not alive.

(8) I'll spend the rest of my life puzzling over my survival. Cancer no longer consumes my life, my thoughts, or my behavior, but the changes it wrought are there in me, unalterable. I've learned that intense movement is a necessary thing in my life, something as fundamental and as simple as breathing. I don't believe I could ride, or live, any differently. Also, I've learned to be more thoughtful, and resist saying the first thing that otherwise might come out of my mouth. Above all, I've learned that if I have a tough week, all I have to do is sit back and reflect. It's easy to say, "These things don't bother me anymore."

(9) So on the night that I lost the gold medal and won the bronze, Kik and I took some of our closest friends on a dinner cruise of Sydney Harbor, and we celebrated the fact that there would be other races. We celebrated my health. And then we went home to Austin as a family, happily.

GO ON TO THE NEXT PAGE

(10) I still ride my bike into the hill country above Austin, and the trucks still blow by. But now a lot of the truck drivers recognize me in my U.S. Postal team jersey. Some wave. Some take a hard look and some still try to run me off the road. I keep riding, into the highest peering hills, up the pitch of a mountainside, where green leaves quiver in the cold sun.

34. Lance Armstrong feels he—

A. beat cancer.
B. survived cancer.
C. surrendered to cancer.
D. still has cancer.

35. Which of the following BEST describes Lance Armstrong's tone in the last paragraph?

A. persuasive
B. humorous
C. optimistic
D. anxious

36. In which sentence from the passage does the narrator acknowledge that some people will still try to thwart his efforts?

A. "And some still try to run me off the road."
B. "It's their good opinion that I desire now."
C. "Eki deserved every ounce of gold in his medal."
D. "No victory or loss could compare to it."

37. In paragraph 7, Lance's wife uses the Latin phrase *Carpe Diem*, which means—

A. Day of the Dead.
B. Seize the Day.
C. All Soul's Day.
D. Buyer Beware.

Read the following article and answer questions 38 through 46.

Wake Up to the Risks of Drowsy Driving

Getting behind the wheel when you're short on sleep is very risky business. The worst-case scenario, falling asleep at the wheel, is surprisingly common. Drowsy driving is blamed for at least 100,000 accidents, 71,000 injuries, and 1,550 deaths in the U.S. each year.

In 2003, New Jersey enacted a first-of-its-kind law stipulating that sleep-deprived drivers who cause fatal accidents can be charged with vehicular homicide. New York is considering an anti-drowsy-driving measure. And other states have prosecuted fatigued drivers under existing laws.

The New Jersey law defines a fatigued driver as one who has gone without sleep for more than 24 hours. But you needn't be that sleep-deprived to court trouble. People who sleep six to seven hours a night—the norm for many Americans—are nearly twice as likely to have a fatigue-related accident as those who sleep eight hours or more, according to a 1999 study of 1,403 drivers by the University of North Carolina's Highway Safety Research Center and School of Medicine.

Like alcohol, fatigue slows reaction time and impairs judgment and vision. Being up for 24 hours is akin to being legally drunk.

Getting enough sleep is the best way to avoid drowsy driving. Aim for eight hours a night. Other factors that can make you drowsy include the following:

Circadian rhythms. Your body's urge to sleep is strongest from about midnight to 5 a.m. and in the midafternoon.

Driving conditions. Late-night driving, long trips, and monotonous roads can make you tired, especially if you're alone.

Alcohol. Even small amounts can exacerbate the effects of fatigue.

Medications. Antianxiety medications, narcotics, and antihistamines can make you drowsy. Also beware of drugs that can disrupt sleep, leaving you tired the next day. Check labels and also ask your doctor or pharmacist whether any of your medications could cause drowsiness or sleep disruption.

Medical disorders. If you're often sleepy or fatigued for no obvious reason, visit a doctor to find out if an underlying disorder, such as sleep apnea, is to blame.

GO ON TO THE NEXT PAGE

If you find yourself fighting fatigue behind the wheel, the two best tactics are to either stop for the night or have someone else take over driving. If you can't, try this short-term fix: Pull over to a safe location, drink two cups of coffee, and take a 15- to 20-minute nap, which gives the caffeine time to enter your bloodstream.

38. **What suggestions does the article make about staying awake on the highway?**

    A. Plan most of your driving to occur after midnight.

    B. Have an alcoholic beverage or two to relax you.

    C. Drink two cups of coffee, take a 20-minute nap, and then continue on your way.

    D. Get a solid six hours of uninterrupted sleep per night.

39. **Driving while fatigued from being up all night is MOST like which of the following activities?**

    A. eating a large meal and then going swimming

    B. being legally drunk

    C. failing to monitor your blood pressure

    D. playing contact sports without proper headgear

40. **New Jersey's decision to charge with vehicular homicide those motorists who cause fatal accidents while driving sleep-deprived indicates—**

    A. the seriousness of the offense.

    B. a desire to enhance the growth of the hotel/motel industry.

    C. a desire to imitate the largely successful law on accidents of this nature in New York.

    D. a response to consumer demand.

41. **Which of the following BEST summarizes the information contained in this article?**

    A. Drivers need to get at least eight hours of sleep per night to be safe on the highways.

    B. The body's circadian rhythms indicate that driving after midnight and before 5 a.m. is the most dangerous time for drivers.

    C. Studies show that sleep disorders are the principal cause of traffic accidents.

    D. Driving while fatigued is dangerous and states are taking steps to prosecute those who cause accidents while doing it.

42. Which of the following about this article would be the MOST appropriate for further research?

   A. how caffeine works on the brain
   B. the effect that the new laws have on reducing the accident, injury, and fatality rates
   C. the role the medical community has on reducing fatigue-related accidents
   D. an examination of other forward-thinking laws enacted or proposed by the New Jersey legislature

43. Read this sentence from the article.

> Being up for 24 hours is akin to being legally drunk.

In this sentence from the article, the word *akin* MOST likely is synonymous with—

   A. the opposite.
   B. similar.
   C. in pain.
   D. normal.

44. Read this sentence from the article.

> The worst-case scenario, falling asleep at the wheel, is surprisingly common.

In this sentence from the article, the word *scenario* means—

   A. something that could happen but hasn't happened yet.
   B. an athletic event.
   C. something a novelist might write.
   D. a type of sleeping disorder.

45. Which of the following best indicates the author's attitude toward driving while fatigued?

   A. It happens to everyone; therefore, it's not serious.
   B. It's rare, and therefore, it's not serious.
   C. It is serious, but it is usually confined to long-distance truckers.
   D. It is extremely serious, common, and dangerous.

46. Which of the following is NOT discussed in the article?

   A. circadian rhythms
   B. drugs that disrupt your sleep, causing you to lose valuable rest
   C. the sentences given to convicted sleep-deprived drivers who cause accidents in New Jersey
   D. medical disorders that rob you of sleep

Practice Test 2

GO ON TO THE NEXT PAGE

The following excerpt is from "My Furthest-Back Person" by Alex Haley. Read the excerpt and answer questions 47 through 52.

My Furthest-Back Person

by Alex Haley

Alex Haley is an African American who turned his family tree into the novel *Roots*, which was later turned into a television mini-series. "My Furthest-Back Person" is the essay that led to *Roots*.

One Saturday in 1965 I happened to be walking past the National Archives building in Washington. Across the interim years I had thought of Grandma's old stories—otherwise I can't think what diverted me up the Archives' steps. And when a main reading room desk attendant asked if he could help me, I wouldn't have dreamed of admitting to him some curiosity hanging on from boyhood about my slave forebears. I kind of bumbled that I was interested in census records of Alamance County, North Carolina, just after the Civil War.

The microfilm rolls were delivered, and I turned them through the machine with a building sense of intrigue, viewing in different census takers' penmanship an endless parade of names. After about a dozen microfilmed rolls, I was beginning to tire, when in utter astonishment I looked upon the names of Grandma's parents: Tom Murray, Irene Murray . . . older sisters of Grandma's as well—every one of them a name that I'd heard countless times on her front porch.

It wasn't that I hadn't believed Grandma. You just *didn't* not believe my Grandma. It was simply so uncanny actually seeing those names in print and in official U.S. Government records.

During the next several months I was back to Washington whenever possible, in the Archives, the Library of Congress, the Daughters of the American Revolution Library. (Whenever black attendants understood the idea of my search, documents I requested reached me with miraculous speed.) In one source or another during 1966 I was able to document at least the highlights of the cherished family story. I would have given anything to have told Grandma, but, sadly, in 1949 she had gone. So I went and told the only survivor of those Henning front-porch storytellers: Cousin Georgia Anderson, now in her 80's in Kansas City, Kan. Wrinkled, bent, not well herself, she was so overjoyed, repeating to me the old stories and sounds; they were like Henning echoes: "Yeah, boy, that African say his name was '*Kin-tay*': he say the banjo was '*ko*,' an' the river '*Kamby*

Bolong,' an' he was off choppin' some wood to make his drum when they grabbed 'im!" Cousin Georgia grew so excited we had to stop her, calm her down. "You go 'head, boy! Your grandma an'all of 'em—they up there watching what you do!"

That week I flew to London on a magazine assignment. Since by now I was steeped in the old, in the past, scarcely a tour guide missed me—I was awed at so many historical places and treasures I'd heard of and read of. I came upon the Rosetta stone in the British Museum, marveling anew at how Jean Champollion, the French archaeologist, had miraculously deciphered its ancient demotic and hieroglyphic texts.[1]

47. **What does Haley do with his family tree information?**

A. share it with his grandma
B. write a book
C. film a mini-series
D. make a movie

48. **How does Haley feel when he sees his ancestors' names in print?**

A. eerie
B. elated
C. sad
D. angry

49. **Why does Haley have such a hard time tracing his roots?**

A. His family told him lies.
B. Archivists would not help him.
C. Africans would not help him.
D. Most of the information he had was oral.

50. **How can Haley's endeavors be compared to Jean Champollion's?**

A. Both men searched for their ancestors.
B. Both men are archaeologists.
C. Both men searched for answers.
D. Both men visited the British Museum.

51. **Read the following sentence from the story.**

> Across the interim years I had thought of Grandma's old stories—otherwise I can't think what diverted me up the Archives' steps.

Based on the context in which it is used in the story, what does *interim* mean?

A. interval
B. specific
C. numerous
D. objective

1 **Demotic and hieroglyphic texts** Ancient Egyptian writing, using symbols and pictures to represent words.

GO ON TO THE NEXT PAGE

52. **Read the following sentence from the story.**

> Since by now I was steeped in the old, in the past, scarcely a tour guide missed me—

Based on the context in which it is used in the story, what does *steeped* mean?

A. an incline
B. deeply absorbed
C. clearly understanding
D. leaving alone

The following is a draft of a paragraph about mountain biking. It may contain errors in grammar, sentence structure, vocabulary, and organization. Some of the questions may refer to underlined or numbered sentences or phrases within the text. Read the draft and answer questions 53 through 57.

Mountain Biking

(1) Mountain biking can help you improve your balance and have greater control when you bike around town. (2) For example, because mountain biking requires you to ride on dirt, snow, grass, and rocky trails, you learn to handle tricky situations, which means you will be less inclined to panic when the unexpected happens on regular city streets. (3) Because you have to conquer more hills and surmount more obstacles, mountain biking strengthens your leg muscles more than road biking. (4) And the muscles in your arms and shoulders will also get built up. (5) With a mountain bike, you can ride on trails and dirt that would damage a regular road bike, and that means greater freedom. (6) One of the best advantages of riding off the road is that you can therefore experience more of nature. (7) I advise you to do some research and invest in a good mountain bike, not a cheap one. (8) Biking in the mountains is actually even safer than biking on a city street because there are no cars or trucks, and if you fall, the landing is softer.

GO ON TO THE NEXT PAGE

53. If inserted before sentence 1, which of the following would be the BEST opening sentence for this paragraph?

    A. Always wear the proper safety gear when mountain biking.

    B. Mountain biking is a popular sport, especially with people under thirty.

    C. As a sport, mountain biking has several advantages over road biking.

    D. Mountain biking is a good way to have fun.

54. Which of the sentences below is the BEST way to combine sentences 3 and 4?

    A. Mountain biking strengthens your leg, arm, and shoulder muscles more than road biking does because you have to conquer more mountains and surmount more obstacles.

    B. Mountain biking strengthens your leg muscles and also your arm and shoulder muscles more than road biking strengthens them because of the fact you have to conquer more hills and surmount more obstacles.

    C. The muscles in your legs will be built up by mountain biking more than road biking because of having to conquer more hills and surmount more obstacles, as well as your arm and shoulder muscles.

    D. Building up your leg, arm, and shoulder muscles will be done better by mountain biking than by road biking because of the many hills you have to conquer and the many obstacles you have to overcome.

55. Which of the following sentences does NOT fit well in this paragraph?

    A. Sentence 4

    B. Sentence 6

    C. Sentence 7

    D. Sentence 8

56. Which of the following points is NOT supported by details?

    A. Mountain biking helps make you a better road biker.

    B. It is a good idea to buy an expensive mountain bike.

    C. A mountain bike allows you more freedom.

    D. Mountain biking is less dangerous than road biking.

57. Of the following, which would probably be the BEST source of information on the characteristics of a good mountain bike?

    A. a sports history book

    B. a guide to off-road biking trails

    C. an almanac

    D. articles in cycling magazines

The following is a draft of a paragraph about Niagara Falls. It may contain errors in grammar, sentence structure, vocabulary, and organization. Some of the questions may refer to underlined or numbered sentences or phrases within the text. Read the paragraph and answer questions 58 through 60.

Niagra Falls—Power and Beauty

(1) Every year thousands of tourists travel to upstate New York and Ontario, Canada, to see Niagara Falls. (2) Visitors can appreciate the waterfall's power and beauty from several angles because <u>there are provided many bridges, towers, and caves from which they can view them.</u> (3) If <u>you</u> prefer to watch the thundering falls from below, steamer rides on the Niagara River are available. (4) Some tourists also take an elevator down over 150 feet to look out from behind the falls. (5) The first bridge built over the Niagara River was the Whirlpool Rapids bridge, which was built in 1897 and is about two miles long. (6) Over the years, both amateur and professional photographers have taken advantage of the different views of the falls to create spectacular pictures.

58. What is the MOST effective way to change the underlined section of sentence 2?

A. of the many bridges, towers, and caves.
B. it is possible to locate yourself on many bridges, towers, and caves.
C. there are to be found many bridges, towers, and caves.
D. Leave as is.

59. Which of the following sentences does NOT fit well in the paragraph?

A. Sentence 4
B. Sentence 5
C. Sentence 3
D. Sentence 6

60. What is the BEST substitution for the underlined word in sentence 3?

A. we
B. people
C. one
D. Leave as is.

GO ON TO THE NEXT PAGE

The following is a draft of a report about the writ of habeas corpus. It may contain errors in grammar, sentence structure, vocabulary, and organization. Read the draft and answer questions 61 through 64.

The Writ of Habeas Corpus

(1) Felix Frankfurter was Justice of the Supreme Court from 1939–1962. (2) He called habeas corpus "the basic safeguard of freedom in the Anglo-American world." (3) Although most people have heard the term, they don't know exactly what it means. (4) What a writ of habeas corpus is is a court order that commands an official who holds someone in custody to bring that person to court. (5) The official then has to justify the legal grounds for detaining the person or denying his personal liberty. (6) A writ of habeas corpus has nothing to do with whether a person is guilty or not guilty of a crime but only whether the person has been given due process of law.

(7) A writ of habeas corpus is now guaranteed in the United States Constitution. (8) Habeas corpus is mentioned as early as the 14th century in England and became the law there in the Habeas Corpus Act of 1679. (9) Like many of our legal practices, therefore, it is borrowed from the English. (10) The colonists in America were very much in favor of habeas corpus, and in fact the refusal of the British to issue the writ was a major complaint before the Revolution.

(11) Writs of habeas corpus have been used throughout the history of the United States. (12) One of the first examples occurred during the Civil War. (13) A civilian was sentenced to death by a court-martial even though the local grand jury had refused to indict him. (14) His life was spared when the Supreme Court granted a writ of habeas corpus. (15) Another example occurred in World War II when a writ of habeas corpus was used to release Americans of Japanese descent from camps where they had been taken against their will. (16) Today, the writ of habeas corpus is still used.

61. Which of the following is the MOST effective way to combine sentences 1 and 2?

A. Felix Frankfurter, who was a Supreme Court Justice from 1939–1962 and who called habeas corpus "the basic safeguard of the Anglo-American world."

B. "The basic safeguard of the Anglo-American world" was what Felix Frankfurter, who was a Supreme Court Justice from 1939–1962, called habeas corpus.

C. Felix Frankfurter was a Supreme Court Justice from 1939–1962, and he called habeas corpus "the basic safeguard of the Anglo-American world."

D. Felix Frankfurter, Supreme Court Justice from 1939 to 1962, called habeas corpus "the basic safeguard of the Anglo-American world."

62. Which of the following is the BEST revision of sentence 4 in paragraph 1?

A. The definition of a writ of habeas corpus is a court order whose purpose is to command an official holding someone in custody to bring the person in custody to court.

B. A writ of habeas corpus is a court order and it commands an official who holds someone in custody to bring that person to court.

C. A writ of habeas corpus is a court order commanding an official to bring a person in custody to court.

D. When an official is holding someone in custody, a writ of habeas corpus commands that the person in custody be brought to court.

63. Which of the following is the BEST placement of sentence 7 in paragraph 2?

A. As the first sentence of paragraph 1.
B. As the last sentence of paragraph 1.
C. As the last sentence of paragraph 2.
D. Leave as is.

64. Which of the following would MOST improve paragraph 3?

A. A current example of the use of a writ of habeas corpus
B. Deleting the example of habeas corpus from the Civil War period
C. A discussion of the arguments against the use of a writ of habeas corpus
D. The specific date when the writ of habeas corpus was first used in the United States

GO ON TO THE NEXT PAGE

Practice Test 2

For questions 65 through 74, choose the answer that is the most effective substitute for each underlined part of the sentence. If no substitution is necessary, choose "Leave as is."

65. Because Sean made the payment early, he received a discount.

   A. Because Sean made the payment early. He
   B. Because, Sean made the payment early, he
   C. Because Sean made the payment early; he
   D. Leave as is.

66. "Where would you like to have dinner, he asked me politely."

   A. "Where would you like to have dinner? He asked me politely."
   B. "Where would you like to have dinner," he asked me politely.
   C. "Where would you like to have dinner?" he asked me politely.
   D. Leave as is.

67. Edgar Allan Poe created a gloomy, melancholy mood in his short stories; and in some of his poetry.

   A. short stories and in some of his poetry.
   B. short stories: and in some of his poetry.
   C. short stories. And in some of his poetry.
   D. Leave as is.

68. Gliding down the snow-covered mountain on a crisp winter day, gave her the feeling of freedom and joy.

   A. Gliding down the snow-covered mountain on a crisp winter day. Gave her the feeling
   B. Gliding down the snow-covered mountain on a crisp winter day gave her the feeling
   C. Gliding down the snow-covered mountain on a crisp winter day; gave her the feeling
   D. Leave as is.

69. The movie according to everyone in our class was much more exciting than the novel, which most of us hadn't even finished.

   A. movie, according to everyone in our class, was much more exciting than the novel which
   B. movie, according to everyone in our class, was much more exciting than the novel, which
   C. movie according to everyone in our class, was much more exciting than the novel which
   D. Leave as is.

70. At the meeting in Philadelphia the head of the company reads the report on our performance and then presented achievement awards.

   A. read the report on our performance and then presented
   B. will have read the report on our performance and then presents
   C. reads the report on our performance and then will have presented
   D. Leave as is.

71. They were carrying a large dog in their arms, which they had found wandering on the side of the highway.

   A. They were carrying a large dog, which they had found wandering on the side of the highway, in their arms.
   B. A large dog which they had found wandering on the side of the highway was being carried by them in their arms.
   C. In their arms they were carrying a large dog, which they had found wandering on the side of the highway.
   D. Leave as is.

72. He gave me a gift that he had purchased at a market in Istanbul.

   A. gives me a gift that he shall have purchased
   B. has gave me a gift that he purchased
   C. had given me a gift that he has purchased
   D. Leave as is.

73. The hikers wanted <u>water, a resting place under our shade trees, and to use a phone.</u>

    A. to have water, a resting place under our shade trees, and using a phone.

    B. water, to rest under our shade trees, and use of a phone.

    C. water, a resting place under our shade trees, and use of a phone.

    D. Leave as is.

74. <u>We bought a used car, from a fast-talking salesperson that broke down within a month.</u>

    A. From a fast-talking salesperson we bought a used car that broke down within a month.

    B. From a fast-talking salesperson was bought a used car that broke down within a month.

    C. We bought from a fast-talking salesperson, a used car that broke down within a month.

    D. Leave as is.

For questions 75 through 79 choose the word or phrase that best completes the sentence.

75. The argument between Mr. Wright and _____ was settled within a few minutes.

    A. he
    B. she
    C. me
    D. they

76. They told _____ that nothing would get in the way of a successful trip.

    A. theyreselves
    B. thereselves
    C. theirselves
    D. themselves

77. Mr. Hollingsworth said that the new community center would _____ children in a positive way.

    A. affect
    B. have an affect on
    C. effect
    D. effects

78. Mrs. Chen's new baby is the _____ child I've ever seen.

    A. happy
    B. happiest
    C. most happiest
    D. happier

79. They waited in the rain for Shana and _____ to finish shopping at the mall.

    A. he
    B. I
    C. us
    D. she

Practice Test 2

END SESSION 2   STOP

Answer Key for Practice Test 2

(WA) Word Analysis   (RC) Reading Comprehension   (LR) Literary Response and Analysis

Session 1

For "Roadwork Ahead"

1. C (RC) ❑   **4.** B (RC) ❑   **6.** D (WA) ❑

2. D (RC) ❑   **5.** A (RC) ❑   **7.** A (RC) ❑

3. B (WA) ❑

For "The Maldive Shark"

8. D (LR) ❑   **9.** A (LR) ❑   **10.** B (LR) ❑

For "On Summer"

11. B (LR) ❑   **13.** D (LR) ❑   **15.** B (WA) ❑

12. A (LR) ❑   **14.** A (LR) ❑

For "New Directions"

16. D (LR) ❑   **18.** C (LR) ❑   **20.** B (WA) ❑

17. A (LR) ❑   **19.** A (LR) ❑   **21.** A (LR) ❑

Session 2

For "Helen Keller and Anne Sullivan"

22. A (LR) ❑   **24.** D (LR) ❑   **26.** C (LR) ❑

23. C (RC) ❑   **25.** B (LR) ❑   **27.** A (WA) ❑

For "Why Are Cable Rates Still Rising?"

28. D (RC) ❑   **30.** A (RC) ❑   **32.** A (WA) ❑

29. C (RC) ❑   **31.** C (RC) ❑   **33.** D (WA) ❑

For "It's Not About the Bike"

34. B (LR) ❏   **36.** A (LR) ❏

35. C (LR) ❏   **37.** B (WA) ❏

For "Wake Up to the Risks of Drowsy Driving"

38. C (RC) ❏   **41.** D (RC) ❏   **44.** A (WA) ❏

39. B (RC) ❏   **42.** B (RC) ❏   **45.** D (RC) ❏

40. A (RC) ❏   **43.** B (WA) ❏   **46.** C (RC) ❏

For "My Furthest-Back Person"

47. B (RC) ❏   **49.** D (RC) ❏   **51.** A (WA) ❏

48. A (LR) ❏   **50.** C (LR) ❏   **52.** B (WA) ❏

For Writing Strategies

53. C ❏   **57.** D ❏   **61.** D ❏

54. A ❏   **58.** A ❏   **62.** C ❏

55. C ❏   **59.** B ❏   **63.** C ❏

56. B ❏   **60.** B ❏   **64.** A ❏

For Writing Conventions

65. D ❏   **70.** A ❏   **75.** C ❏

66. C ❏   **71.** C ❏   **76.** D ❏

67. A ❏   **72.** D ❏   **77.** A ❏

68. B ❏   **73.** C ❏   **78.** B ❏

69. B ❏   **74.** A ❏   **79.** C ❏

Reviewing Practice Test 2

Review your simulated CAHSEE English-Language Arts Practice Test by following these steps:

1. Check the answers you marked on your answer sheet against the Answer Key. Put a check mark in the box following any wrong answer.
2. Fill out the Review Char below.
3. Read all the explanations (pp. 215–221). Go back to review any explanations that are not clear to you.
4. Fill out the Reasons for Mistakes chart below.
5. Have your essay evaluated using the checklist that is included.
6. Go back to the review sections and review any materials necessary before taking the next practice test.

Don't leave out any of these steps. They are very important in learning to do your best on the CAHSEE English-Language-Arts.

Review Chart

Use your marked Answer Key to fill in the following Review Chart for the multiple-choice questions.

	Possible	Completed	Right	Wrong
Word Analysis (WA) (7)	12			
Reading Comprehension (RC) (18)	19			
Literary Response and Analysis (LR) (20)	21			
Writing Strategies (WS) (12)	12			
Writing Conventions (WC) (15)	15			
Totals	79			

The numbers in ( ) are the actual number of each type that count toward your score.

Reasons for Mistakes

Fill out the following chart only after you have read all the explanations that follow. This chart will help you spot your strengths and weaknesses and your repeated errors or trends in types of errors.

	Total Missed	Simple Mistake	Misread Problem	Lack of Knowledge
Word Analysis (WA)				
Reading Comprehension (RC)				
Literary Response and Analysis (LR)				
Writing Strategies (WS)				
Writing Conventions (WC)				
Totals				

Examine your results carefully. Reviewing the above information will help you pinpoint your common mistakes. Focus on avoiding your most common mistakes as you practice. The "Lack of Knowledge" column will help you focus your review. If you are missing a lot of questions because of "Lack of Knowledge," you should go back and spend extra time reviewing the basics.

Explanations for Practice Test 2

Session 1

For "Roadwork Ahead"

1. **C.** Choice **A** is good advice and is contained in the article, but it is a detail and not really the main point of the passage. Choice **B** is also good advice but is not contained anywhere in the article. Choice **C** is mentioned in the opening paragraph. It serves as a lead-in informing the reader of exactly what this passage is going to be about. The article clearly states in the next-to-the last paragraph that a good driver will vary speed to match road conditions, eliminating **D** as an answer. **(Reading Comprehension)**

2. **D.** Choices **A**, **B** and **C** are all mentioned in the text as being sound driving practices. While **D** may be a good idea, it is not mentioned as such in the article. **(Reading Comprehension)**

3. **B.** Choices **A** and **C** may be true but are not responsive to the question. Choice **D** is simply not true, nor is it mentioned anywhere in the article. **(Word Analysis)**

4. **B.** Choice **A** suggests an analysis of new cars. Choice **C** sounds autobiographical, while **D** is a do-it-yourself manual. Only **B** suggests the safe-driving theme. **(Reading Comprehension)**

5. **A.** The author talks at length about constantly checking mirrors and the traffic around you and positioning yourself to have an escape route away from other vehicles. You should avoid being hemmed in by other cars and seek to follow them from a distance. Choice **B** is not the answer because driving slowly is not necessarily a bad thing. Choice **C** is clearly absurd. Choice **D** is not mentioned in the article. **(Reading Comprehension)**

6. **D.** While a telegraph is a device that sends messages via electrical impulses, the word is used metaphorically here. The actions of other drivers (if carefully observed) can tell you what they are going to do precious seconds before they do it. **(Word Analysis)**

7. **A.** Becoming a better driver is clearly the ultimate goal of this article. Choice **D** is mentioned as a detail. Choice **C** is true but not mentioned. Techniques of race drivers are mentioned, but only as they apply to safer driving. **(Reading Comprehension)**

For "The Maldive Shark"

8. **D.** The relationship between the pilot-fish and the shark is a living arrangement between two organisms in which both derive some benefit from the other—mutual benefit. In this case, the shark benefits because the pilot-fish lead it to prey; the pilot-fish benefit because they can "find asylum," that is, a safe place, in the shark's jaws. They aren't indifferent to one another (**A**) because they obviously both want the benefits provided by the arrangement. The large shark certainly wouldn't fear the pilot-fish (**B**), nor do the small fish fear the shark, which provides them with safety. And the trust isn't *misplaced* (**C**); the pilot-fish can trust that they will be kept safe by the shark's presence. **(Literary Response and Analysis)**

9. **A.** Alliteration is the repetition of a sound (usually a beginning consonant sound) in two or more words, in this case, the *g* sound in *glittering gates.* So this phrase is an example of alliteration, and it does describe the teeth of the shark, which are specifically named in the preceding line. Choice **C** is incorrect because it isn't the entire shark that is compared to the gate, but only its teeth. **(Literary Response and Analysis)**

10. **B.** An ironic situation is one in which the appearance is different from our recognition of the reality. In this case, one could speak of the entire poem as being ironic because it concerns these small pilot-fish, which live in harmony with this killer of the seas, the shark. Of the lines given, however, only **C** directly deals with this fact. These small fish "there find a haven," a safe place, right in the mouth of this predator, amid its teeth. The irony lies in the fact that normally one would think, upon seeing a small animal in the mouth of the large animal, that the small one was about to be eaten—which is not the case here at all. Choice **A** simply describes the pilot-fish; **C** describes the shark's meal; and **D** describes the shark itself. **(Literary Response and Analysis)**

For "On Summer"

11. **B.** Choice **B** encompasses much of Hansberry's argument. Choices **A, C,** and **D** overstate by suggesting "no purpose," "adolescents" in general, and "always too hot." (**Literary Response and Analysis**)

12. **A.** Imagery uses words that appeal to the five senses. The phrases are not metaphors or similes because nothing is being compared. (**Literary Response and Analysis**)

13. **D.** The narrator states the initial reason she was displeased with summer; therefore, **D** is correct. The tone of the passage was set in the first paragraph, so **A** is incorrect. The narrator never uses language that is persuasive, so **B** is incorrect. Although the passage might serve to describe an aspect of the narrator's personality, that is too limited a purpose to apply to the entire paragraph. (**Literary Response and Analysis**)

14. **A.** Nature is an inanimate object that is given the human quality of getting *carried away*; therefore, it is an example of personification. (**Literary Response and Analysis**)

15. **B.** Hansberry just discussed all of the contradictions that encompass summer. She specifically discusses how items are too bright or too dark or too loud. Choice **B** is the correct answer because it encompasses all of her ideas about summer being overpowering, as is the case with the shadows being too pronounced or the light too blinding. Choice **A** is incorrect because she is clear about her feelings, **C** is incorrect because it only addresses one aspect of her thoughts and **D** is incorrect because she does not feel close to the season at all. (**Word Analysis**)

For "New Directions"

16. **D.** The essay discusses the courage it took for Annie to make changes in her life. In the last paragraph, the narrator discusses the roads each of us takes and that we have the responsibility to assess the roads and make any changes necessary. (**Literary Response and Analysis**)

17. **A.** Metaphors are direct comparisons and the Annie is comparing her life to a road. (**Literary Response and Analysis**)

18. **C.** The sentence states why Annie had to be creative in order to make money instead of just taking domestic work. Choice **B** is incorrect. Just because Annie needs money and has few skills, doesn't explain why she would be motivated to open her own business. (**Literary Response and Analysis**)

19. **A.** Annie is determined to change her life for the better. She practices her job before she actually attempts it, and she works out a good business plan to get several different customers. (**Literary Response and Analysis**)

20. **B.** While **A, C,** and **D** may be true statements, **B** is the only one that picks up on the implication that Mr. Johnson is leaving his wife for another woman. That fact is not explicitly stated, but there is no other reason to mention the "friendly, unmarried daughter." (**Word Analysis**)

21. **A.** If Annie were the narrator, we'd have to be careful about opinionated statements as opposed to factual ones. Since Annie is not the narrator, we can assume that the information is more likely to be objective. (**Literary Response and Analysis**)

Have an English teacher, tutor, or someone else with good writing skills read and evaluate your essay using the checklist below.

Checklist for Response to Writing Prompt

Does your letter . . .

❑ Provide a thoughtful, well-written letter that addresses the writing task?

❑ Use specific supporting details and examples?

❑ Demonstrate a clear focus and tone?

❑ Show coherent, logical organization?

❑ Clearly address the intended audience?

❑ Use precise, descriptive language?

❑ Use a variety of sentence types?

❑ Contain almost no errors in grammar, punctuation, spelling, capitalization and usage?

❑ Clearly state a position and make a case for that position?

❑ Defend the position with specific relevant evidence?

❑ Address the reader's potential misunderstandings, biases, and expectations?

❑ Use the proper letter format and spacing?

Session 2

For "Helen Keller and Anne Sullivan"

22. **A.** Helen refers to the act as "finger play" and "monkey-like imitation" that she did not comprehend, but that she did enjoy. (**Literary Response and Analysis**)

23. **C.** Helen states that she was like a ship in the fog before her education began. She "had no way of knowing how near the harbor was" because she couldn't hear or speak. (**Reading Comprehension**)

24. **D.** Fingers do not have a consciousness; that is a human characteristic. (**Literary Response and Analysis**)

25. **B.** The entire passage is about Miss Sullivan teaching Helen about words. Helen states several times that before she met Miss Sullivan she was in the dark; therefore, if Miss Sullivan had not come into her life, Helen would have remained unable to communicate all her life. (**Literary Response and Analysis**)

26. **C.** Helen is looking back on her childhood and commenting on or evaluating it. That is the definition of retrospect. (**Literary Response and Analysis**)

27. **A.** Even if you don't know what *languor* means, substitute in the other answers. By process of elimination, **B** and **D** don't make much sense. Since the last few lines are about Helen's restlessness and passionate struggle, *lethargy* or *listlessness* makes the most sense. (**Word Analysis**)

For "Why Are Cable Rates Still Rising?"

28. **D.** While **A** is suggested as a possible solution to the problem of rising prices, there is no hint that the cable companies are preparing to embrace such a solution. Choice **B** is wrong because the article doesn't support the idea of cable companies bargaining with customers. The first paragraph states that cable prices have soared, not decreased in recent years, ruling out **C**. (**Reading Comprehension**)

29. **C.** The other three answer choices are not mentioned anywhere in the article. Paragraphs 2 and 3 mention costs, increased channels, and more customer service as the reasons for the spiral in cable prices. (**Reading Comprehension**)

30. **A.** This answer is contained in lines 38–40. None of the other answer choices is stated or even implied. (**Reading Comprehension**)

31. C. The author lists the responses of the cable industry, but also cites other, contradictory information. The author certainly isn't depressed (**B**). Humor is not a part of a largely informational text and strong emotions like anger are completely absent. **(Reading Comprehension)**

32. A. The phrase *keep a lid on* something means to prevent it from rising higher. Choice **B** is a way this might happen, but is not an explanation of the term. Choices **C** and **D** are not mentioned in the text. **(Word Analysis)**

33. D. Although **B, C,** and **D** are all meanings of the word *stake* (and **A,** the homonym *steak*) only **D** fits the context created by the sentence. **(Word Analysis)**

For "It's Not About the Bike"

34. B. In paragraph 7, Lance Armstrong states "We remind ourselves that it's a myth to say that I beat cancer . . . I just survived it." **(Literary Response and Analysis)**

35. C. Lance Armstrong states that no matter what, he keeps riding higher and higher. This is a metaphor for never giving up. **(Literary Response and Analysis)**

36. A. No matter what Lance does, some truckers try to run Lance off the road. This statement ties into the metaphor from the last question. Lance will never give up, even when people try to run him off the road. **(Literary Response and Analysis)**

37. B. *Carpe Diem* means *seize the day.* **(Word Analysis)**

For "Wake Up to the Risks of Drowsy Driving"

38. C. Choice **A** is incorrect because your body's urge to sleep is the strongest after midnight and before 6 a.m. Clearly **B** is wrong because alcohol enhances the effects of fatigue and it is illegal to drive while under the influence. Choice **D** isn't the answer because people who sleep six hours a night are nearly twice as likely to have a fatigue-related accident as those who get eight hours or more. **(Reading Comprehension)**

39. B. While choices **A, C,** and **D** may be dangerous to your health and well being, only **B** is both dangerous *and* illegal. It is also mentioned in paragraph 4 as analogous to driving after being up for 24 hours. **(Reading Comprehension)**

40. A. Clearly, killing someone while driving fatigued is a serious offense that the new law recognizes. Answer **B** lacks support in the article. There is no indication that consumers are clamoring for a new law on this subject, ruling out **D.** New York is *considering* a law on this issue, so **C** is not the answer. **(Reading Comprehension)**

41. D. Choices **A, B,** and **C** are details, not summaries that capture the entire argument. The correct answer, **D,** encompasses both the physiological and legal aspects of this article. **(Reading Comprehension)**

42. B. The article is primarily about fatigue-related accidents and attempts to reduce them by passing stricter laws. It is legitimate to find out if those laws are actually working. Are they reducing the number of accidents, injuries, and fatalities caused by people driving while fatigued? Choice **A,** while perhaps interesting, is far too narrow a part of the article to be a candidate for further research relevant to this article. The medical community has a role in prescribing medications that may make people drowsy but ultimately the responsibility falls on the patient to use the drugs as directed and avoid driving while drowsy, ruling out Choice **C.** Choice **D** is too broad to be relevant. **(Reading Comprehension)**

43. B. The word *akin* means similar to. **(Word Analysis)**

44. A. *Scenario* means that which hasn't happened but could. If you plug in any of the other choices, the sentence becomes nonsensical. **(Word Analysis)**

45. D. Driving while fatigued is very common (see paragraph 1) and extremely dangerous, ruling out **A** and **B.** The fact that so many people experience it rules out the idea that it is a problem only for long-distance truckers. **(Reading Comprehension)**

46. C. Circadian rhythms are discussed in paragraph 6. Drugs are discussed under the heading "Medications," and medical disorders like sleep apnea are mentioned in the next-to-the–last paragraph. While the laws and charges pertaining to sleep-deprived drivers are discussed, no sentences are mentioned. **(Reading Comprehension)**

For "My Furthest-Back Person"

47. B. The introductory paragraph states that Haley turns the information into a book. (**Reading Comprehension**)

48. A. Haley states that he had an *uncanny* feeling. *Uncanny* means strange or eerie. (**Literary Response and Analysis**)

49. D. While many people are willing to help him, most of his information is from his ancestors' stories. (**Reading Comprehension**)

50. C. Haley is trying to piece together information to discover his roots. Champollion pieced together information from the Rosetta stone to discover the meanings behind previously undecipherable languages. (**Literary Response and Analysis**)

51. A. Even if you don't know what *interim* means, try substituting in the other words as answers. Since this part of the story is about his wandering thoughts and how they lead him up the steps, **A** is the best answer. (**Word Analysis**)

52. B. As in the previous question, even if you don't know what *steeped* means, or you are confused by the context, try substituting in the other answers. Choice **B** is the only answer that makes sense when you substitute in the words. (**Word Analysis**)

For Writing Strategies

53. C. Choice **C** is best. The paragraph compares mountain biking to road biking, emphasizing the advantages of mountain biking. Choice **A** is a detail and would be out of place as an opening sentence. Choices **B** and **D** may be true, but they do not introduce the subject covered by the paragraph.

54. A. Choice **A** is best. It doesn't include unnecessary words and is less awkward than **B.** The best answer in this type of question is usually the one that expresses the idea most simply and directly. Choices **C** and **D** both use the passive voice of the verb. Whenever possible, the active voice is a better choice. Choice **C** also includes a confusingly placed phrase ("as well as your arm and shoulder muscles").

55. C. Choice **C** is the best answer. It is the only sentence that does not deal with the advantages of mountain biking. It is related to a different topic, i.e., selecting a mountain bike to buy.

56. B. Choice **B** is the best answer. The reasons to buy an expensive bike are not covered in this paragraph, whereas **A, C,** and **D** are.

57. D. The best choice is **D.** Cycling magazines are most likely to cover the factors that make a good mountain bike. A guide to trails, (**B**), might include some information (but probably not). Choice **A** might mention mountain biking but would not give information about characteristics of a good mountain bike, and **C** is irrelevant to the topic.

58. A. Choice **A** is the best answer. It conveys the meaning and is not wordy, as are **B, C,** and **D.**

59. B. The best answer is Choice **B.** This sentence presents a historical fact, which changes the focus of the paragraph. Choices **A** and **C** fit in the paragraph because they are about ways to view the waterfall, and **D** is an appropriate concluding sentence.

60. B. The best choice is **B.** The paragraph uses plural nouns ("tourists," "visitors"), making "people" appropriate here. **A, C,** and **D** are all pronouns that don't agree with the plural nouns.

61. D. The best choice is **D.** The sentences are combined by turning the phrase "Justice of the Supreme Court from 1939 to 1962" into an appositive referring to Justice Frankfurter. This is the most efficient way to combine these sentences without changing meaning. Choice **A** creates a sentence fragment, the "was what" construction in **B** is awkward, and the use of "and" to combine the sentences is much less effective than **D.**

62. C. Choice **C** is the best answer. Once again, the simplest, least wordy version of the sentence is the most clear and effective. Choices **A** and **D** unnecessarily repeat words, and **B** unnecessarily creates a compound sentence.

63. **C.** The best answer is **C**. The paragraph, except for the first sentence, treats habeas corpus chronologically. The second-best answer is **D**, but because of the historical order of the facts, **C** is a better choice. Choices **A** and **B** are not good locations for this sentence.

64. **A.** The best choice is **A**. The paragraph would be better if the point in sentence 16 was supported by an example. Choice **C** is beyond the scope of the paragraph, **D** is trivial, and **B** is definitely not a good idea. Examples and details are important in an essay.

For Writing Conventions

65. **D.** The sentence is correct as it is (**D**). "Because Sean made the payment early" isn't a complete thought. (What happened because Sean made the payment early?) Clauses like this are called subordinate clauses. If a period or a semicolon separated this clause from the main clause ("he received a discount"), as in choices **A** and **C**, it would be a sentence fragment, and in Choice **B**, the comma is incorrectly placed after "Because."

66. **C.** "Where would you like to have dinner?" is the question in this sentence, and therefore the question mark should follow "dinner." Also, because this is a quotation, the mark should be inside the quotation marks (**C**). In the original sentence, the question mark is missing and the second set of quotation marks is in the wrong place. Choice **A** also has the quotation marks in the wrong place; in **B**, while the quotation marks are correct, the question mark is missing.

67. **A.** "And in some of his poetry" is a phrase, not a sentence. Therefore, it can't follow a semicolon, a colon, or a period. Those marks would make it a sentence fragment. One way to correct the sentence is to simply delete the semicolon, as in Choice **A**.

68. **B.** "Gliding" may look like a verb, but it is acting as a noun here. (Words like this are called gerunds.) In this sentence, "Gliding down the snow-covered mountain on a crisp winter day" is a gerund phrase and is actually acting as the subject of the sentence. In its simplest form, the sentence would be "Gliding gave her the feeling of freedom and joy." No punctuation is needed in this sentence because a subject and a predicate ("gliding" and "gave") shouldn't be separated by a comma. Therefore, Choice **B** is correct.

69. **B.** The main idea of this sentence is "The movie was much more exciting than the novel." "According to everyone in our class" is a phrase that adds information, but it is parenthetical and could be removed. Phrases like this should be enclosed in commas. Another comma should follow "novel" because "which most of us hadn't even finished" also adds information that isn't necessary to the main idea. Choice **B** uses the best punctuation.

70. **A.** Choice **A** is best because both verbs are in the past tense ("read," "presented"). Keep verb tenses consistent within a sentence. Choice **B** uses future perfect ("will have read") and present tenses ("presents"), as does Choice **C**, though in the opposite order ("reads," "will have presented"). The original sentence uses present and past tense ("reads," "presented").

71. **C.** In this sentence a modifying clause is misplaced. Is it their arms that they found wandering on the side of the highway, as the original sentence suggests? Of course not. The clause "which they had found wandering on the side of the highway" belongs next to "large dog," as in Choice **C**. Choice **C** is much smoother than **A** (although **A** is not incorrect), in which "in their arms" is distant from "They were carrying." Choice **B**, which does not have a misplaced clause, is still not a good choice because of the wordiness of the passive voice ("was being carried by them").

72. **D.** Both the past tense ("gave") and the past perfect tense ("had purchased") are used in this sentence. The two actions occurred in the past, but the past perfect indicates that the action of purchasing the gift occurred before the giving of the gift, which makes sense. Choice **D** is the best answer.

73. **C.** The three things that the hikers wanted should be in the same grammatical form. In grammar, this is called parallel structure. Choice **C** is correct; "water," "resting place," and "use" are all nouns. Choices **A** and **B** as well as the original sentence all contain faulty parallelism. The original sentence uses two nouns ("water," "resting place") and an infinitive phrase ("to use a phone"). Choice **A** uses an infinitive phrase ("to have water"), a noun ("resting place") and a gerund ("using a phone"). In **B**, there are two nouns ("water," "use") and an infinitive phrase ("to rest").

74. A. Once again a modifying clause is misplaced. The original sentence suggests that the salesperson broke down within a month. For clarity, "that broke down within a month" should follow "car." Choice **B** uses the passive voice ("was bought") and is awkward. Choice **C** is also awkward, and a comma shouldn't follow "salesperson." The best answer here is **A.**

75. C. The only answer that is correct here is **C.** "Between" is a preposition and should be followed by an object, in this sentence the objective case of the pronoun. All of the choices except **C** are in the subjective case. One of the most common mistakes people make is using the phrase "Between you and I." It should always be "Between you and me."

76. D. "Theirselves," (**C**), is sometimes used for "themselves," but in fact it isn't grammatical or even a word. Neither are choices **A** and **B**.

77. A. The right word here is "affect" (**A**). As a verb, it means to influence. "Affect" and "effect" are often confused. "Effect" as a verb means "to cause to happen," but it is usually used as a noun meaning result ("The effect of the decision was significant"). In most cases, if you can put "the" or "an" in front of the word, it is probably "effect"; if you can't, it is probably "affect." Although Choice **B** does use the word "affect", the phrasing in choice B requires the noun "effect" instead.

78. B. "Happiest," not "most happiest" (**C**), is the correct superlative. The sense of the sentence requires the superlative form, but **A** simply uses the positive "happy" rather than the superlative. "Happier" **D** is the comparative form used when two things are compared ("John is happier than Bill"). Here, however, the baby is compared to all the children the speaker has seen.

79. C. The only pronoun that will work here is the objective case "us" (**C**). It is the object of the preposition "for." The other three pronouns ("he," "I," and "she") are in the subjective case. A quick way to see the correct answer here is to drop "Shana." You wouldn't say "waited for he," "waited for I," or "waited for she."

Answer Sheets for Practice Test 3

(Remove This Sheet and Use It to Mark Your Answers)

Session 1

1 (A) (B) (C) (D)
2 (A) (B) (C) (D)
3 (A) (B) (C) (D)
4 (A) (B) (C) (D)
5 (A) (B) (C) (D)
6 (A) (B) (C) (D)
7 (A) (B) (C) (D)
8 (A) (B) (C) (D)
9 (A) (B) (C) (D)
10 (A) (B) (C) (D)
11 (A) (B) (C) (D)
12 (A) (B) (C) (D)
13 (A) (B) (C) (D)
14 (A) (B) (C) (D)
15 (A) (B) (C) (D)
16 (A) (B) (C) (D)
17 (A) (B) (C) (D)
18 (A) (B) (C) (D)
19 (A) (B) (C) (D)
20 (A) (B) (C) (D)
21 (A) (B) (C) (D)

Session 2

22 (A) (B) (C) (D)
23 (A) (B) (C) (D)
24 (A) (B) (C) (D)
25 (A) (B) (C) (D)
26 (A) (B) (C) (D)
27 (A) (B) (C) (D)
28 (A) (B) (C) (D)
29 (A) (B) (C) (D)
30 (A) (B) (C) (D)
31 (A) (B) (C) (D)
32 (A) (B) (C) (D)
33 (A) (B) (C) (D)
34 (A) (B) (C) (D)
35 (A) (B) (C) (D)
36 (A) (B) (C) (D)
37 (A) (B) (C) (D)
38 (A) (B) (C) (D)
39 (A) (B) (C) (D)
40 (A) (B) (C) (D)
41 (A) (B) (C) (D)
42 (A) (B) (C) (D)
43 (A) (B) (C) (D)
44 (A) (B) (C) (D)
45 (A) (B) (C) (D)
46 (A) (B) (C) (D)
47 (A) (B) (C) (D)
48 (A) (B) (C) (D)
49 (A) (B) (C) (D)
50 (A) (B) (C) (D)

51 (A) (B) (C) (D)
52 (A) (B) (C) (D)
53 (A) (B) (C) (D)
54 (A) (B) (C) (D)
55 (A) (B) (C) (D)
56 (A) (B) (C) (D)
57 (A) (B) (C) (D)
58 (A) (B) (C) (D)
59 (A) (B) (C) (D)
60 (A) (B) (C) (D)
61 (A) (B) (C) (D)
62 (A) (B) (C) (D)
63 (A) (B) (C) (D)
64 (A) (B) (C) (D)
65 (A) (B) (C) (D)
66 (A) (B) (C) (D)
67 (A) (B) (C) (D)
68 (A) (B) (C) (D)
69 (A) (B) (C) (D)
70 (A) (B) (C) (D)
71 (A) (B) (C) (D)
72 (A) (B) (C) (D)
73 (A) (B) (C) (D)
74 (A) (B) (C) (D)
75 (A) (B) (C) (D)
76 (A) (B) (C) (D)
77 (A) (B) (C) (D)
78 (A) (B) (C) (D)
79 (A) (B) (C) (D)

CUT HERE

Essay

On the actual exam you will have **over two pages to write your essay.** Use another sheet of lined paper to complete your essay for this practice test.

CUT HERE

Practice Test 3

Session 1

Read the following poem and answer questions 1 through 5.

George Gray

by Edgar Lee Masters

Edgar Lee Masters is best known for his collection of poems titled *Spoon River Anthology*. The poems are about various people who used to live in Spoon River. They no longer "live" there because they are dead.

I have studied many times

The marble which was chiseled for me—

A boat with a furled sail at rest in a harbor.

In truth it pictures not my destination

(5)   But my life.

For love was offered me and I shrank from its disillusionment;

Sorrow knocked at my door, but I was afraid;

Ambition called to me, but I dreaded the chances.

Yet all the while I hungered for meaning in my life.

(10)   And now I know that we must lift the sail

And catch the winds of destiny

Wherever they drive the boat.

To put meaning in one's life may end in madness,

But life without meaning is the torture

(15)   Of restlessness and vague desire—

It is a boat longing for the sea and yet afraid.

GO ON TO THE NEXT PAGE

1. **What is the marble that was chiseled for George Gray?**

    A. a statue
    B. his tombstone
    C. a stone
    D. a boat

2. **Which statement BEST describes the speaker's life?**

    A. full and rich
    B. meaningful
    C. filled with fear
    D. filled with hope

> A boat with a furled sail at rest in a harbor.

3. **What does *furled* mean in the above line from the poem?**

    A. open
    B. folded
    C. holy
    D. mysterious

4. **What lesson has the speaker learned?**

    A. You must be willing to take chances.
    B. Life is meaningless.
    C. Life is filled with restlessness.
    D. You must be ambitious.

5. **Because the narrator is dead, what tone is set for the poem?**

    A. nostalgia
    B. regret
    C. anger
    D. fear

Read the following section from a high school handbook and answer questions 6 through 11.

Internet Acceptable Use Policy

Valid signatures from students and their parents are required for permission to use the Internet. Permission must be renewed each year of the student's enrollment at Southport High School. Students cannot be allowed access to the Internet unless they have received a sticker on their ID card from the library.

Student and staff Internet use shall be legal, efficient, and consistent with school purposes and with general standards of decency. All Internet users are expected to show consideration and respect for other users communicating on-line, as well as respect for equipment and school property.

The school holds the following activities as just cause for taking disciplinary action, up to and including dismissal, revoking network privileges, and/or making referral to legal authorities:

- Gaining intentional access to obscene or inappropriate files
- Using the network for any illegal activity, including violation of copyright or other licenses or contracts
- Accessing "chat lines" which are not a part of a class activity directly under the supervision of a teacher
- Using objectionable language in either public or private messages
- Posting anonymous messages
- Causing undue congestion of the network through lengthy downloads of files or by engaging in idle activities
- Vandalizing the data of another user
- Gaining unauthorized access to resources or files
- Identifying one's self with another person's name
- Using an account or password of another user without authorization
- Using the network for financial or commercial gain
- Theft of data, equipment, or intellectual property
- Invading the privacy of individuals

GO ON TO THE NEXT PAGE

6. Who is the intended audience for this document?

   A. vandals

   B. computer hackers looking to access school files via the Internet

   C. interested parties who work in the computer industry

   D. students seeking to use the Internet in school and their parents

7. What does the word *valid* mean in the following sentence?

> Valid signatures from students and their parents are required for permission to use the Internet.

   A. noteworthy

   B. valuable

   C. true

   D. well-written

8. Based on information contained in the document, which of the following statements about the acceptable use of the Internet is NOT true?

   A. Obtaining access to inappropriate files is just cause for disciplinary action.

   B. A student has to have a signature from his/her parent to use the Internet.

   C. Using another person's name to access the Internet or using another's account or password is just cause for disciplinary action.

   D. Posting anonymous messages is just cause for disciplinary action.

9. Based on information contained in the document, using the school's Internet facility to sell one's collection of baseball cards would be considered a violation of the Acceptable Use Policy because—

   A. it would violate copyright laws.

   B. it would constitute using the school's Internet connection and equipment for commercial gain.

   C. it would make the school liable for customer service problems regarding the sale.

   D. selling baseball cards without parental permission is illegal.

10. What does the word *revoking* mean in the following sentence?

> The school holds the following activities as just cause for taking disciplinary action, up to and including dismissal, revoking networking privileges, and/or making referral to legal authorities.

   A. canceling

   B. rewriting

   C. linking together

   D. reaffirming

11. The document provides the LEAST information on—

   A. what legal authorities might do upon receiving a referral from a school regarding a student who has violated the Acceptable Use Policy.

   B. what a student has to do to access the Internet at this school.

   C. what actions are considered liable to subject the student to disciplinary action.

   D. how often a student has to renew his/her permission to use the Internet at this school.

Read the following selection and answer questions 12 through 15.

Into Thin Air

by Jon Krakauer

In April 1996, writer Jon Krakauer joined an expedition to the top of Mount Everest. Krakauer survived to write a book about his experience, but before the trip was over, eight climbers had lost their lives. Here, Krakauer describes one of the terrifying ordeals of his climb.

If the Icefall required few orthodox climbing techniques, it demanded a whole new repertoire of skills in its stead—for instance, the ability to tiptoe in mountaineering boots and crampons[1] across three wobbly ladders lashed end to end, bridging a heart-stopping chasm. There were many such crossings, and I never got used to them.

At one point I was balanced on an unsteady ladder in the predawn gloaming, stepping tenuously from one bent rung to the next, when the ice supporting the ladder on either end began to quiver as if an earthquake had struck. A moment later came an explosive roar as a large serac[2] somewhere close above came crashing down. I froze, my heart in my throat, but the avalanching ice passed fifty yards to the left, out of sight, without doing any damage. After waiting a few minutes to regain my composure I resumed my herky-jerky passage to the far side of the ladder.

The glacier's continual and often violent state of flux added an element of uncertainty to every ladder crossing.

As the glacier moved, crevasses would sometimes compress, buckling ladders like toothpicks; other times a crevasse might expand, leaving a ladder dangling in the air, only tenuously supported, with neither end mounted on solid ice. Anchors securing the ladders and lines routinely melted out when the afternoon sun warmed the surrounding ice and snow. Despite daily maintenance, there was a very real danger that any given rope might pull loose under body weight.

1 **crampons** (kram' penz) n. iron spikes on shoes to prevent slipping.
2 **serac** (se rak') n. high, pointed mass of ice.

GO ON TO THE NEXT PAGE

But if the Icefall was strenuous and terrifying, it had a surprising allure as well. As dawn washed the darkness from the sky, the shattered glacier was revealed to be a three-dimensional landscape of phantasmal beauty. The temperature was six degrees Fahrenheit. My crampons crunched reassuringly into the glacier's rind. Following the fixed line, I meandered through a vertical maze of crystalline blue stalagmites.[3] Sheer rock buttresses seamed with ice pressed in from both edges of the glacier, rising like the shoulders of a malevolent god. Absorbed by my surroundings and the gravity of the labor, I lost myself in the unfettered pleasures of ascent, and for an hour or two, actually forgot to be afraid.

Three-quarters of the way to Camp One, Hall remarked at a rest stop that the icefall was in better shape than he'd ever seen it: "The route's a bloody freeway this season." But only slightly higher, at 19,000 feet, the ropes brought us to the base of a gargantuan, perilously balanced serac. As massive as a twelve-story building, it loomed over our heads, leaning 30 degrees past vertical. The route followed a natural catwalk that angled sharply up the overhanging face; we would have to climb up and over the entire off-kilter tower to escape its threatening tonnage.

Safety, I understood, hinged on speed. I huffed toward the relative security of the serac's crest with all the haste I could muster, but since I wasn't acclimatized my fastest pace was no better than a crawl. Every four or five steps I'd have to stop, lean against the rope, and suck desperately at the thin, bitter air, searing my lungs in the process.

I reached the top of the serac without it collapsing and flopped breathless onto its flat summit, my heart pounding like a jackhammer. A little later, around 8:30 A.M., I arrived at the top of the Icefall itself, just beyond the last of the seracs. The safety of Camp One didn't supply much peace of mind, however; I couldn't stop thinking about the ominously tilted slab a short distance below, and the fact that I would have to pass beneath its faltering bulk at least seven more times if I were going to make it to the summit of Everest. Climbers who snidely denigrate this as the Yak Route, I decided, had obviously never been through the Khumbu Icefall.

---

3 **stalagmites** (ste lag' mits') n. cone-shaped mineral deposits.

12. The author's use of the words *tiptoe*, *wobbly*, and *heart stopping* in paragraph 1 suggest a feeling of—

   A. anxiety.
   B. terror.
   C. surprise.
   D. pleasure.

13. At what point does Krakauer shift from discussing ice climbing's negative aspects to ice climbing's positive aspects?

   A. "I froze, my heart in my throat, but the avalanching ice passed fifty yards to the left, out of sight, without doing any damage."
   B. "There were many such crossings, and I never got used to them."
   C. "Three-quarters of the way to Camp One, Hall remarked at a rest stop that the icefall was in better shape than he'd ever seen it. . . ."
   D. "But if the icefall was strenuous and terrifying, it had a surprising allure as well."

14. Which of the following is an example of figurative language?

   A. "The temperature was six degrees Fahrenheit."
   B. "rising like the shoulders of a malevolent god."
   C. "I resumed my herky-jerky passage. . . ."
   D. "Anchors securing the ladders and lines routinely melted out when the afternoon sun warmed the surrounding ice and snow."

15. In which sentence from the passage does the narrator criticize those who ridicule an aspect of climbing?

   A. "Climbers who snidely denigrate this as the Yak Route . . . had obviously never been through the Khumbu Icefall."
   B. "The safety of Camp One didn't supply much peace of mind. . . ."
   C. "But if the Icefall was strenuous and terrifying, it had a surprising allure as well."
   D. "Despite daily maintenance, there was a very real danger that any given rope might pull loose under body weight."

GO ON TO THE NEXT PAGE

The following article discusses two different types of workout equipment. Read the article and answer questions 16 through 21.

The Weights Debate

by Marnell Jameson
(special to *The Times*)

Which is better, machines or free weights? Progressive fitness trainers and coaches see advantages to working both into your regimen.

In the beginning were free weights. Then, in the 1970s, Arthur Jones invented the Nautilus® weight machine. For years afterward, the question of which is better—free weights or machine weights—was hotly debated among strength coaches and bodybuilders. Today, most exercise experts agree that both free weights and machines have their place.

The stubborn few who still hold that one system is better than the other may be missing out on the best possible workout.

"Anyone who tells you that working out only with free weights or only with machine weights is better is lying," says Mark Wateska, director of athletic performance for Indiana University and former lead strength and conditioning coach for Stanford University. "Today, most progressive coaches see a place for both."

Free weights usually take the form of barbells or dumbbells and can be moved freely through space.

Machines guide weights on a preordained track. To the muscle, which can't see where the resistance is coming from, both types of equipment feel like work. When used correctly, both can produce a great result, says Wateska, who oversees strength and training regimens for 24 sports.

Still, each system has advantages and disadvantages. For beginners, machines are the best place to start, many experts say. They're safer and easier to learn to use properly. Free weights require more skill, particularly more coordination and balance.

Another advantage of machines is efficiency. If you have only 30 minutes to devote to your weight-training session, you might not want to waste minutes loading barbells and finding a spotter, Wateska says. Exercisers thinking of buying a set of dumbbells for their home gym should consider whether they have a spotter around in case they get pinned while doing a bench press.

One more plus for machines is their cam, a kidney-shaped wheel on most machines that allows them to adjust their resistance so lifters get a consistent load throughout the full range of motion. With free weights, lifters can only work the load when pushing it against gravity. The cam device also eliminated the sticking point, the point in the range of motion in which lifters are at the greatest biomechanical disadvantage.

Free weights, on the other hand, are more versatile. A barbell can be used to do several exercises—a bench press, a dead lift, a squat, to name a few—while machines are generally limited to only one or two exercises.

The biggest argument in the weight room today centers on the isolation—and the integration—of muscles.

Because machines are so good at isolating muscles, they've been favored by those wanting deep definition. Now more people are seeking the integrated muscle strength that free weights build, says Cedric Bryant, chief exercise physiologist for the American Council on Exercise in San Diego.

Exercises performed using weight machines tend to work isolated muscles and muscle groups. When people lift free weights, they tend to recruit more muscles to assist and stabilize. For example, lifting a barbell over the head requires help from the legs and hips; this isn't the case when using a machine. Thus, some say lifting free weights better mimics the strength requirements of real life.

"If there's a trend in weight lifting, it's toward a resurgence of people who want to lift so they can feel stronger for everyday tasks, and fewer who just have to have those great cuts," Bryant says.

However, muscle isolation makes machines a good choice when the goal is to rehabilitate a muscle post-injury or to strengthen a deficient muscle, he adds.

Machines can also help prevent re-injury. Wateska recommends, for example, that a player with a history of back injury do leg presses on a machine rather than squats with free weights. Machines are easier on the joints, Wateska says, which is why during the season he has his players do 75% of their strength training on machines and 25% on weights. Off season, he flips that ratio.

Working both into an exercise regimen can yield real gains. "Free weights are great because they bring in the assisted muscle groups, but certain exercises—like a leg extension or curl or a lat pull-down—you can only do on machines; you can't replicate them with free weights," Wateska says.

"A good trainer is like a master craftsman who uses a variety of tools," adds Bryant. "Free weights and machines are just different tools. A good trainer will look at what the goals are and use the appropriate tools for the job."

GO ON TO THE NEXT PAGE

Bridging the two weight-lifting worlds is a new generation of weight machines, which some call free-motion machines. These hybrids, already in many gyms, incorporate cable pulleys so lifters get a greater variety of freedom. The machines offer the freedom of free weights along with the safety, ease, and consistency of machines.

Whether they'll truly deliver the best of both worlds, only time and debate will tell.

16. **What information supports the idea that machines are more efficient?**

   A. There is no time-consuming changing of weights and the person doesn't need a spotter.
   B. Trainers like them better.
   C. Machines integrate the entire body's musculature.
   D. Machines can help prevent reinjuring a damaged muscle or joint.

17. **The article provides information about all of the following EXCEPT—**

   A. what a sticking point is.
   B. the versatility of free weights.
   C. whether free weights or machines are better for those seeking greater muscle definition.
   D. the use of performance enhancing drugs to build strength.

18. **According to the article, which of the following people would probably realize the greatest strength gains?**

   A. a person who worked out exclusively on machines three times a week
   B. a person who worked out exclusively with free weights three times a week
   C. a person who incorporated both free weights and machines into her workout
   D. a person who did stretching and cardiovascular work only

19. **This article provides the MOST information on—**

   A. the protein requirements for muscle building.
   B. how the cam in machines works to overcome the body's natural sticking points.
   C. why definition is important to today's weight trainee.
   D. why a combination of both free weights and machines used together is best for muscular development.

20. Which of the following statements from the article BEST summarizes the author's main point?

A. Free weights, on the other hand, are more versatile.

B. "Anyone who tells you that working out only with free weights or only with machines is better is lying . . . Today, most progressive coaches see a place for both."

C. Exercises performed using weight machines tend to work isolated muscles and muscle groups.

D. Free weights require more skill, particularly more coordination and balance.

21. What does the word *rehabilitate* mean in the following sentence?

> However, muscle isolation makes machines a good choice when the goal is to rehabilitate a muscle post-injury or to strengthen a deficient muscle.

A. to change a muscle

B. to restore something to a former condition

C. to re-create something that once existed in the distant past

D. to lessen the pain of a person injured while performing an athletic event

GO ON TO THE NEXT PAGE

Essay

Write your essay on the pages provided in your answer document. You may only use a No. 2 pencil. Do not use pen. You may use the blank space in your test booklet to make notes before you begin writing. Any notes you make in the test booklet will NOT be considered when your essay is scored.

Reminder

- Be sure to write your response to the writing prompt given below.
- You may place a title on your essay if you would like, but it is not necessary.
- No dictionary may be used. If you have trouble spelling a word, sound the word out and do the best you can.
- You may write in cursive or print.
- Write clearly! Any changes, erasures, or strikethroughs should be made as neatly as possible.

Writing Task

> By the time students finish high school, they have seen, met, or read about many people with extraordinary skills or qualities they admire. Sometimes these people become their role models or heroes.
>
> Write an essay in which you discuss someone who has become your role model or hero. Describe the skills or qualities that you admire most. Explain why this person is your role model or hero. Use specific details or examples.

Checklist for Your Writing

The following checklist will help you. Always make sure that you:

- ☐ Read the task or tasks carefully.
- ☐ Organize your writing by including a strong introduction, body, and conclusion.
- ☐ Always support your ideas with specific details and examples.
- ☐ Write to your audience by using appropriate words.
- ☐ Use words that are appropriate for your purpose.
- ☐ Make your writing interesting to read by varying your sentences.
- ☐ Check carefully for mistakes in grammar, usage, spelling, punctuation, capitalization, and sentence structure.

END SESSION 1

Session 2

Read the following excerpt and answer questions 22 through 26.

The Mail-Order Catalogue

by Harry Crews

"The Mail-Order Catalogue" is an excerpt from Crews's autobiography *A Childhood: The Biography of a Place*. Crews grew up during the Depression in a very poor town. Here he discusses his simple life there.

In the minds of most people, the Sears, Roebuck catalogue is a kind of low joke associated with outhouses. God knows the catalogue sometimes ended up in the outhouse, but more often it did not.

The Sears, Roebuck catalogue was much better used as a Wish Book, which it was called by the people out in the country, who would never be able to order anything out of it, but could at their leisure spend hours dreaming over.

Willalee Bookatee and I used it for another reason. We made up stories out of it, used it to spin a web of fantasy about us. Without that catalogue our childhood would have been radically different. The federal government ought to strike a medal for the Sears, Roebuck company for sending all those catalogues to farming families, for bringing all that color and all that mystery and all that beauty into the lives of country people.

I first became fascinated with the Sears catalogue because all the people in its pages were perfect. Nearly everybody I knew had something missing, a finger cut off, a toe split, an ear half-chewed away, an eye clouded with blindness from a glancing fence staple. And if they didn't have something missing, they were carrying scars from barbed wire or knives or fishhooks. But the people in the catalogue had no such hurts. They were not only whole, had all their arms and legs and toes and eyes on their unscarred bodies, but they were also beautiful. Their legs were straight and their heads were never bald and on their faces were looks of happiness, even joy, looks that I never saw much of in the faces of the people around me.

Young as I was, though, I had known for a long time that it was all a lie. I knew that under those fancy clothes there had to be scars, there had to be swellings and boils of one kind or another because there was no other way to live in the world. And more than that, at some previous,

GO ON TO THE NEXT PAGE

unremembered moment, I had decided that all the people in the catalogue were related, not necessarily blood kin, but knew one another, and because they knew one another there had to be hard feelings, trouble between them off and on, violence, and hate between them as well as love. And it was out of this knowledge that I first began to make up stories about the people I found in the book.

22. What does the Sears, Roebuck catalogue symbolize to the farmers in the story?

   A.   necessities

   B.   all that they can have

   C.   mystery and beauty

   D.   a low joke

23. Read this sentence from story.

> We made up stories out of it, used it to spin a web of fantasy about us.

Used it to spin a web of fantasy about us is an example of—

   A.   figurative language.

   B.   alliteration.

   C.   allusion.

   D.   simile.

24. According to the narrator, what is the difference between the people in the catalogue and the people he knows?

   A.   The people in the catalogue lie and the people he knows do not.

   B.   The people in the catalogue don't know each other and the people he knows do.

   C.   The people in the catalogue lead fascinating lives and the people he knows do not.

   D.   The people in the catalogue are perfect and the people he knows are not.

25. Based on the context in which it is used in the story, what does *radically* mean?

> Without that catalogue our childhood would have been radically different.

   A.   positively

   B.   traditionally

   C.   superficially

   D.   extremely

26. Based on the context in which it is used in the story, what does *glancing* mean?

> Nearly everybody I knew had something missing, a finger cut off, a toe split, an ear half-chewed away, an eye clouded with blindness from a glancing fence staple.

    A. to look at quickly
    B. to hit at an angle
    C. to miss entirely
    D. to shine brightly

GO ON TO THE NEXT PAGE

Read the following excerpt and answer questions 27 through 32.

Excerpt from "Four Skinny Trees"

by Sandra Cisneros

Sandra Cisneros is a Mexican-American author who writes about her childhood memories. "Four Skinny Trees" is an essay about her feelings on growing up.

They are the only ones who understand me. I am the only one who understands them. Four skinny trees with skinny necks and pointy elbows like mine. Four who do not belong here but are here. Four raggedy excuses planted by the city. From our room we can hear them, but Nenny just sleeps and doesn't appreciate these things.

Their strength is secret. They send ferocious roots beneath the ground. They grow up and they grow down and grab the earth between their hairy toes and bite the sky with violent teeth and never quit their anger. This is how they keep.

Let one forget his reason for being, they'd all droop like tulips in a glass, each with their arms around the other. Keep, keep, keep, trees say when I sleep. They teach.

When I am too sad and too skinny to keep keeping, when I am a tiny thing against so many bricks, then it is I look at trees. When there is nothing left to look at on this street. Four who grew despite concrete. Four who reach and do not forget to reach. Four whose only reason is to be and be.

27. Which statement BEST describes the lesson that the narrator learns from the trees?

   A. rely on others
   B. reach out to others
   C. stand tall
   D. never give up

28. "Four skinny trees with skinny necks and pointy elbows like mine" is an example of—

   A. alliteration.
   B. allegory.
   C. personification.
   D. alliteration.

29. Why does the narrator identify with the trees?

   A. The trees are a part of nature and she loves nature.
   B. The trees are the only pretty things on the street, and she is the only pretty girl in the neighborhood.
   C. The trees grow despite hardships, and she grows despite hardships.
   D. The trees are unappreciated and she is unappreciated.

30. The narrator compares herself to the trees. Based on the connotation of such words as *skinny* and *pointy* that she uses to describe the trees, how does the narrator feel about herself?

   A. She feels she is attractive.
   B. She feels she is disfigured.
   C. She feels she is smart and aggressive.
   D. She feels she is awkward and unattractive.

31. "Four Skinny Trees" can best be described as—

   A. a monologue.
   B. a tragedy.
   C. a comedy.
   D. a drama.

32. Based on the connotation with which it is used in the story, what does *ferocious* mean?

   > They send ferocious roots beneath the ground.

   A. angry
   B. fierce
   C. dilapidated
   D. calm

GO ON TO THE NEXT PAGE

Read the following article and answer questions 33 through 39.

Greening the World's Most Popular Fruit

by Christine Mlot

(1) THE BANANA has a huge fan base. Babies and the elderly love its easy-to-eat-and-digest sweetness, athletes gulp it for potassium-rich quick energy, and comedians have worked its shape and packaging into endless gags. The banana is popular worldwide, with more that 25 pounds consumed annually per capita in the United States, most eaten straight out of the wrapper. In East Africa, where bananas and their plantain cousins are dietary staples, consumption is seven times that amount.

(2) What the banana lacks, though, is a huge genetic base. The familiar yellow fruit—botanically, a berry—is largely derived from a single variety known as Cavendish grown on plants that are essentially cuttings, or clones, of the same stock. The birds and the bees have nothing to do with cultivated bananas, and this lack of sexual reproduction, with its mixing genes, leaves the crop vulnerable to diseases and pests such as fungi, viruses, bacteria, insects, and roundworms, some of which have become epidemic in recent years.

(3) This means that conventional banana production depends heavily on pesticides—and lots of them. Fungicides, for example, may be applied 40 times a year, even though the chemicals lose their effectiveness with overuse. Worse, these highly toxic compounds often drift or run off of farm fields, posing a threat to fish, birds, and other species—including humans. Even more poisonous to people and the environment are the nematicides typically used to control roundworm pests. And conventional banana production generates a host of other problems as well—from rivers polluted with eroded sediment and plastic waste to tropical forests razed to carve out new plantations.

(4) These environmental problems, along with historically poor conditions for banana workers, have prompted several organizations to create certification and seals of approval for producers that meet certain environmental and social standards. In addition, a small but growing number of exporters are harvesting organically grown bananas, eschewing agrochemicals altogether. The result: Consumers today have a much greater opportunity to purchase bananas that are friendly to the environment than even a decade ago.

(5) The Better Banana Project, sponsored by the New York-based Rainforest Alliance, is one of the oldest certification efforts. Launched in 1991, it required producers to maintain health and safety standards for workers and to demonstrate reduced pesticide use and other sound

environmental practices such as soil conservation and proper waste disposal. Today 15 percent of all bananas traded are certified by the project.

(6) One major global producer, Chiquita Brands International, has converted all of its Latin American farms to meet the project's standards. According to David McLaughlin, the company's senior environmental director, about two-thirds of the Chiquita bananas sold in North America come from these certified farms.

(7) The Better Banana Project has "improved conditions on all Chiquita plantations greatly," says Robert Mack, an organic agriculture consultant to small-scale farmers in Costa Rica. The use of toxic nematicides, for example, has been halved on certified farms, and tons of blue plastic bags and twine, which once littered virtually all banana farms, have been recycled through the program. In addition, pay and other benefits for workers have improved greatly. Thanks to efforts of project participants, "the banana industry is making a long slow 180-degree turn," says the Rainforest Alliance's Chris Wille, one of the project's founders. "Now there's even competition among workers to get jobs on certified farms and competition between farms to see who can have the cleanest and greenest one."

(8) Besides Chiquita, the Favorita Fruit Company, an Ecuadorian producer that supplies some European markets, has also achieved 100 percent certification of its farms.

Eco-certified bananas are even grown in the United States: The Mauna Kea Banana Company in Hawaii markets these creamy, mildly tart apple bananas by mail order.

(9) For pesticide-free fruit, one can choose organic bananas. Though less than one percent of the bananas sold in the United States now are organic, that fraction is growing by more than 20 percent per year nationally and by 30 percent globally, according to the United Nations Food and Agriculture Organization.

(10) Certified organic bananas are taking root throughout Latin America, often in drier habitats where harmful fungi don't occur. The Dominican Republic is the region's biggest exporter of organic bananas, followed by Mexico and Colombia. Small- and medium- scale growers are even managing to grow organic bananas in Costa Rica, where the fungal disease black sigatoka is a constant problem for large producers. By planting bananas in the shade in combination with other marketable crops such as cacao, these producers can get a modest but pesticide-free crop that commands a premium price. U.S. consumers looking for organic bananas can often find them in natural food stores and even main grocery chains for just slightly more than conventionally grown bananas.

(11) The fruit that sustains hundreds of millions of people is itself slowly becoming a more sustainable crop.

GO ON TO THE NEXT PAGE

33. What is the main purpose of this article?

    A. to discuss the genetic origins of bananas

    B. to discuss some recent successes the banana industry has had in dealing with environmental and social problems

    C. to explore the reasons why bananas should be part of every healthy diet

    D. to introduce the work of The Better Banana Project to the reader

34. The article mentions the fact that bananas are largely derived from a single variety through cloning with the result that—

    A. a banana vulnerable to many diseases.

    B. great uniformity in color and taste.

    C. an industry dependent on a single source in Costa Rica for its entire product.

    D. poor working conditions for banana workers.

> The banana is popular worldwide, with more than 25 pounds consumed annually per capita in the United States, most eaten straight out of the wrapper.

35. The word *wrapper* in the sentence MOST likely means—

    A. a gaily-decorated holiday gift paper.

    B. a sleeve used to enhance the appeal of the fruit.

    C. a specially-designed covering that retards spoilage.

    D. the skin.

36. Based on the article, which of the following statements is true?

    A. Organic bananas, once popular, are now gradually disappearing from grocers' shelves.

    B. Black sigatoka is a fungal disease that attacks bananas in Costa Rica.

    C. Botanically, the banana is a type of grain.

    D. Chemicals used as fungicides do not lose their effectiveness over time.

37. Read this sentence from the article.

> "And conventional banana production generates a host of other problems as well—from rivers polluted with eroded sediment and plastic waste to tropical forests razed to carve out new plantations."

What does the word *razed* mean in the article?

    A. shaved

    B. burned

    C. taken down

    D. polluted

38. Which of the following statements BEST summarizes the information contained in the article?

    A. Certification programs add high costs to banana production.

    B. Banana production is hampered by environmental concerns.

    C. Certification programs help workers and benefit the environment with less pollution and pesticide use.

    D. Because of its lack of genetic diversity, the banana faces almost insurmountable problems in the future.

39. Which of the following most accurately describes the author's attitude toward the subject?

    A. The author is positive about the effect that certification programs are having on the environmental and social problems of the banana industry.

    B. The author is most interested in the effects that a narrow genetic base is having on the future of the banana crop.

    C. The author is primarily concerned with maintaining the lowest possible price for the consumer.

    D. The author is fearful that continued applications of nematicides will severely damage the roundworm population.

Read the following article and answer questions 40 through 46.

Beauty with Brains

by Doug Stewart

Butterflies have long enchanted us with their good looks; now scientists are discovering that the insects' abilities are even greater than we think.

Watching the butterfly zigzag aimlessly across a meadow on a sunny morning, you could easily take it for nature's most carefree vagabond—unhurried, unburdened, even a little dizzy. You'd be mistaken. Butterflies are purposeful, aggressive, sexually driven and smarter than you think. Most of us, however, enchanted as we are by the butterfly's flamboyant good looks and rollicking flight path, are unaware of these traits. That's understandable, says Georgetown University biologist Martha Weiss, an expert on butterfly behavior.

"Unlike honeybees, which have a reputation as the intellectuals of the insect world," Weiss says, "butterflies spend their time basking in the sun and sipping nectar from beautiful flowers. It's easy to think they're a bit indolent."

Much of a butterfly's behavior is hardwired, of course, not learned by trial and error. Consider the caterpillar. "The lifestyle of all insect larvae is risky," says long-time butterfly researcher Thomas Eisner, a professor of chemical ecology at Cornell University. "They can't fly. They're slow. So they have a lot of interesting strategies to defend themselves."

When attacked, some caterpillars pop foul-smelling tentacles, or osmeteria, from their thoraxes and brandish them menacingly. Young swallowtail caterpillars disguise themselves as bird droppings (not very scary, perhaps, but distinctly inedible). In a later molt, the same caterpillars can resemble snakes—eyes, patterning and all. "Some caterpillars feed on toxic plants, then they vomit," Eisner says. "It's a way to use the plant's toxins for their own defense." Other caterpillars, notably the monarch, incorporate the toxins they consume in their own tissues, rendering them poisonous to predators even as adults; a bird takes a bite and immediately drops the caterpillar, which often survives the encounter.

Butterflies help pollinate many flowering plants, even if more ostentatiously hardworking bees and wasps get the credit for this. The yellow-fringed orchid (*Platanthera ciliaris*) found throughout the eastern United States is pollinated only by a swallowtail butterfly. "The flowers have a very long nectar spur that only a long-tongued butterfly can

GO ON TO THE NEXT PAGE

get all the nectar out of," says Don Harvey, a lepidopterist at the Smithsonian's National Museum of Natural History. Rather than dusting the visitor with pollen grains, the orchid sticks a whole packet of pollen on to the swallow-tail's body. The insect then transfers it—precisely if unintentionally—to just the right spot on the next orchid.

Learning Curve

Uniquely, butterflies of the tropical genus *Heliconius* (which in the United States includes the zebra longwing and the gulf fritillary) have evolved a taste for pollen as a food, which supplements their nectar intake. As a result, the insects spend less time as a carbo-loading caterpillar bulking up for the future and more time as pollen-feeding adults, according to Lawrence Gilbert, a population biologist at the University of Texas—Austin. Over time, he says, natural selection has favored *Heliconius* butterflies with longer life spans and more brainpower. He found that foraging *Heliconius* butterflies learn to follow precise routes from flower to flower, visiting the same plant at the same time, day after day. As old flowers close and new flowers open, the insects learn new routes. Younger butterflies have even been observed following older butterflies as though they were apprentices.

Legally Blind

Further evidence of the insects' learning ability: *Heliconius* butterflies that used to escape from Gilbert's greenhouses in Austin would behave strangely. "They would fly out the door into the open," he says, "and they'd fly only as high as the roof and back down again. They seemed to learn the dimensions of the greenhouse as part of their home range. They never bashed their wings on the walls like most butterflies." They also seemed to memorize the location of spider webs; butterflies new to a greenhouse were most likely to be snared. In the wild, *Heliconius* butterflies will even avoid spots where in the past they've been netted.

Gilbert has evidence that these butterflies use visual landmarks, not scent or other signals, to plot their routes. Whatever landmarks they use, they are probably big ones. The compound eyes of butterflies are large and impressive, but the insects are nearsighted all the same. "By human standards, butterflies have 20-1,000 vision, which means they're legally blind," says Ron Rutowski, a behavioral ecologist at Arizona State University. The butterflies that size up one another notice brightness and movement but probably not much visual detail. This would explain why males occasionally court a dead leaf fluttering in the wind.

When one's adulthood is measured in weeks, finding a mate is obviously a matter of some urgency. Males take the initiative. In some *Heliconius* species, they save time by perching on a female's chrysalis and copulating with her as she emerges. During mating, males pass a spermatophore, a large case containing sperm and nutrients, to the female as a sort of paternal gift. Some females may rely on the nutrients for the draining chore of egg-production. To produce this costly gift, males of some species have to round up salts and nitrogen compounds not found in nectar. This explains the bizarre phenomenon known as puddling, in which male butterflies congregate by the thousands to insert their proboscises into patches of muddy ground. Mineral-starved males will also partake of carrion, dung and urine.

Frantic or sedate, the very act of fluttering is one of a butterfly's most characteristic traits. Its wing beat is relatively slow for an insect. A monarch will flap its wings 5 to 12 beats a second, for example, while some flies beat their wings 1,000 times a second. A skipper can travel in bursts at nearly 50 miles an hour, approaching dragonfly speed, but most butterflies' progress is slower and more erratic. Not that butterflies are clumsy: they're masters of the pinpoint landing, alighting on flower petals with their tongues uncoiled and ready to drink.

Aerodynamically, butterflies have much larger wings than necessary for staying aloft. Their oversized wings, in fact, are responsible for their herky-jerky trajectory. Eisner believes the butterfly evolved its clumsy-looking flight style as a defense. "Their erratic flight tells birds, 'I'm not worth pursuing. I'm too hard to catch, and I'm

not much of a meal,'" he says. "Butterflies are colorful and visible at a great distance, but they're all wrapper, no candy." He believes birds end up discriminating against them as a group compared to other prey.

On the Fly

Migration in butterflies is triggered by environmental conditions, not a genetic compulsion, so members of a single species can behave in widely different ways. Monarchs in the United States that emerge in mid-summer don't migrate at all. They're too short-lived to worry about winter. Those emerging in late summer and early fall are the ones that head south.

Taylor has flown from Kansas to Washington, D.C., with monarchs in his carry-on luggage to see which way the insects would try to migrate when they got there. "For about 48 hours, they still think they're in Kansas. Then they get acclimated and pick up the new orientation that the local butterflies have." He suspects they sense a mix of local environmental cues, including the Earth's magnetic field, to chart their course.

"If you think about it, this is what migrating butterflies have to do whenever they're blown off course. They have to reorient themselves." The details of how they do it remain a mystery, but somehow those little butterfly brains have it all worked out.

GO ON TO THE NEXT PAGE

40. According to the article, butterflies do all of the following things to protect themselves EXCEPT—

   A. disguise themselves as bird droppings.

   B. incorporate plant toxins into their own tissues.

   C. learn details about their home range.

   D. watch the surrounding areas carefully, using their excellent vision.

41. What does the word *indolent* mean in the following sentence?

> "Unlike honeybees, which have a reputation as the intellectuals of the insect world, . . . butterflies spend their time basking in the sun and sipping nectar from beautiful flowers. It's easy to think they're a bit indolent."

   A. ineffective

   B. lazy

   C. flowery

   D. beautiful

42. Which of the following statements BEST summarizes the information contained in the article?

   A. Butterflies' seemingly carefree manner disguises an insect that is purposeful, aggressive, and intelligent.

   B. Butterflies use many different behaviors to protect themselves.

   C. Butterflies probably use the Earth's magnetic field to orient themselves.

   D. Butterflies are more aggressive than any other insect.

43. According to the article, migration in the butterflies is—

   A. genetically hardwired into every butterfly.

   B. determined by their desire to reproduce.

   C. triggered by environmental conditions.

   D. done because of changes in the numbers of predators present in a given area.

44. Based on the article, which of the following statements about butterflies is MOST accurate?

   A. Butterflies rarely pollinate plants.

   B. Butterflies are able to see things in remarkably vivid detail.

   C. Most butterflies' wing beats are slow compared to other insects.

   D. Butterflies have small wings compared to other flying insects.

45. The word *apprentices* in the sentence below MOST likely means—

> As old flowers close and new flowers open, the insects learn new routes. Younger butterflies have even been observed following older butterflies as though they were apprentices.

   A. fellow travelers.

   B. those working with others in order to learn a trade.

   C. fearful individuals.

   D. individuals who have lost their way.

46. The document provides the LEAST information on—

   A. how butterflies migrate.

   B. the vision of butterflies.

   C. the mating habits of butterflies.

   D. why butterflies have such short adult lives.

Gary Soto is a Mexican American who grew up in Fresno. "The Talk" is about his and his best friend's hopes for the future. Read the following story and answer questions 47 through 52.

The Talk

by Gary Soto

My best friend and I knew that we were going to grow up to be ugly. On a backyard lawn—the summer light failing west of the mulberry tree where the house of the most beautiful girl on the street stood—we talked about what we could do: shake the second-base dirt from our hair, wash our hands of frog smells and canal water, and learn to smile without showing our crooked teeth. We had to stop spitting when girls were looking and learn not to pile food onto a fork and into a fat cheek already churning hot grub.

We were twelve, with lean bodies that were beginning to grow in weird ways. First, our heads got large, but our necks wavered, frail as crisp tulips. The eyes stayed small as well, receding into pencil dots on each side of an unshapely nose that cast remarkable shadows when we turned sideways. It seemed that Scott's legs sprouted muscle and renegade veins, but his arms, blue with ink markings, stayed short and hung just below his waist. My gangly arms nearly touched my kneecaps. In this way, I was built for picking up grounders[1] and doing cartwheels, my arms swaying just inches from the summery grass.

We sat on the lawn, with the porch light off, waiting for the beautiful girl to turn on her bedroom light and read on her stomach with one leg stirring the air. This stirred us, and our dream was a clean dream of holding hands and airing out our loneliness by walking up and down the block.

When Scott asked whom I was going to marry, I said a brown girl from the valley. He said that he was going to marry a strawberry blonde who would enjoy Millerton Lake, dirty as it was. I said mine would like cats and the sea and would think nothing of getting up at night from a warm, restless bed and sitting in the yard under the icy stars. Scott said his wife would work for the first year or so, because he would go to trade school[2] in refrigeration. Since our town was made with what was left over after God made hell, there was money in air conditioning, he reasoned.

I said that while my wife would clean the house and stir pots of nice grub, I would drive a truck to my job as a carpenter, which would allow me to use my long arms. I

2 **trade school** School in which students specialize in learning one set of skills for a particular profession.

1 **picking up grounders** Catching balls as they bounce along the ground.

GO ON TO THE NEXT PAGE

would need only a stepladder to hand a fellow worker on the roof a pinch of nails. I could hammer, saw, lift beams into place, and see the work I got done at the end of the day. Of course, she might like to work, and that would be okay, because then we could buy two cars and wave at each other if we should see the other drive by. In the evenings, we would drink Kool-Aid and throw a slipper at our feisty dog at least a hundred times before we went inside for a Pop-Tart and hot chocolate.

Scott said he would work hard too, but now and then he would find money on the street and the two of them could buy extra things like a second TV for the bedroom and a Doughboy swimming pool for his three kids. He planned on having three kids and a ranch house on the river, where he could dip a hand in the water, drink and say, "ahh, tastes good."

But that would be years later. Now we had to do something about our looks. We plucked at the grass and flung it into each other's faces.

"Rotten luck," Scott said. "My arms are too short. Look at 'em."

"Maybe we can lift weights. This would make up for our looks," I said.

"I don't think so," Scott said, depressed. People like people with nice faces."

He was probably right. I turned onto my stomach, a stalk of grass in my mouth. "Even if I'm ugly, my wife's going to be good-looking," I said. "She'll have a lot of dresses and I'll have more shirts than I have now. Do you know how much carpenters make?"

Then I saw the bedroom light come on and the beautiful girl walk into the room drying her hair with a towel. I nudged Scott's short arm and he saw what I saw. We flicked the stalks of grass, stood up, and walked over to the fence to look at her scrub her hair dry. She plopped onto the bed and began to comb it, slowly at first because it was tangled. With a rubber band, she tied it back, and picked up a book that was thick as a good-sized sandwich.

Scott and I watched her read a book, now both legs in the air and twined together, her painted toenails like red petals. She turned the pages slowly, very carefully, and now and then lowered her face into the pillow. She looked sad but beautiful, and we didn't know what to do except nudge each other in the heart and creep away to the front yard.

"I can't stand it anymore. We have to talk about this," Scott said.

"If I try, I think I can make myself better looking," I said. "I read an article about a girl whitening her teeth with water and flour."

So we walked up the street, depressed. For every step I took, Scott took two, his short arms pumping to keep up. For every time Scott said, "I think we're ugly," I said two times, "Yeah, yeah, we're in big trouble."

47. As a child, the narrator valued what trait in girls?

A. strength

B. intelligence

C. humor

D. beauty

48. By referring to the town as what "was made with what was left over after God made hell," Soto implies that his town was—

A. evil.

B. pleasant.

C. hot.

D. religious.

49. Which of these lines from the selection is an example of a simile?

A. "frail as crisp tulips"

B. "my arms swaying"

C. "she might like to work"

D. "nudge each other in the heart"

> . . . on her stomach with one leg stirring the air.
> This stirred us, . . .

50. In these lines from the selection, the meanings of the words *stirring* and *stirred*—

A. differ because the first means "mixing" and the second means "affected emotionally."

B. are similar because they both refer to an action performed by the girl.

C. are meant to suggest the ugliness of the boys.

D. are slang rather than standard English.

51. This selection is BEST described as—

A. monologue.

B. historical fiction.

C. autobiography.

D. a chapter of a larger work.

GO ON TO THE NEXT PAGE

52. Which sentence best describes the theme of this selection?

   A. Children who think themselves ugly should change the way they look.

   B. Boys' dreams for their future may not be realistic.

   C. Planning for a job is more important than planning for a marriage.

   D. Our childhood friends may not be our friends when we are adults.

The following is a draft of a report about wolves. It may contain errors in grammar, sentence structure, vocabulary, and organization. Some of the questions may refer to underlined or numbered sentences or phrases within the text. Read the essay and answer questions 53 through 57.

Wolves

(1) One of the most interesting things about wolves is that they are social animals. (2) They do almost everything together because they are programmed by their genes to cooperate with each other. (3) From the beginning of their lives mutual affection and loyalty are demonstrated by wolves. (4) These are the same traits we look for in dogs. (5) Wolves are, after all, the original dogs. (6) Wolves usually have bushier fur and bigger feet.

(7) Because of their social nature, wolves live and travel in packs. (8) These packs vary in size. (9) What determines the size of the pack is factors such as how many wolves are needed to bring down large prey, how many can feed at a single kill, and what social stresses develop when packs reach a certain size. (10) The maximum recorded number of wolves in a pack is 36. (11) Usually the wolves in a pack are related by blood because the strongest bonds are between parents and their pups and among brothers and sisters. (12) Most packs consist of a breeding pair (the "alpha" male and female), a middle layer of subdominant wolves, the pups of the season, and sometimes a few low-ranking wolves at the bottom. (13) The term "lone wolf" refers to young animals who compete too hard for breeding and feeding rights, wolves who are socially rejected by the pack, wolves who are orphaned by some catastrophe, or old wolves who have lost their mates. (14) The fact is, wolves are almost never alone by choice. (15) They want to be part of a pack.

GO ON TO THE NEXT PAGE

53. Which is the MOST effective substitution for sentence 3?

   A. From the beginning of their lives wolves demonstrate mutual affection and loyalty.

   B. Mutual affection and loyalty are demonstrated by wolves from the beginning of their lives.

   C. Mutual affection and loyalty, from the beginning of their lives, are demonstrated by wolves.

   D. It is clear that from the beginning of their lives mutual affection and loyalty are demonstrated by the wolves.

54. Which of the following sentences does NOT fit well in the paragraph where it is found?

   A. Sentence 2

   B. Sentence 6

   C. Sentence 9

   D. Sentence 14

55. What is the BEST version of sentence 9?

   A. What determines the size of the pack is a lot of things, including factors such as how many wolves are needed to bring down large prey, how many can feed at a single kill, and do social stresses develop when packs reach a certain size.

   B. The size of the pack is determined by factors such as how many wolves are needed to bring down large prey, how many can feed at a single kill, and what social stresses develop when packs reach a certain size.

   C. Factors such as how many wolves are needed to bring down large prey, how many can feed at a single kill, and what social stresses developed when packs reach a certain size are the things that determine the size of the pack.

   D. Determining the size of the pack are factors such as how many wolves are needed to bring down large prey, how many can feed at a single kill, and that social stresses may develop when packs reach a certain size.

56. Which of the following points is supported by details in the report?

   A. Dogs and wolves have much in common.

   B. Wolves are dangerous when attacked.

   C. "Lone wolves" don't survive as long as wolves in packs.

   D. The size of a wolf pack varies, depending on circumstances.

57. Which of the following words is the BEST way to express the meaning of the words *brothers and sisters* in sentence 11?

   A. kin

   B. siblings

   C. relatives

   D. blood relations

The following is a draft of the first paragraph of an essay about roller coasters. It may contain errors in grammar, punctuation, sentence structure, vocabulary, and organization. Some of the questions may refer to underlined or numbered sentences or phrases within the text. Read the paragraph and answer questions 58 through 61.

Roller Coasters

(1) Roller coasters go back to something called a "Russian Mountain," which Russian <u>high-class</u> people used for recreation in the 1400's. (2) The "mountain" was built on a wooden frame, and <u>sleds would be carried by people to the top and then they would be ridden to the bottom</u>, powered by gravity. (3) These aren't like our coasters today. (4) In many languages "Russian Mountain" is still a common term for a roller coaster.

58. Which of the following sentences, if inserted before sentence 1, would make the MOST effective opening sentence?

- **A.** Riding roller coasters is a lot of fun, and the scarier the better.
- **B.** Many different kinds of roller coasters have been created over the centuries, and most people agree that they appeal to young and old alike.
- **C.** Although roller coasters may seem as American as apple pie, they originated in Russia before America was discovered.
- **D.** In this essay the early history of the roller coaster and its development into one of the main attractions at amusement parks will be examined.

59. Which of the following is the BEST way to express the meaning of the underlined word *high-class* in sentence 1?

- **A.** rich people
- **B.** nouveau-riche
- **C.** upper-class
- **D.** wealthy

60. Which of the following is the MOST effective substitution for the underlined part of sentence 2?

- **A.** people would carry sleds to the top and then ride to the bottom.
- **B.** sleds would be carried to the top and then would be ridden to the bottom by people.
- **C.** people, who would have carried their sleds to the top, would then ride the sleds to the bottom.
- **D.** Leave as is.

61. Which of the following is the BEST way to combine sentences 3 and 4?

- **A.** These aren't like our coasters today, however in many languages "Russian Mountain" is still a common term for a roller coaster.
- **B.** These aren't like our coasters today, and in many languages "Russian Mountain" is still a common term for a roller coaster.
- **C.** These aren't like our coasters today, and therefore in many languages "Russian Mountain" still means roller coaster.
- **D.** These aren't like our coasters today, although in many languages "Russian Mountain" is still a common term for a roller coaster.

GO ON TO THE NEXT PAGE

The following is a draft of a paragraph about the world's food supply. It may contain errors in grammar, sentence structure, vocabulary, and organization. Some of the questions may refer to underlined or numbered sentences or phrases within the text. Read the paragraph and answer questions 62 through 64.

The World's Food Supply

(1) The newspapers carry stories about serious famines in certain parts of the world. (2) Does this mean that there is just not enough food on earth to feed the world's growing population? (3) Right now there probably is, but distribution of it is ineffective and often made worse by political problems and by natural disasters such as droughts and flooding. (4) Before long, however, if the world population continues to grow at its present rate, we may have to change our eating habits and eat less meat and more grain. (5) Earth can only produce so much grain, and currently much of it is eaten by cattle instead of humans. (6) If humans ate the grain instead of eating the cattle, the calories would be twenty times more efficient than the calories from eating the beef. (7) Many relief agencies send food to countries during times of famine, but local corruption can keep the food from getting to the people who most need it.

62. Which is the BEST placement of sentence 7 in the paragraph?

   A. before sentence 1
   B. following sentence 1
   C. following sentence 3
   D. following sentence 5

63. Which of the following ideas is supported in the paragraph?

   A. Most famines occur in Africa.
   B. Grain is a more efficient food source than meat.
   C. Natural disasters cause most famines in the world.
   D. If governments would cooperate, famines could be eliminated.

64. To get more information about food production, the writer of the paragraph might consult all of the following sources EXCEPT—

   A. government reports.
   B. newspaper articles.
   C. a thesaurus.
   D. an encyclopedia of world geography.

For questions 65 through 74, choose the answer that is the most effective substitute for each underlined part of the sentence. If no substitution is necessary, choose "Leave as is."

65. A sleek, black limousine pulled into the restaurant parking lot <u>at nine o'clock. Stopping just</u> long enough for the famous couple to emerge and run past the photographers.

   A. at nine o'clock. Stopped just
   B. at nine o'clock, it stopped just
   C. at nine o'clock, stopping just
   D. Leave as is.

66. The teacher asked everyone to bring the <u>following to class, a pen, a pencil, a three-ring binder,</u> and a pair of scissors.

   A. following to class: a pen, a pencil, a three-ring binder,
   B. following to class. A pen, a pencil, a three ring-binder,
   C. following to class a pen, a pencil, a three-ring binder,
   D. Leave as is.

67. The explorers made the <u>fateful decision to continue</u> up the river until they could go no farther.

   A. fateful decision; to continue
   B. fateful decision. To continue
   C. fateful decision. Continuing
   D. Leave as is.

68. <u>Nicholas wrote letters to everyone who had been on the ship when the incident occurred. Because he thought they would have observations he could use in his research paper.</u>

   A. Nicholas wrote letters to everyone who had been on the ship when the incident occurred because he thought they would have observations he could use in his research paper.
   B. Because he thought they would have interesting observations he could use in his research paper. Nicholas wrote letters to everyone who had been on the ship when the incident occurred.
   C. Because he thought they would have interesting observations he could use in his research paper; Nicholas wrote letters to everyone who had been on the ship when the incident occurred.
   D. Leave as is.

69. The <u>lecturer said "that he felt we should provide a clean water source and places for shelter if we wanted to encourage wildlife in our habitat."</u>

   A. lecturer said: "That he felt we should provide a clean water source and places for shelter if we wanted to encourage wildlife in our habitat."
   B. lecturer said 'that he felt we should provide a clean water source and places for shelter if we wanted to encourage wildlife in our habitat.'
   C. lecturer said that he felt we should provide a clean water source and places for shelter if we wanted to encourage wildlife in our habitat.
   D. Leave as is.

70. We <u>added the second coat of paint and then leave it</u> to dry overnight.

   A. added the second coat of paint and then will leave it
   B. added the second coat of paint and then left it
   C. add the second coat of paint and then left it
   D. Leave as is.

GO ON TO THE NEXT PAGE

71. <u>While talking on the telephone, the smoke alarm went off in the kitchen.</u>

    A. While I was talking on the telephone, the smoke alarm went off in the kitchen.
    B. The smoke alarm in the kitchen went off while talking on the telephone.
    C. In the kitchen, while talking on the telephone, the smoke alarm went off.
    D. Leave as is.

72. My sister likes <u>to gossip with her friends, shop at the mall, dancing, and to sleep late in the morning.</u>

    A. to gossip with her friends, shopping at the mall, dancing, and sleeping late in the morning.
    B. gossiping with her friends, to shop at the mall, to dance, and to sleep late in the morning.
    C. gossiping with her friends, shopping at the mall, dancing, and sleeping late in the morning.
    D. Leave as is.

73. As of next month Charlie <u>will have been in Japan</u> for five years.

    A. will be in Japan
    B. will be staying in Japan
    C. is in Japan
    D. Leave as is.

74. <u>The woman wore a rose in her dark hair that she had found in our garden.</u>

    A. In her dark hair the woman wore a rose that she had found in our garden.
    B. In her dark hair a rose was worn by the woman that she had found in our garden.
    C. A rose that she wore in her dark hair was found by the woman in our garden.
    D. Leave as is.

For questions 75 through 79 choose the word or phrase that best completes the sentence.

75. Mr. Williams and _____ checked in the equipment after the game was over.

    A. me
    B. myself
    C. me, we
    D. I

76. All of the men _____ planning to go to the meeting next week.

    A. was not
    B. was
    C. were
    D. wasn't

77. If the manager had helped, Jennifer _____ finished her work on time.

    A. would of
    B. could of
    C. can have
    D. could have

78. You _____ to go to Europe next summer.

    A. ought
    B. had ought
    C. oughten
    D. ought'en

79. They sang the songs _____ because of all the practice sessions.

    A. real well
    B. real good
    C. very good
    D. very well

END SESSION 2

Answer Key for Practice Test 3

(WA) Word Analysis   (RC) Reading Comprehension   (LR) Literary Response and Analysis

Session 1

For "George Gray"

1. B (LR)   ❑   **3.** B (WA)   ❑   **5.** B (LR)   ❑

2. C (LR)   ❑   **4.** A (LR)   ❑

For "Internet Acceptable Use Policy"

6. D (RC)   ❑   **8.** A (RC)   ❑   **10.** A (WA)   ❑

7. C (WA)   ❑   **9.** B (RC)   ❑   **11.** A (RC)   ❑

For "Into Thin Air"

12. A (WA)   ❑   **14.** B (LR)   ❑

13. D (LR)   ❑   **15.** A (LR)   ❑

For "The Weights Debate"

16. A (RC)   ❑   **18.** C (RC)   ❑   **20.** B (RC)   ❑

17. D (RC)   ❑   **19.** D (RC)   ❑   **21.** B (WA)   ❑

Session 2

For "The Mail-Order Catalogue"

22. C (LR)   ❑   **24.** D (LR)   ❑   **26.** B (WA)   ❑

23. A (LR)   ❑   **25.** D (WA)   ❑

For "Four Skinny Trees"

27. D (LR)   ❑   **29.** C (LR)   ❑   **31.** A (LR)   ❑

28. C (LR)   ❑   **30.** D (LR)   ❑   **32.** B (WA)   ❑

For "Greening the World's Most Popular Fruit"

33. B (RC) ❑
34. A (RC) ❑
35. D (WA) ❑

36. B (RC) ❑
37. C (WA) ❑

38. C (RC) ❑
39. A (RC) ❑

For "Beauty with Brains"

40. D (RC) ❑
41. B (WA) ❑
42. A (RC) ❑

43. C (RC) ❑
44. C (RC) ❑

45. B (WA) ❑
46. D (RC) ❑

For "The Talk"

47. D (LR) ❑
48. C (LR) ❑

49. A (LR) ❑
50. A (WA) ❑

51. C (LR) ❑
52. B (LR) ❑

For Writing Strategies

53. A ❑
54. B ❑
55. B ❑
56. D ❑

57. B ❑
58. C ❑
59. C ❑
60. A ❑

61. D ❑
62. C ❑
63. B ❑
64. C ❑

For Writing Conventions

65. C ❑
66. A ❑
67. D ❑
68. A ❑
69. C ❑

70. B ❑
71. A ❑
72. C ❑
73. D ❑
74. A ❑

75. D ❑
76. C ❑
77. D ❑
78. A ❑
79. D ❑

Reviewing Practice Test 3

Review your simulated CAHSEE English-Language Arts Practice Test by following these steps:

1. Check the answers you marked on your answer sheet against the Answer Key. Put a check mark in the box following any wrong answer.
2. Fill out the Review Chart below.
3. Read all the explanations (pp. 263–269). Go back to review any explanations that are not clear to you.
4. Fill out the Reasons for Mistakes chart below.
5. Have your essay evaluated using the checklist that is included.
6. Go back to the review sections and review any materials necessary.

Don't leave out any of these steps. They are very important in learning to do your best on the CAHSEE English-Language-Arts.

Review Chart

Use your marked Answer Key to fill in the following Review Chart for the multiple-choice questions.

	Possible	Completed	Right	Wrong
Word Analysis (WA) (7)	13			
ReadingComprehension (RC) (18)	19			
Literary Response and Analysis (LR) (20)	20			
Writing Strategies (WS) (12)	12			
Writing Conventions (WC) (15)	15			
Totals	79			

The numbers in ( ) are the actual number of each type that count towards your score.

Reasons For Mistakes

Fill out the following chart only after you have read all the explanations that follow. This chart will help you spot your strengths and weaknesses and your repeated errors or trends in types of errors.

	Total Missed	Simple Mistake	Misread Problem	Lack of Knowledge
Word Analysis (WA)				
Reading Comprehension (RC)				
Literary Response and Analysis (LR)				
Writing Strategies (WS)				
Writing Conventions (WC)				
Totals				

Examine your results carefully. Reviewing the above information will help you pinpoint your common mistakes. Focus on avoiding your most common mistakes as you practice. The "Lack of Knowledge" column will help you focus your review. If you are missing a lot of questions because of "Lack of Knowledge," you should go back and spend extra time reviewing the basics and the question explanations.

Explanations for Practice Test 3

Session 1

For "George Gray"

1. **B.** The introduction sets up the fact that the speaker is dead. The second line makes reference to "the marble which was chiseled for me." The marble chiseled for a dead person would most likely be a tombstone. (**Literary Response and Analysis**)

2. **C.** The poem discusses all the missed opportunities for the speaker. Lines six through eight are about all he could have done but didn't, and lines nine through sixteen are about the lesson he has learned from those missed opportunities. (**Literary Response and Analysis**)

3. **B.** Even if you don't know what *furled* means, if you read the word in context, *folded* makes sense. The boat is "at rest in a harbor" and he "now [knows] that [he] must lift the sail and catch the winds of destiny," implying that up to this point he had not done so. Therefore, a closed sail must be what is chiseled on the marble because that would make sense in representing "not [his] destination/ But [his] life." (**Word Analysis**)

4. **A.** The entire poem is leading up to the lesson he has learned, but he states that "we must lift the sail" and "put meaning in one's life" because "life without meaning is the torture." So even though he spent his life taking no chances, he now sees that we must if we are going to live life to its fullest. (**Literary Response and Analysis**)

5. **B.** The speaker spends the poem discussing all of his missed opportunities, and although he has since learned that we must take chances, it is too late for him because he is dead. (**Literary Response and Analysis**)

For "Internet Acceptable Use Policy"

6. **D.** There are certainly warnings against vandalism, but we cannot suppose that vandals or potential vandals are the sole audience for this document. Likewise, computer hackers cannot be considered to be the target audience. This is simply a school policy statement designed to delineate the proper use of the Internet while in school. The first sentence of the document gives the intended audience. (**Reading Comprehension**)

7. **C.** The definition of the word *valid* is that which is true and legal. (**Word Analysis**)

8. **A.** The key word omitted in answer **A** is *intentional*. A student may access inappropriate or obscene files accidentally and that would not be considered a violation of the acceptable use policy. The others are all mentioned in the document as violations. (**Reading Comprehension**)

9. **B.** It is expressly forbidden to use the schools equipment and Internet connections for commerce or for financial gain. (**Reading Comprehension**)

10. **A.** The word *revoke* means to cancel. (**Word Analysis**)

11. **A.** While it is mentioned that contacting legal authorities is one of the things the school might do regarding a student violation of the acceptable use policy, there is nothing stated about what the authorities have done or might do. The document details what students need to do to use the Internet (**B**) and what actions are considered subject to disciplinary action (**C**) and tells us that the student has to renew his or her permission to use the Internet annually (**D**). (**Reading Comprehension**)

For "Into Thin Air"

12. **A.** Choice **A** best explains the connotation of the words as used by the author. Choice **B** has such a negative connotation that it is too strong to express how Krakauer feels. He isn't filled with "terror" because he does continue to climb mountains and he loves it. Choices **C** and **D** have a pleasant connotation that negates the fact that there is even a problem, which there certainly is. Therefore, **A** is correct. (**Word Analysis**)

13. D. It is the only one that discusses the fact that the icefall is "strenuous and terrifying," yet it holds "a surprising allure." (**Literary Response and Analysis**)

14. B. "rising like the shoulders of a malevolent god" is a simile. A simile is a type of figurative language. The other answers are simply descriptive . (**Literary Response and Analysis**)

15. A. He discusses climbers who make snide remarks and insult the route they are taking and then goes on to say that such people have obviously never actually attempted the route. (**Literary Response and Analysis**)

For "The Weights Debate"

16. A. Choice **B** is incorrect. Some trainers might like them better, but the consensus today is that a blend of free weights and machines is optimal. Choice **C** is incorrect. Free weights actually force the individual to recruit more of the body's muscles. Choice **D** is true but is obviously limited to those people who are injured. (**Reading Comprehension**)

17. D. This article is about exercise equipment, not the use of drugs. The others are all discussed in the text: **A** in paragraph 7, **B** in paragraph 8, **C** in paragraph 10. (**Reading Comprehension**)

18. C. The point of this article is that a combination of both free weights and machines offers the best strength workout. Choice **D** is not mentioned in the article and would probably build endurance and flexibility but not large amounts of strength. (**Reading Comprehension**)

19. D. Diet is not mentioned anywhere in the text. Likewise the physics of the cam and the reasons for the fascination with definition are not mentioned in the text. Choice **D** summarizes the main idea of the passage. (**Reading Comprehension**)

20. B. The main idea of this passage is that free weights and machines have both advantages and disadvantages. Using both is the best way to maximize muscular gains. All the other choices are far too specific. (**Reading Comprehension**)

21. B. *Rehabilitate* means to restore something to a previous condition. The muscle might be changed (**A**) and pain might be reduced (**D**), but those are not the primary meaning of the word. (**Word Analysis**)

Have an English teacher, tutor, or someone else with good writing skills read and evaluate your essay using the checklist below.

Checklist for Response to Writing Prompt

Does your essay . . .

❑ Provide a thoughtful, well-written composition that addresses the writing task?

❑ Use specific supporting details and examples?

❑ Demonstrate a clear focus and tone?

❑ Show coherent, logical organization?

❑ Clearly address the intended audience?

❑ Use precise, descriptive language?

❑ Use a variety of sentence types?

❑ Contain almost no errors in grammar, punctuation, spelling, capitalization and usage?

❑ Clearly state a position and make a case for that position?

❑ Defend the position with specific relevant evidence?

❑ Address the reader's potential misunderstandings, biases, and expectations?

Session 2

For "The Mail-Order Catalogue"

22. **C.** The author says that the catalogue brought "all that color and all that mystery and all that beauty into the lives of country people." Choice **A** isn't mentioned. The people dream over the catalogue but we aren't told that they feel they need the merchandise. The author doesn't state that country people are so optimistic that they believe they can attain the goods one day (**B**). **(Literary Response and Analysis)**

23. **A.** The line is a metaphor that compares spinning a web to creating a fantasy. Metaphors are a type of figurative language. **(Literary Response and Analysis)**

24. **D.** The narrator says that the people in the catalogue aren't missing any body parts and they have no scars. The other answers are never stated. **(Literary Response and Analysis)**

25. **D.** Even if you don't know what *radically* means, or you think you know, but your meaning doesn't seem to make sense, substitute in the other words in place of *radically*. The only one that makes sense is *extremely*. **(Word Analysis)**

26. **B.** In this context, *glancing* means to hit at an angle. Since the surrounding lines are about how people got scarred, Choices **A, C,** and **D** don't make sense since none of those actions would directly result in a scar. **(Word Analysis)**

For "Four Skinny Trees"

27. **D.** The speaker spends the essay discussing how the trees, although awkward and out of place, never die. They continue to grow and sometimes even thrive in their environment. She looks at the trees and learns that she must "keep keeping." **(Literary Response and Analysis)**

28. **C.** Trees don't have necks and elbows, people do. Personification is the assigning of human characteristics to inanimate objects; therefore, **C** is correct. **(Literary Response and Analysis)**

29. **C.** The speaker discusses the fact that the trees rip into the ground and grab on ferociously with their roots and grow despite the concrete. This is a metaphor for the speaker's life and how she hangs on even when it is difficult and grows despite the concrete or hardships in her life. **(Literary Response and Analysis)**

30. **D.** Used in this context, *skinny* and *pointy* are negative terms. If you imagine what a skinny and pointy tree looks like, and then apply that to what a girl would look like if she describes herself that way, that translates into an awkward and unattractive girl. Choices **A** and **C** are positive traits that don't fit the connotation of the words, and **B** is too strong a statement. **(Literary Response and Analysis)**

31. **A.** The passage is one person speaking about her thoughts and feelings. That is the definition of a monologue. **(Literary Response and Analysis)**

32. **B.** Substituting in the answers would help you eliminate **C** and **D** since the paragraph refers to *strength, violent teeth,* and *anger. Angry* does have a negative connotation but is not the definition of *ferocious*. A person may be ferocious because he is angry, but based on the context of the word, **A** doesn't fit. **(Word Analysis)**

For "Greening the World's Most Popular Fruit"

33. **B.** Choice **A** is a detail that introduces the need for the many pesticides and fungicides used on bananas. Choice **C** may be true but is not germane to this discussion. The Better Banana Project is one of the oldest certification efforts and as such is important but as a detail. **(Reading Comprehension)**

34. **A.** Lacking genetic diversity, the banana is subject to many diseases that require the use of pesticides and fungicides. Choice **B** is probably true but is not mentioned. Choice **C** is false; Costa Rica is but one of many places where bananas are grown. Choice **D** is incorrect because there isn't a direct link between a lack of genetic diversity in the banana and the poor working conditions of the workers. **(Reading Comprehension)**

35. **D.** Bananas are typically eaten right out of their skin. The word wrapper is used metaphorically here. The other choices are either not suggested or are too far-fetched to be correct. **(Word Analysis)**

36. **B.** Choice **B** is mentioned in the text. Choice **A** is not the answer because although still small, the sale of organic bananas is growing. The banana is a type of berry, not a grain, ruling out answer **C.** Choice **D** is incorrect because the pesticides *are* losing their effectiveness as is stated in the third paragraph. **(Reading Comprehension)**

37. **C.** The word *razed* means to take down, or level to the ground. The trees are cut down in order to make room for the bananas. **(Word Analysis)**

38. **C.** Certification programs do add costs but the increases are not regarded as extreme, ruling out **A.** The environmental concerns are there (**B**), but this choice gives part of the problem without mentioning the solution. Choice **C** is the best answer because it details the issues of pollution, pesticides, and workers' welfare and the certification programs. The article clearly regards the certification programs as the best chance for correcting the ills inherent in the world of banana production. The language in choice **D** is extreme; nowhere are the problems called insurmountable. **(Reading Comprehension)**

39. **A.** The article focuses on the problems inherent in the banana industry. The author seems hopeful that the best long-term solution to these problems lies in the proliferation of certification efforts like The Better Banana Project. Choice **B** is incorrect because it describes a detail that is not discussed in the article. The author is not concerned solely with price, ruling out **C,** and **D** is incorrect because nematicides *are designed* to severely damage the roundworm population. **(Reading Comprehension)**

For "Beauty with Brains"

40. **D.** Butterflies have poor vision. The others are all mentioned in the text as things butterflies do to protect themselves. **(Reading Comprehension)**

41. **B.** *Indolent* means lazy, a word you might have guessed in the comparison between the hardworking honeybee and the butterfly relaxing in the sun and sipping nectar. **(Word Analysis)**

42. **A.** The entire article is about the discrepancy between what we perceive to be the nature of the butterflies and their true nature. Choices **B** and **C** are true but too narrow to be a good summation of the entire article. Choice **D** is simply not true. **(Reading Comprehension)**

43. **C.** Butterflies migrate because of environmental conditions—nothing else. This is stated in the article. **(Reading Comprehension)**

44. **C.** The article states that butterflies beat their wings from 5 to 12 beats per second, while flies beat their wings over a 1000 beats per second. The other choices are false; butterflies do pollinate plants, they have poor eyesight, and their wings are larger than what is aerodynamically necessary. **(Reading Comprehension)**

45. **B.** An apprentice is someone who agrees to work with another in order to be instructed in a specific trade. The younger butterfly follows the older ones around in hope of learning the routes to the flowers, which metaphorically speaking, is the trade of the butterfly, that is, what he does to live and eat. **(Word Analysis)**

46. **D.** Mating, migration, and vision are explored in the text; while the life span of an adult butterfly, although mentioned as being very short, is not discussed in any detail. **(Reading Comprehension)**

For "The Talk"

47. **D.** The narrator specifically says "Even if I'm ugly, my wife's going to be good-looking," and he focuses on the beauty of the girl in the window. He doesn't, however, discuss any of the other qualities listed as answers. The best answer is **D. (Literary Response and Analysis)**

48. **C.** The narrator, immediately after this comment, mentions that this is why his friend believes he'll be successful if he goes into the air conditioning business. That's a business most likely to do well in a very hot climate. The best answer is **C. (Literary Response and Analysis)**

49. **A.** A simile uses *like* or *as* in a comparison. Choice **C** is not correct because although it uses the word *like*, the meaning of the word in this case is *enjoy*, not *similar to*. The best answer is **A. (Literary Response and Analysis)**

50. A. Probably, by placing these two words, used in very different ways, near one another the author intends the reader to think about their difference in meaning. In the first case, the girl they see through the window is *stirring* the air with her leg. This is a very visual description—her leg is described as having the motion of a spoon that is stirring something in a bowl. And watching that motion *stirred* the boys—that is, they experienced an emotional reaction by watching her. The best answer is **A. (Word Analysis)**

51. C. Autobiography is an author's account of his or her own life. (Biography is an account of someone else's.) In this case, reading the comment that appears before the selection, about the author and about this piece, would give you the correct answer. Don't forget to read any extra information given along with a selection. The piece *could* be a chapter from a larger work, but nothing in the selection or the extra information suggests that it is, so we don't know, and the selection does seem to be complete in itself. The best answer is **C. (Literary Response and Analysis)**

52. B. Many of the specifics of the boys' dreams of their futures are somewhat unrealistic, based undoubtedly on their lack of knowledge of realities at this point in their lives. For example, Scott suggests that his future wife will "enjoy Millerton Lake, dirty as it was." The narrator sees himself and his wife as adults enjoying Kool-Aid and Pop-Tarts, snack items more suitable to a child's taste than a grownup's. And he thinks that because his arms seem too long for his body now that he would "only need a stepladder to hand a fellow worker on the roof a pinch of nails," not realizing that many young people seem not quite "put together" right at this growth-spurt time of their lives. And there are many other instances of this unrealistic dreaming in the selection. The best answer is **B. (Literary Response and Analysis)**

For Writing Strategies

53. A. Choice **A** uses the active voice of the verb, which is more effective and less wordy than the passive voice. The other answers use the passive voice. Choice **D** adds an unnecessary clause ("It is clear"). Try to avoid phrases and clauses that add nothing to the meaning.

54. B. Although sentence 5 mentions dogs, the paragraph is not a comparison between dogs and wolves, and thus sentence 6 changes the focus (which is the social nature of wolves). All of the other sentences fit better in their locations than sentence 6 does.

55. B. The point is made more directly in **B** than in the other choices, and this answer is also grammatically correct. Choice **A** includes an unnecessary phrase: "a lot of things" and the elements of the series are not parallel in structure. (The third element—"do social stresses"—is in question format.) Choice **C** is awkward and wordy. Notice the unnecessary phrase "are the things that". "Things" is a vague repetition of the idea in "Factors." Choice **D** includes faulty parallelism; the clause "that social stresses . . . ." is not parallel to the other two elements in the series.

56. D. See sentence 9. Choices **A** and **C** may seem good choices, but neither of these points is made in the essay, though dog and "lone wolf" are mentioned. Choice **B** is not covered at all.

57. B. *Siblings* means brothers and sisters, and it is the term most appropriate when writing about animals. Choice **A** is informal and not as specific, and **C** and **D** are also less precise than *siblings*.

58. C. This sentence connects most logically to what follows, that is, a description of the first roller coaster. Choice **A** may be true, but it isn't the subject of this paragraph. Choice **B** may seem a good first sentence, but its second part sets up a different subject from the one in the paragraph. Choice **D** is a clumsy opening.

59. C. *High-class* is a slang term; *upper-class* is more acceptable. Choices **A**, **B**, and **D** are all related to money, and the emphasis here is on class.

60. A. Choice **A** is the best version of the underlined part of this sentence. It is in the active voice and is direct and to the point. Choice **B** and the original version (**D**) both use the passive voice, which is less effective. Choice **C** is unnecessarily wordy and less direct.

61. D. *Although* makes the most sense in joining the two parts of this sentence. "However" would be satisfactory, too, but "however" should be preceded by a period or a semicolon. Otherwise, it creates a run-on sentence (**A**), which "although" does not. Answers **B** and **C** are poor choices because neither "and" nor "therefore" is a logical connector. The sentence requires a contrast, that is, the early roller coasters aren't like ours today but in many languages "Russian Mountain" still means roller coaster.

62. **C.** Sentence 7 directly supports the statement in sentence 3, that is, the difficulties of food distribution. It would not be a good opening sentence (**A**) nor does it logically belong after sentence 1 (**B**) or after sentence 5 (**D**), which is about the world's grain supply.

63. **B.** Choice **B** is supported in the paragraph. See sentence 6. Choices **A, C,** and **D** might or might not be true, but none of these statements is supported in this paragraph.

64. **C.** A thesaurus is a book that gives synonyms for words, and it would not be useful in researching famines. All of the other choices could be good sources of information.

For Writing Conventions

65. **C.** "Stopping just long enough . . ." is a participial phrase, not a sentence. Choice **C** is the best answer. The phrase (which modifies "limousine") is separated from the main clause with a comma. If it were separated from the main clause by a period, it would be a sentence fragment (Choice **D**). Choice **A** is also a fragment because the verb "stopped" has no subject. Choice **B** adds a subject ("it stopped") but then the original sentence becomes two sentences run together with a comma (a run-on sentence).

66. **A.** The correct punctuation here is a colon (**A**). Colons are used to introduce a list, and the words "as follows" or "following" are clear indications that a colon is appropriate. A period is too strong and creates a fragment (**B**), while no punctuation (**C**) or a comma (**D**) is too weak.

67. **D.** The sentence is correct as it is (**D**). "To continue up the river . . ." is an infinitive phrase which explains the word "decision." It should be written in the same sentence with the word it explains, and no punctuation is needed. The other three choices create sentence fragments.

68. **A.** The original sentence creates a fragment (the subordinate clause beginning with "because"). Changing the order of the sentence doesn't help; in choices **B** and **C,** the clause remains a fragment because of incorrect punctuation. Choice **A** is the best answer. No punctuation is needed when the subordinate clause follows the main (or independent) clause.

69. **C.** Quotation marks are used for direct quotations. This sentence, however, is indirect discourse, that is, the person speaking is reporting what another person (the lecturer) said, not directly quoting him or her. Therefore, the correct answer is choice **C.**

70. **B.** Both verbs should be in the same tense. Choice **B** is the best answer because both "added" and "left" are past tense verbs. In the other choices the tenses of the two verbs are inconsistent.

71. **A.** Was the smoke alarm talking on the telephone? Placement of the modifying phrase "While talking on the telephone" makes it sound as if this were the case. It is a dangling modifier. Choices **B** and **C** don't solve this problem. Adding "I was" to this phrase is one way to correct the problem (Choice **A**). Other ways would be "While talking on the telephone, I heard the smoke alarm go off in the kitchen," or "The smoke alarm in the kitchen went off while I was talking on the telephone." These choices are not offered, however.

72. **C.** Items in a series should be expressed in the same form. This is called parallel construction. The best choice here is **C** ("gossiping," "shopping," "dancing," and "sleeping"). All of the elements match (using the "-ing" form of the word). In the other choices, the items in the series vary: in Choice **A**, "to gossip" is out of place; in Choice **B**, "gossiping" is out of place; and in Choice **D** (the original sentence) "dancing" is out of place. Choice **D** has another problem with parallel structure. "Shop at the mall" isn't parallel to "to gossip" or "to sleep" because it is missing the "to."

73. **D.** The sentence is correct as it is (**D**). "As of next month" refers to the future. But Charlie has lived in Japan for awhile, an action begun in the past but which will be continuing in the future. This calls for the future perfect tense: "will have been." Choices **A** and **B** are simple future tenses, and **C** is present tense.

74. **A.** In this sentence a modifying clause ("that she had found in our garden") is in the wrong place. Did the woman find her dark hair in the garden? Of course not. She found a rose in the garden. Choice **A** changes sentence order to correctly place "that she found in our garden" next to "rose." Choice **B** doesn't correct the problem, and Choice **C** awkwardly uses the passive voice of the verb ("was found by the woman").

75. D. If "Mr Williams and" is eliminated from this sentence, the right answer (Choice **D**) is clear. You wouldn't say "Me checked in the equipment" or" "Myself checked in the equipment." A common mistake is using the objective case ("me," "him," "her, "us" or "them") when a sentence has two subjects ("Mr. Williams and I"). Repeating the subject ("Mr. Williams and me, we checked in the equipment", Choice **C**) just makes things worse.

76. C. A verb should agree with its subject. In this sentence "All of the men" is the complete subject. Therefore, the verb should be plural (Choice **C**). The other three choices are all singular. A special note: "All" can take a singular verb. For example, "All is well" is correct if the "all" means "everything." "All are well" can also be correct, meaning "All (of the men) are well."

77. D. Choice **D** is correct. In "could of" (Choice **B**), "of" is incorrectly substituted for the verb "have," perhaps because, when spoken quickly, "have" may sound like "of." This is a common mistake also with "should of" for "should have" and "would of" for "would have."

78. A. "Ought" (Choice **A**) is correct here. Choices **C** and **D** are not actual words, and adding "had" as in Choice **B** is ungrammatical. Don't use "had" with "ought."

79. D. "Good" is an adjective used to modify a noun: "That was a good dinner." "Well" is an adverb used to modify a verb: "He ate well." Don't mix them up. In this sentence, "well" is the right choice because it describes how they sang the songs. In addition, "very," not "real" is the correct intensifier. We use "real" in everyday language ("He sings real well"), but avoid using it in writing. Therefore, the best choice for this question is **D.**

PART IV

FINAL PREPARATION AND SOURCES

The Final Touches

1. Make sure that you are familiar with the areas covered on the test.

2. Spend the last week of preparation on a general review of the areas covered with emphasis on strengthening your weak areas.

3. Don't cram the night before the exam. It is a waste of time!

4. Start off crisply, working the questions you know first, then going back and trying to answer the others.

5. Try to eliminate one or more choices before you guess, but make sure that you fill in all the answers. There is no penalty for guessing!

6. Underline key words in questions. Write out important information and make notations. Take advantage of being permitted to write in the test booklet.

7. Make sure that you answer what is being asked.

8. Use an elimination strategy. Cross out incorrect choices immediately: This can keep you from reconsidering a choice that you have already eliminated.

9. Don't get stuck on any one question. They are all of equal value.

10. The key to getting a good score on the CAHSEE is keeping up with your school work, reviewing properly, practicing, and getting the questions right that you can and should get right. A careful review of parts I and II of this book will help you focus during the final week before the exam.

A Comprehensive List of Prefixes, Suffixes, and Roots (for Reference)

Do not try to memorize this list. It is for reference only.

Common Prefixes		
Prefix	*Meaning*	*Examples*
a-	without, not	atypical—not typical
ab-, abs-	away from	abhor—to withdraw from in fear or disgust
		abscond—to run away
ad-, a-, ac-, af-, ag-, an-, ap-, ar-, as-, at-	to; toward	adapt—to fit to
		accede—to agree to
ambi-	both	ambivalent—having two feelings
amphi-	on both sides; around	amphibian—an animal that lives first in the water then adapts to land life
		amphitheater—a theater with seats all around
ante-	before	anterior—before in time; prior
anti-	against	antifreeze—a substance added to a liquid to prevent freezing
auto-	self	automobile—a self-propelled vehicle
bi-	two	bifocals—glasses with lenses for two focuses
circum-	around	circumscribe—to draw around
com-, con-, co-, col-	with; together	combine—to bring together
		conjoin—to join together
		co-worker—one who works with
contra-, contro-, counter-	against	contradict—to say the opposite
		counteract—to act against
de-	away from; down; the opposite of	depart—to go away from
		decline—to turn down
		deactivate—to make inactive
di-	twice	dioxide—an oxide with two atoms of oxygen in a molecule
dia-	across, through	diagonal—across or through a figure
		diagnose—to determine what is wrong through knowledge
dis-	apart; not	disperse—to scatter widely
		dishonest—not honest

(continued)

Common Prefixes (continued)		
Prefix	**Meaning**	**Examples**
dys-	bad; ill	dysfunction—a poor functioning
epi-	upon	epitaph—an inscription upon a tombstone (upon burial)
equi-	equal; equally	equitable—fair
ex-, e-, ef-	out; from	excavate—to hollow out
		eject—to throw out
		effuse—to pour out
extra-	outside; beyond	extraordinary—outside the usual
fore-	before; in front of	foresee—to anticipate
geo-	earth	geology—the study of the earth
homo-	same; equal; alike	homonym—a word with the same pronunciation as another word
hyper-	over; too much	hypertension—unusually high tension
hypo-	under; too little	hypodermic—under the skin
in-, il-, ig-, ir-, im-	not	inactive—not active
		illegal—not legal
		ignoble—not noble
		irreverent—not reverent
		improbable—not probable
in-, il-, ir-, im-	in; into	inject—to put in
		illuminate—to light up
		irradiate—to shine on
		implant—to fix firmly in
inter-	between; among	interurban—between cities
intra-, intro-	within, inside of	intravenous—directly into a vein
		introvert—one who looks inside himself
mal-, male-	bad; wrong; ill	malfunction—to fail to function correctly
		malevolent—wishing harm to others
mis-	wrong; badly	mistreat—to treat badly
mis-, miso-	hatred	misanthrope—one who hates people
mono-	one; alone	monologue—a speech by one person
neo-	new	neologism—a new word or a new meaning for an old word
non-	not; the reverse of	nonsense—something that makes no sense
omni-	all; everywhere	omnipresent—present everywhere

Prefix	Meaning	Examples
pan-	all	pandemic—existing over a whole area
per-	by; through; throughout	pervade—to be present throughout
poly-	many	polygon—a many-sided plane figure
post-	after	postwar—after the war
pro-	forward; going ahead of; supporting	proceed—to go forward prowar—supporting war
re-	again; back	retell—to tell again retroactive—applying to things that have already taken place
se-	apart	secede—to withdraw
semi-	half; partly	semicircle—half a circle semiliterate—able to read and write a little
sub-	under; less than	submarine—underwater subconscious—beneath the consciousness
super-	over; above; greater	superimpose—to put something over something else superstar—a star greater than the others
syn-, sym-, syl-, sys-	with; at the same time	synchronize—to make things agree symmetry—balance on the two sides of a dividing line
tele-	far	telepathy—communication by thought alone
trans-	across	transcontinental—across the continent
un-	not	unhelpful—not helpful

Common Suffixes

Suffix	Meaning	Examples
-able, -ible, -ble	able to, capable of being	viable—able to live edible—capable of being eaten
-acious, -cious	having the quality of	tenacious—holding firmly
-al	of; like	nocturnal—of the night
-ance, -ancy	the act of; a state of being	performance—the act of performing truancy—the act of being truant
-ant, -ent	one who	occupant—one who occupies respondent—one who responds
-ar, -ary	connected with; concerning	ocular—pertaining to the eye beneficiary—one who receives benefits

(continued)

Common Suffixes *(continued)*		
Suffix	**Meaning**	**Examples**
-ence	the act, fact, or quality of	existence—the quality of being
-er, -or	one who does	teacher—one who teaches
		visitor—one who visits
-ful	full of; having qualities of	fearful—full of fear
		masterful—having the qualities of a master
-fy	to make	deify—to make into a god
-ic, -ac	of; like; pertaining to	cryptic—hidden
		cardiac—pertaining to the heart
-il, -ile	pertaining to	civil—pertaining to citizens
		infantile—pertaining to infants
-ion	the act or condition of	correction—the act of correcting
-ism	the philosophy, act, or practice of	patriotism—support of one's country
-ist	one who does, makes, or is occupied with	artist—one who is occupied with art
-ity, -ty, -y	the state or character	unity—the state of being one
		novelty—the quality of being novel or new
-ive	containing the nature of; giving or leaning toward	pensive—thoughtful
-less	without; lacking	heartless—cruel; without a heart
-logue	a particular kind of speaking or writing	dialogue—a conversation or interchange
-logy	a kind of speaking; a study or science	eulogy—a speech or writing in praise of someone
		theology—the study of God and related matters
-ment	the act of ; the state of	alignment—the act of aligning
		retirement—the state of being retired
-ness	the quality of	eagerness—the quality of being eager
-ory	having the nature of, a place or thing for	laudatory—showing praise
		laboratory—a place where work is done
-ous, -ose	full of, having	dangerous—full of danger
		verbose—wordy
-ship	the art or skill of; the state or quality of being	leadership—the ability to lead
-some	full of; like	troublesome—full of trouble
-tude	the state or quality of	servitude—slavery or bondage
-y	full of, somewhat; somewhat like	musty—having a stale odor
		chilly—somewhat cold
		willowy—like a willow

Common Roots		
Root	**Meaning**	**Examples**
acr	sharp, bitter	acrid—sharp, bitter
act, ag	to do; to act	activity—action
		agent—one who does
acu	sharp; keen	acuity—keenness
alt	high	exalt—to raise or lift up
anim	life; mind	animate—to make alive
ann	year	annual—yearly
anthrop	man, mankind	misanthrope—one who hates people
apt	fit	adapt—to fit to
arch	to rule	patriarch—a father and ruler
aud	to hear	audience—those who hear
bas	low	debase—to make lower
belli	war	bellicose—hostile, warlike
ben, bene	well; good	benevolent—doing or wishing good
bio	life	biology—the study of living things
brev	short	abbreviate—to shorten
cad, cas	to fall	cadence—the fall of the voice in speaking, movement in sound
		cascade—a small waterfall
cap, capt, cip, cept, ceive, ceit	to take or hold	captive—one who is caught and held
		receive—to take
cav	hollow	excavate—to hollow out
cede, ceed, cess	to go; to give in	precede—to go before
		access—a means of giving to
chrom	color	chromatic—having color or colors
chron, chrono	time	synchronize—to make agree in time
		chronology—the order of events
cid, cis	to cut, to kill	incisive—cutting into, sharp
		homicide—the killing of a man by another
clin	to lean, to bend	decline—to bed or turn downward
clud, clus, clos, claud, claus	to close, to shut	exclude—to shut out
		claustrophobia—fear of closed places

(continued)

Common Roots (continued)

Root	Meaning	Examples
cogn, cognit	to know, to learn	cognizant—aware
		recognition—knowing on sight
cor, cord	heart	accord—agreement
corp, corpor	body	corporal—bodily
cred, credit	to believe	credible—believable
crypt	hidden	cryptic—with hidden meaning
cum	to heap up	cumulative—increasing by additions
cur	to care	accurate—careful and precise
curr, curs, cours	to run	current—the flow of running water
da, date	to give	date—a given time
dem, demo	people	demography—a statistical study of the population
di	day	diary—a daily record
dic, dict	to say	diction—wording; verbal expression
		indict—to make a formal accusation
doc, doct	to teach	doctrine—something taught
dol	grief, pain	doleful—sorrowful
domin	to rule, to master	dominion—rule; a ruled territory
dorm	to sleep	dormant—sleeping, inactive
duc, duct	to lead	induce—to lead to action
		aqueduct—a pipe or waterway
dynam	power	dynamite—a powerful explosive
ego	I	egocentric—seeing everything in relation to oneself
eu	good, beautiful	euphonious—having a pleasant sound
fac, fact, fic, fec, fect	to make, to do	facile—easy to do
		artifact—an object made by man
		fiction—something that has been made up
fer, ferr, lat	to carry, to bring or bear	refer—to carry to something or somebody else
fid	faith; trust	confide—to tell a trusted person
fin	end; limit	final—coming at the end
fort, force	strong	fortitude—strength
		enforce—to give strength to

Root	Meaning	Examples
frag, fract	to break	fragment—a part broken from the whole
gen	birth	generate—give birth to
gen, gener	kind; race	general—applying to a whole class or kind
		gender—classification of words by sex
gnos	to know	agnostic—one who believes people cannot know whether God exists
grad, gress	to step, to go	graduate—to go from one state to another
		progress—to move forward
graph, gram	writing	graphic—relating to writing
		telegram—a written message sent over a distance
helio	sun	heliolatry—sun worship
hydro	water	hydrant—a pipe from which one draws water
jac, jact, jec, ject	to throw	trajectory—the path of an object that has been thrown or shot
		project—to propose; to put forward
junct	to join	junction—a joining
jur	to swear	perjure—to lie under oath
labor	to work	elaborate—worked out carefully
leg, lect	to gather, to choose	legion—a large number gathered together
		elect—to choose
leg	law	legislate—to make laws
liber	book	library—a book collection
liber	free	liberation—freedom
loc	place	dislocate—to displace
loqu, locut	to talk	loquacious—talkative
		elocution—style of speaking
luc	light	elucidate—to clarify ("throw light on")
magna	great	magnanimous—of noble mind; generous
		magnate—an important person
man, mani, manu	hand	manipulate—to work with hands
		manuscript—a document written by hand
mar	the sea	maritime—having to do with the sea
medi	middle	intermediate—in the middle

(continued)

Common Roots (continued)

Root	Meaning	Examples
meter, metr, mens	to measure	thermometer—an instrument to measure temperature
		symmetry—similarity of measurement on both sides
		immense—very large (immeasurable)
micro	very small	microbe—an organism too small to be seen with the naked eye
min, mini	small	minute—very tiny
		miniature—a small copy of something
mit, mitt, miss	to send	admit—to allow in
		missile—a projectile
mon, monit	to advise, warn, remind	monument—a plaque, statue, building, etc., set up to remind of someone or something
		premonition—an advance warning
mort ,morti	to die	mortal—destined to die
		moribund—dying
mov, mot, mob	to move	remove—to move away
		emotion—strong (moving) feelings
		immobile—not movable
mut	to change	immutable—never changing
nat, nasc	born	prenatal—before birth
		nascent—coming into being; being born
nav	ship	circumnavigate—to sail around
nocturn	night	nocturnal—taking place at night
nomy	law, arranged order	astronomy—the science of the stars
nov, novus	new	innovation—something new
onym	name	anonymous—without a name
oper	to work	operative—capable of working
pac	peace	pacify—to calm
par	equal	disparate—not alike; distinct
pars, part	part	depart—to go away from
pater, patr	father	paternal—fatherly
		patriarch—a father and a ruler

Root	Meaning	Examples
path, pat, pas	feeling, suffering	empathy—"feeling with" another person patient—suffering without complaint passion—strong emotion
ped, pede, pod	foot	pedestal—the bottom of a statute, column, etc. impede—to hinder podium—a platform on which to stand
pel, puls	to drive	expel—to drive out repulse—to drive out
pend, pens	to hang; to weigh; to pay	pendulous—hanging loosely pensive—thoughtful pension—a payment to a person after a certain age
pet, petit	to seek	impetus—a motive petition—to request
phil, philo	loving	philanthropy—a desire to help mankind philosophy—a love of knowledge
phobia	fear	hydrophobia—fear of water
phon, phone	sound	symphony—harmony of sounds telephone—an instrument for sending sound over a distance
plac	to please	placate—to stop from being angry
polis	city	metropolis—a major city
pon, pos, posit, pose	to place	proponent—a person who makes a suggestion or supports a cause
port, portat	to carry	porter—one who carries transportation—a means of carrying
psych, psycho	mind	psychology—the science of the mind
quer, quisit	to ask	query—to question inquistion—a questioning
quies	quiet	acquiesce—to agree without protest
radi	ray	irradiate—to shine light on
rid, ris	to laugh	ridiculous—laughable risible—causing laughter

(continued)

	Common Roots (continued)	
Root	**Meaning**	**Examples**
rog, rogate	to ask	prerogative—a prior right interrogate—to question
rupt	to break	disrupt—to break up
sat, satis	enough	satiate—to provide with enough or more than enough satisfy—to meet the needs of
schis, schiz	to cut	schism—a split or division schizophrenia—a mental disorder characterized by a separation of the thoughts and emotions
sci	to know	science—knowledge
scop	to watch, to view	telescope—an instrument for seeing things at a distance
scrib, script	to write	describe—to tell or write about transcript—a written copy
sec, sect	to cut	sectile—cutable with a knife bisect—to cut in two
sed, sess, sid	to sit	sediment—material that settles to the bottom (in liquid) session—a meeting preside—to have authority
sent, sens	to feel, to think	sentiment—feeling sensitive- responding to stimuli
sequ, secu, secut	to follow	sequence—order consecutive—one following another
solv, solut	to loosen	absolve -to free from guilt solution—the method of working out an answer
soph	wise, wisdom	sophisticate—a worldly-wise person
spec, spect,	to look, to appear	specimen—an example inspect—to look over
spir, spirit	to breathe	expire—to exhale; to die spirit—life
sta, stat	to stand	stable—steady stationary—fixed, unmoving
stru, struct	to build	construe—to explain or deduce the meaning structure—a building

Root	Meaning	Examples
suas, suad	to urge	persuasive—having the power to cause something to change
		dissuade—to change someone's course
sum, sumpt	to take	assume—to take on
		resumption—taking up again
tact, tang	to touch	tactile—able to be touched or felt
		intangible—unable to be touched
tempor	time	temporal—lasting only for a time; temporary
ten, tent, tain	to hold	untenable—unable to be held
		retentive—holding
		maintain—to keep or keep up
tend, tens	to stretch	extend—to stretch out or draw out
		tension—tautness
terr	land	territory—a portion of land
the, theo	god	atheist—one who believes there is no God
		theocracy—rule by God or by persons claiming to represent Him
thermo	heat	thermal—having to do with heat
tract	to draw	attract—to draw
trud, trus	to thrust	protrude—to stick out
		intrusive—pushing into or upon something
un, uni	one	unanimous—of one opinion
		uniform—of one form
urb	city	suburb—a district near a city
ut, util	to use; useful	utile—the quality of being useful
vac	empty	vacuum—empty space
ven, vent	to come	convene—to meet together
		advent—an arrival
ver	true	verify—to prove to be true
vert, vers	to turn	advert—to turn away
vi, via	way	deviate—to turn off the prescribed way
		via—by way of
vid, vis	to see	evident—apparent; obvious
		invisible—unable to be seen

(continued)

285

Common Roots *(continued)*		
Root	**Meaning**	**Examples**
vinc, vict	to conquer	convince—to overcome the doubts of victory—an overcoming
vit, viv	to live	vital—alive vivacious—lively
voc, voke, vocat	to call	vocal—spoken or uttered aloud invoke—to call on vocation—a calling
void	empty	devoid—without
volv, volut	to roll or turn around	evolve—to develop by stages, to unfold
vol	to fly	volatile—vaporizing quickly

Sources

I would like to give a special "thank you" to the following authors and publishing companies who have given me permission to reprint excerpts from their fine works:

Pages 9–10; 12–13: "The Coming Climate" by Thomas R. Karl, Neville Nicholls, and Jonathan Gregory. Reprinted by permission of the authors.

Pages 26–28: "Marked for Extinction" by Kim Clark, © 2004. *U.S. News and World Report*. L.P. Reprinted with permission.

Pages 35–36: "Boy on a Dolphin" by Horace E. Dobbs from *Animal Stories*. Octopus Books Limited. Copyright 1980, by Horace E. Dobbs.

Page 38: "Those Winter Sundays" from *Collected Poems of Robert Hayden*, Liveright Publishing Corporation. Copyright by Robert Hayden.

Pages 40–42: "Eleven" by Sandra Cisneros. Reprinted by permission of Susan Bergholz.

Pages 74–76: "One Foot on the Ground" by Glen F. Stillwell. From *Humorous Stories*. A Lantern Press Book. Pocket Books, New York.

Pages 129–131: "Gaining on the Men" by Martin Miller. Los Angeles Times. Reprinted by permission of TMS Reprints.

Pages 133–134: "Susan Allen Toth (1940 –)" by Susan Allen Toth. Ballantine Books.

Pages 143–144: "Our Finest Hour" from *The Osgood Files* by Charles Osgood. G.P. Putnam's Sons, a division of Penguin Group (USA) Inc. © Charles Osgood.

Pages 149–150: "To the Residents of A.D. 2029" by Bryan Woolley. Copyright by Bryan Woolley. Reprinted by permission.

Page 152: From "The Boxer's Heart" by Kate Sekules, copyright © 2000 by Kate Sekules. Used by permission of Villard Books, a division of Random House, Inc.

Pages 175–177: "Roadwork Ahead" by John Dinkel. Published by *WESTWAYS*. Reprinted by permission of John Dinkel.

Page 181: "On Summer" by Lorraine Hansberry. PLAYBILL® Used by permission.

Pages 183–184: "New Directions" from *Wouldn't Take Nothing for My Journey Now* by Maya Angelou. Copyright 1993 by Maya Angelou. Used by permission of Random House, Inc.

Pages 194–196: "It's Not About the Bike: My Journey Back to Life" by Lance Armstrong. © 2000 by Lance Armstrong. Used by permission of G.P. Putnam's Sons, a division of Penguin Group (USA) Inc.

Pages 200–201: "My Furthest-Back Person" by Alex Haley. Copyright © 1972 by Alex Haley. Reprinted by permission of John Hawkins and Associates, Inc.

Page 225: "George Gray" by Edgar Lee Masters from *Spoon River Anthology* in *Elements of Literature*. Holt, Rinehard and Winston Inc. 1989.

Pages 229–230: From "Into Thin Air" by Jon Krakauer copyright © 1997 by Jon Krakauer. Used by Permission of Villard Books, a division of Random House, Inc.

Pages 232–234: "The Weights Debate" by Marnell Jameson, Los Angeles Times. Reprinted by permission of TMS Reprints.